VOTING AND COLLECTIVE CHOICE

SOME ASPECTS OF THE THEORY OF GROUP DECISION-MAKING

VOTING AND COLLECTIVE CHOICE

SOME ASPECTS OF THE THEORY OF GROUP DECISION-MAKING

PRASANTA K. PATTANAIK

Senior Research Fellow, Nuffield College, Oxford

CAMBRIDGE

AT THE UNIVERSITY PRESS

1971

Published by the Syndics of the Cambridge University Press
Bentley House, 200 Euston Road, London N.W.1
American Branch: 32 East 57th Street, New York, N.Y.10022

© Cambridge University Press 1971

Library of Congress Catalogue Card Number: 75–152 630

ISBN: 0 521 07961 6

Printed in Great Britain
at the University Printing House, Cambridge
(Brooke Crutchley, University Printer)

To Shree Ma

CONTENTS

PREFACE

This is the revised version of a dissertation written at the Delhi School of Economics under the supervision of Professor A. K. Sen, and approved for a Ph.D. degree by the University of Delhi in 1968. A part of the work was done while I was at Harvard University, and was financed by a grant from the National Science Foundation.

It is impossible to express my indebtedness to Professor A. K. Sen with any adequacy. At every stage of my work I have freely encroached on his time, and have received his valuable help. I am also grateful to Professor K. J. Arrow, Professor J. Bhagwati, Professor S. Chakravarty, Dr Padma Desai, Professor F. H. Hahn, Professor S. A. Marglin, Professor K. A. Naqvi, and Professor K. N. Raj for the help and encouragement I received from them. Needless to say, any error that remains is mine.

Finally, I would like to thank the publishers of the *Economic Journal*, *Econometrica*, the *Journal of Economic Theory*, the *Journal of Political Economy*, and the *Review of Economic Studies* for kind permission to use here material from my articles and notes already published in these journals.

PRASANTA K. PATTANAIK

Nuffield College, Oxford

INTRODUCTION

The purpose of this study is to examine some recent developments in the theory of social choice. In particular, emphasis is
given on the set of problems which have been brought to light
by Arrow[1], and which have provoked a considerable volume
of contributions to the field especially from economists. The
central theorem of Arrow[1] which has aroused so much interest
is negative in its impact. Essentially, what it demonstrates is
this: certain value judgments which we might find reasonable
to incorporate in the criterion for social choice, are logically
incompatible. The paradoxical feature of this conclusion arises
from the fact that the value judgments proposed by Arrow all
seem—at first sight at least—highly appealing. It is this problem
of ethical consistency which constitutes the subject of this study.

In the first chapter I lay down the formal framework of my
analysis. Chapter 2 is devoted to some methodological problems
relating to value judgments. This may seem otiose unless we re-
member that in the past not a little confusion has been created in
certain branches of study (e.g., Welfare Economics) because of
methodological ambiguities regarding value judgments. I believe
that methodology, though it may not help us to discover any
profound truths, may yet help us to avoid deep-seated errors.
Accordingly, in Chapter 2 I have tried to clarify certain basic
issues regarding value judgments and their place in the theory of
social choice. In particular, drawing upon some recent works in
Ethics, I have tried to outline the types of rational argument that
can be used with respect to the value judgments used in a
normative theory of social choice. In Chapter 3 I discuss
Arrow's[1] approach to the problem of social decisions and the
paradox it leads to. The subsequent chapters deal with some of
the different methods suggested for resolving Arrow's paradox.

Three different methods of solving the problem are considered.
Firstly, Arrow is concerned with a social decision process which
can derive a complete social ordering from any logically possible
set of individual orderings. If the sets of individual orderings in
actual life exhibit certain properties, the question can be raised

whether we should not be satisfied with a social decision process which is otherwise satisfactory and which arrives at a complete social ordering for all sets of individual orderings possessing these properties even though it cannot derive a complete social ordering from every logically possible set of individual orderings. Secondly, the requirement of a complete social ordering itself may be regarded as too demanding. For policy recommendation it would seem enough if we can always pick up a 'best' alternative, i.e., an alternative which is socially considered to be at least as good as every other alternative under consideration. Thirdly, one of Arrow's value judgments rules out the possibility of taking into account the intensities of individual preferences. One can question the desirability of this condition and try to solve Arrow's problem by introducing preference intensities as one of the factors that should influence social choice.

The first two methods are discussed in Chapters 4–8 and the third method is discussed in Chapter 9. Chapter 4 gives certain alternative interpretations of necessary and sufficient conditions in terms of restrictions on individual preferences, for a social decision procedure to yield socially best alternatives or complete social orderings. Chapter 5 deals with necessary and sufficient conditions in terms of restricted individual preferences for the existence of a 'best' alternative under majority decisions. Chapter 6 establishes similar conditions for the existence of a 'best' alternative under some wider classes of social decision rules. In Chapter 7 necessary and sufficient conditions are established for the existence of a complete social ordering under some of the methods of social decision already discussed in Chapters 5 and 6 in connection with the existence of a best alternative. One of the basic assumptions underlying Arrow's analysis as well as most of mine is that individuals have complete preference orderings defined over the set of alternatives under consideration. Some implications of relaxing this assumption, for this analysis, are discussed in Chapter 8. Chapter 9 deals with the possibility of introducing cardinal individual utility functions as the basis of social choice; in particular, I discuss the model of Goodman and Markowitz, and those of Vickrey, and Harsanyi ([1], [2]) in this chapter. I conclude in Chapter 10 with a general review of the discussion.

1

INDIVIDUAL PREFERENCES
AND SOCIAL DECISION

1.1. *Introduction*

Every individual is constantly faced with the problem of choice—a choice out of several alternative actions. The range of actions that are available to him will be determined by his environment, but given this range he has to decide the course of action to be adopted. Similarly, every society is faced with the problem of choice out of a range of alternative social states available at any given time. Like the individual society also cannot escape the burden of taking decisions. This may not be always obvious; in the economists' model of a perfectly competitive economy, for example, a large number of producers and consumers take their decisions individually on the basis of prices prevailing in the market, and the state of the economy emerges as the result of interactions of myriads of individual decisions. But even in this type of decentralized economy a social choice is implied; the choice here takes the form of accepting the result of decentralized decisions of individual producers and consumers.

Given a set of alternative social states, how should social choice be made? One possible answer might be to choose a social state that maximizes social welfare. But this really states the problem in a different form. For, saying that choice of the social state *x* maximizes social welfare implies that *x* should be chosen rather than the other alternatives under consideration; it only invites the further question as to how we determine what maximizes social welfare. It will be generally accepted that social choice from among the alternative social states should, in some sense or other, be grounded on the attitudes of the individuals constituting the society, towards these social states. However, given this 'individualistic' approach, the problem still remains how from the individual attitudes we pass on to social choice. If the preference as between the different social states were identical for all individuals, then this would not be a difficult problem. For, then the preference pattern common to all individuals could reasonably be adopted as the social preference pattern, and choice be made accordingly. The real difficulty in aggregating the individual preferences so as to arrive at a social preference pattern arises because of the diversity in individual preferences. In this book, I shall discuss some of the issues that arise in this context; but first I shall formulate in a more precise form, the problem of aggregation mentioned above.

1.2. *Individual Preferences*

Suppose we have a well defined group of individuals. I shall assume this group to be the society. There could be other possible interpretations of the group. For example, the group could refer to the parliament, the city council, the board of directors of a company and so on. These alternative interpretations will not change the formal structure of this analysis though the substantive content will change.

The set of all alternatives that could possibly be presented for social choice will be indicated by S. The elements of S will usually be indicated by lower-case letters such as x, y, z, w, a, b, and c. There can be several interpretations of these alternatives. They can be interpreted as alternative candidates in an election, or they may be interpreted as alternative social policies, and so on. I shall, however, interpret the elements of S as alternative social states, a social state being a complete specification of the conditions prevailing in the society through time. One can assume these specifications to be as detailed as one likes though in actual practice social states are likely to be visualized in terms of a limited number of features characterizing the society.[1] The elements of S are defined in such a way as to make them mutually exclusive: society cannot choose more than one social state simultaneously. Also, since S is the set of all possible alternatives, society has to choose one element of S; not choosing any element of S is not a feasible alternative. Note that S is not necessarily the set of available alternatives. The alternative social states available to the society at any given time will constitute a subset (most likely a proper subset) of S.

[1] For further discussion of the concept of a social state see Arrow [1].

Individual Preferences and Social Decision

Every individual has a certain preference pattern with respect to the alternatives belonging to S. Later on I shall discuss some problems associated with the interpretation of individual preferences, but at this stage we can simply consider the individual preferences as expressing the individual's liking and disliking for the alternative social states. In particular, it may be useful to point out that we are not assuming anything about the degree of egoism or altruism reflected in these individual preferences.

The weak preference of the ith individual will be indicated by R_i, i.e., for all x and y belonging to S, xR_iy will indicate that the ith individual considers x to be at least as good as y. Thus R_i stands for the relation of 'being better than or indifferent to, according to the ith individual's preferences'. R_i is a *binary* relation, i.e., it is a relation holding between two objects, the objects in this case being elements of S.[1] For all x and y belonging to S, $[xP_iy \leftrightarrow \{xR_iy \ \& \sim (yR_ix)\}]$ and $[xI_iy \leftrightarrow (xR_iy \ \& \ yR_ix)]$. In other words, x stands in the relation of P_i to y if and only if the ith individual considers x to be at least as good as y, but does not consider y to be at least as good as x; x stands in the relation I_i to y if and only if the ith individual considers x to be at least as good as y and also considers y to be at least as good as x. P_i and I_i can thus be interpreted as referring to the strict preference and indifference of the ith individual.

It will be assumed that for every individual i, the weak preference relation R_i defined over S is known. This assumption bypasses several important difficulties. It is well-known that individuals may not always express their preferences sincerely. Strategic considerations may induce them to present only a distorted version of their preferences to the outside world.[2] Even if strategic considerations are not important, it may be difficult to find a practical procedure which will accurately record the preferences of individuals. Voting—the most common device used for recording people's preferences—may not help since there may not be a one-to-one correspondence between the

---

[1] A binary relation defined over any set A can be expressed as a set of ordered pair of elements belonging to A. Suppose, $A = \{x, y\}$, and we have a binary relation T defined over A such that $xTx \ \& \ yTy \ \& \sim (xTy) \ \& \sim (yTx)$. Then the binary relation T can be represented by the set of ordered pairs $\{[x, x], [y, y]\}$. On this, see Suppes, Chapter 10.

[2] See Majumdar [1], and also Rothenberg.

pattern of voting behaviour and people's preferences.[1] I shall, however, ignore these problems and assume that the 'true' preferences of the individuals are known somehow or other.

When I want to indicate simply a weak preference relation without specifying whose preference it is, I shall use the notation $\bar{R}_i$ and also $\bar{R}$. In particular, it may be worth emphasizing that $\bar{R}_i$ does not necessarily refer to the weak preference of the ith individual, or to any individual preference at all. The same is true of $\bar{R}$ also. $\bar{P}_i$ and $\bar{I}_i$ will stand for the strict preference and indifference relations corresponding to $\bar{R}_i$. Thus $x\bar{P}_i y$ if and only if $[x\bar{R}_i y \,\&\sim (y\bar{R}_i x)]$; and $x\bar{I}_i y$ if and only if $[x\bar{R}_i y \,\& \, y\bar{R}_i x]$. Similarly, for $\bar{P}$ and $\bar{I}$.

Like R_i, $\bar{R}_i$ and $\bar{R}$ are also binary relations defined over S. I now define certain properties of binary relations.[2]

DEFINITION 1.1.   *Let T be any binary relation defined over S.*

(i)   *T is reflexive over S if and only if for all x belonging to S, xTx.*

(ii)   *T is connected over S if and only if for all x and y $(x \neq y)$ belonging to S, $[xTy \lor yTx]$.*

(iii)   *T is transitive over S if and only if for all x, y, and z belonging to S, $[(xTy \,\& \, yTz) \to xTz]$.*

(iv)   *T is quasi-transitive over S if and only if for all x, y, and z belonging to S, $[\{xTy \,\&\sim (yTx)\} \,\& \,\{yTz \,\&\sim (zTy)\}]$ implies $\{xTz \,\&\sim (zTx)\}$.*

(v)   *T is asymmetrical over S if and only if for all x and y belonging to S, $[xTy \to \,\sim (yTx)]$.*

(vi)   *T is anti-symmetric over S if and only if for all x and y belonging to S, $(xTy \,\& \, yTx)$ implies $(x = y)$.*

(vii)   *T is a complete ordering (or, in short, an ordering) over S if and only if it is reflexive, connected and transitive over S.*

(viii)   *T is a complete linear ordering (or, in short, a linear ordering) over S if and only if it is reflexive, connected, transitive, and anti-symmetric over S.*

When T is interpreted as a weak preference relation $\bar{R}_i$, the intuitive meaning of these properties becomes obvious. Two points, however, deserve some comment. By the definitions of quasi-transitivity and $\bar{P}_i$ it follows that $\bar{R}_i$ is quasi-transitive over

---

[1] See Sen[2].   [2] See Suppes, Chapter 10.

S if and only if $\bar{P}_i$ is transitive over S. Again, by the definitions of antisymmetry and the indifference relation $\bar{I}_i$ it follows that $\bar{R}_i$ is antisymmetric if and only if the indifference relation $\bar{I}_i$ does not hold between any two *distinct* elements belonging to S.

Throughout this book (except for Chapter 8) it will be assumed that every individual weak preference relation is a complete ordering over S, i.e., for all i, R_i satisfies reflexivity, connectedness, and transitivity over S. These assumptions should be regarded as descriptions of individual preferences as they actually are; they are not to be interpreted in any normative sense. In other words, they are meant to be approximations of reality rather than rules of *rational* behaviour of individuals. The relevance of these assumptions will be discussed in Chapter 8 where also I shall consider certain implications of relaxing the assumption of transitive individual preferences.

The following lemma is due to Sen [7]:

LEMMA 1.1. *Let $\bar{R}_i$ be any binary, reflexive, and connected weak preference relation defined over S. Then*

(i) *$\bar{R}_i$ is transitive over S if and only if $\bar{R}_i$ is quasi-transitive and $\bar{I}_i$ is transitive over S.*

(ii) *$\bar{R}_i$ is quasi-transitive over S if and only if for all x, y, and z belonging to S, $[(x\bar{P}_i y \ \& \ y\bar{R}_i z) \to x\bar{R}_i z)]$.*

1.3. *Social Preferences*

Let N be the total number of individuals in the society. For each individual we have a complete ordering of the alternatives in S. Thus we have a set of N individual orderings $\{R_1, ..., R_N\}$. These orderings are to be aggregated so as to arrive at the social preferences. Let R stand for the social weak preference relation. For all x, and y belonging to S, xRy indicates that x is socially at least as good as y. xPy if and only if $[xRy \ \& \sim (yRx)]$; and xIy if and only if $[xRy \ \& \ yRx]$. P and I are thus the strict preference and indifference relations corresponding to R. Given our premise that social decision should be based on individual preferences, R should, in some sense or other, be determined by individual preferences. This relation between R and the individual preferences is what I seek to make precise through the following definitions.

DEFINITION 1.2. *A Rule is a functional relation f the range of which is a set of binary weak preference relations defined over S and the domain of which is a class of ordered sets of binary weak preference relations defined over S.* The following notation will be adopted:

$$\bar{R} = f(\bar{R}_1, ..., \bar{R}_n).$$

DEFINITION 1.3. *A group decision Rule is a Rule f the range of which is a set of social weak preference relations and the domain of which is a class of ordered sets of individual weak preference relations (one weak preference relation for each individual).*[1] We write

$$R = f(R_1, ..., R_N).$$

Thus given a set of individual weak preference relations (one relation for each individual) the group decision Rule specifies one and only one social weak preference relation. When it is clear from the context that it is a group decision Rule that is under consideration, I shall simply speak of a Rule without the qualifying phrase.

Note that no restriction has been imposed on the binary weak preference relations belonging to the range of a group decision Rule. For example, some R in the range of a group decision Rule may violate connectedness, i.e. for some x and y we may have $[\sim (xRy)\ \&\sim (yRx)]$. In other words, for certain sets of individual orderings, x and y may be non-comparable under a group decision Rule. In such a case, the group decision Rule does not provide any basis for social choice when the set $\{x, y\}$ is the set from which choice is to be made. Again, R may be connected but we may have $[xPy\ \&\ yPx\ \&\ zPx]$. Here also the group decision Rule does not provide any guidance regarding social choice out of the set $\{x, y, z\}$ since for every alternative in $\{x, y, z\}$, there exists a socially better alternative in the same set. To avoid these difficulties we may require our group decision Rule to define socially best alternatives for every non-empty subset of the set of alternatives S. The following definition makes precise the notion of a socially best alternative in a given set.

[1] See Sen [7].

DEFINITION 1.4. *For any given subset A of S, the choice set $C(A)$ is defined as follows:*

$$(\forall x)\,[\{x \in C(A)\} \leftrightarrow \{(x \in A)\ \&\ (\forall y)\,((y \in A) \rightarrow xRy)\}].^{[1]}$$

Thus $C(A)$ is a subset of A and every element of $C(A)$ is socially at least as good as every element in A. In other words, $C(A)$ is the set of socially best alternatives in A. The concept of a choice set needs to be distinguished from the concept of a maximal set.

DEFINITION 1.5. *For any given subset A of S, the maximal set $M(A)$ is defined as follows:*

$$(\forall x)\,[\{x \in M(A)\} \leftrightarrow \{(x \in A)\ \&\ (\forall y)\,((y \in A) \rightarrow\ \sim (yPx))\}].$$

Thus $M(A)$ is the set of alternatives in A such that there does not exist any socially better alternative in A. For example if we have $[\sim (xRy)\ \&\ \sim (yRx)]$ then $M(\{x, y\}) = \{x, y\}$ since neither x is better than y nor y is better than x. $C(\{x, y\})$, however, is empty in this case.

LEMMA 1.2. *For any given R and any subset A of the set S*
  (i) $C(A) \subset M(A)$.
  (ii) $C(A) = M(A)$ *if R is reflexive and connected over A.*
  PROOF:
  (i) Let $x \in C(A)$. Then by definition of $C(A)$, $x \in A$ and also xRy for all y belonging to A. It follows that for all y belonging to A, $\sim (yPx)$. Hence $x \in M(A)$. Since this is true for all x belonging to $C(A)$, it follows that $C(A) \subset M(A)$.
  (ii) Let R be reflexive and connected over S. Let $x \in M(A)$. Then $(\forall y)\,[(y \in A) \rightarrow\ \sim (yPx)]$. By the reflexivity and connectedness of R, it follows that $(\forall y)\,[(y \in A) \rightarrow xRy]$. Therefore $x \in C(A)$. Since this is true for all x belonging to $M(A)$, it follows that if R is reflexive and connected then $M(A) \subset C(A)$. But we have seen that $C(A) \subset M(A)$. Therefore, if R is reflexive and connected $C(A) = M(A)$.   Q.E.D.
  I shall be mainly concerned with choice sets and not with maximal sets. The existence of a non-empty maximal set in itself does not give any definite basis for social choice. To take the example considered earlier, let $A = \{x, y\}$. Let

$$[\sim (xRy)\ \&\ \sim (yRx)].$$

---

[1] See Arrow [1], p. 15.

Here $M(A) = A = \{x, y\}$. However, we do not know which of the two alternatives is to be chosen since they are socially non-comparable. Only the existence of a non-empty choice set provides a clear basis for social decision. The maximal set is of interest in so far as the elements of the choice set are to be searched for among the elements of the maximal set.

DEFINITION 1.6. *Let A be any subset of S. A social choice function (SCF) defined over A is a functional relation that defines a non-empty choice set for every non-empty subset of A.*[1]

When from the context it is clear that it is a social choice function that is being referred to, I shall simply use the phrase 'choice function' omitting the term 'social'.

If we have a social choice function defined over S, then no matter which subset of S may be available to choose from, an unambiguous social decision can be made.[2] Therefore, it is desirable that every R in the range of a group decision Rule should generate a choice function, i.e., a group decision Rule should define socially best alternatives for every non-empty subset of S. Such a group decision Rule will be called a social decision function.

DEFINITION 1.7. *A social decision function (SDF) is a group decision Rule such that every social weak preference relation in its range generates a social choice function over S.*

It is clear that if R violates reflexivity or connectedness over S, then no social choice function could possibly be generated by R. Suppose, for some x belonging to S, $\sim (xRx)$. Then $C(\{x\})$ will be empty. Again, suppose for some x and y $(x \neq y)$ belonging to S, $[\sim (xRy)\ \&\ \sim (yRx)]$. In this case $C(\{x, y\})$ will be empty. Thus no choice function can be generated by R if it violates reflexivity or connectedness. However, reflexivity and connectedness of R are not sufficient for R to generate a social choice function. This can be easily seen by taking a reflexive R under which

$$(xPy\ \&\ yPz\ \&\ zPx).$$

---

[1] See Arrow [1], pp. 15–16.

[2] It is true that if the choice set $C(A)$ for the available set of alternatives A, has more than one element, then there still remains the problem as to which element of $C(A)$ should be chosen. This, however, is not a serious problem. *Any* element of $C(A)$ may be chosen since from the social point of view any element of $C(A)$ is just as good as any other.

R satisfies both reflexivity and connectedness over $\{x, y, z\}$. However, $C(\{x, y, z\})$ is empty and therefore R does not define a choice function over $\{x, y, z\}$. The following results lead to a necessary and sufficient condition for R to generate a choice function over S.

DEFINITION 1.8. *Let T be any binary relation defined over S.*

(i) *A T-cycle occurs in a subset A of S if and only if for some finite number of alternatives a_1, a_2, ..., a_n all belonging to A, we have $(a_1 T a_2$ & $a_2 T a_3$ & ... & $a_{n-1} T a_n$ & $a_n T a_1)$.*

(ii) *T is acyclic over a subset A of S if and only if no T-cycle occurs in A.*

(iii) *T is founded over a subset A of S if and only if there does not exist an infinitely long descending chain of the type*
$$(\dots \text{ & } a_3 T a_2 \text{ & } a_2 T a_1)$$
where ..., a_3, a_2, a_1 all belong to A.[1]

LEMMA 1.3. *Let T be a binary relation defined over S.*

(i) *T is founded over a subset A of S only if it is acyclic over A but the converse is not necessarily true.*

(ii) *If A is a finite subset of S, then T is founded over A if and only if it is acyclic over A.*

PROOF:

(i) Suppose a T-cycle occurs in A. Then for some finite number of alternatives $x_1, x_2, ..., x_n$ belonging to A we have $(x_1 T x_2$ & $x_2 T x_3$ & ... & $x_{n-1} T x_n$ & $x_n T x_1)$. We can now construct an infinitely long descending chain of the type
$$(\dots \text{ & } a_3 T a_2 \text{ & } a_2 T a_1)$$
by starting from the end of the chain and repeating the T-cycle $(x_1 T x_2$ & ... & $x_n T x_1)$ again and again:
$$[\dots \text{ & } (x_1 T x_2 \text{ & } \dots \text{ & } x_n T x_1) \text{ & } (x_1 T x_2 \text{ & } \dots \text{ & } x_n T x_1)].$$
Thus violation of acyclicity implies the violation of foundedness. Therefore R is founded over A only if it is acyclic over A. That the converse is not necessarily true follows from the fact that if A is an infinite set then we can have an infinitely long chain of the type $(\dots \text{ & } a_3 P a_2 \text{ & } a_2 P a_1)$ without any T-cycle being involved.

(ii) Suppose A is finite and T is acyclic over A. We shall show that T will be founded over A.

---

[1] See Quine, p. 141.

Suppose T violates foundedness over A. Then we have an infinitely long descending chain of the type $(\dots \,\&\, x_3 T x_2 \,\&\, x_2 T x_1)$, where $x_1, x_2, x_3, \dots$ all belong to A. But A being finite, there cannot be an infinite number of distinct alternatives $x_1, x_2, x_3, \dots$ all belonging to A. Therefore the infinitely long chain

$$(\dots \,\&\, x_3\, T x_2 \,\&\, x_2\, T x_1)$$

must have a finite segment $(x_n T x_{n-1} \,\&\, x_{n-1} T x_{n-2} \,\&\, \dots \,\&\, x_{r+1} T x_r)$ where $x_r = x_n$. This implies a T-cycle.

Thus if A is finite, T will be acyclic over A only if it is founded over A. Since by Lemma 1.3 (i) foundedness implies acyclicity, Lemma 1.3 (ii) follows. Q.E.D.

THEOREM 1.1. *A necessary and sufficient condition for R to generate a non-empty maximal set for every non-empty subset of S is that P should be founded over S.*

PROOF:

Sufficiency. Let P be founded over S. Let A be any subset of S. Consider first the case where A is a finite set. Suppose $M(A)$ is empty. Then for every alternative in A there exists a socially better alternative in A. Take any element of A and call it x_1. By hypothesis there exists a socially better alternative than x_1 in A. Take one such alternative and call it x_2. Clearly $x_2 \neq x_1$. For if $x_2 = x_1$, then by our hypothesis that $x_2 P x_1$, we shall have $x_1 P x_2$. In this case P will violate acyclicity, and, therefore, by Lemma 1.3 (i) it will violate foundedness. Now take x_3 such that $x_3 \in A$ and $x_3 P x_2$. Since $M(A)$ is empty such an x_3 exists. Also x_3 must be distinct from x_2 and x_1. For if x_3 is identical with x_2 or x_1, then it can be easily checked that P will violate acyclicity and therefore foundedness over S. Proceeding in this fashion, since A is finite we shall exhaust all the elements of A. Let the last element considered in this sequence be x_n. By the hypothesis that $M(A)$ is empty and by the foundedness of P, there must be an element of A which is socially better than A and which is distinct from $x_1, x_2, \dots, x_n$. But this is impossible since we have already exhausted all the elements of A. This contradiction shows that if A is finite and P is founded over A, then $M(A)$ must be non-empty.

Now consider the case where A is an infinite set. Take an element of A and call it x_1. By the same type of argument that was used in the earlier case, there exists x_2 in A such that x_2 is distinct from x_1 and $x_2 P x_1$. Similarly there exists x_3 in A such that x_3 is distinct from x_1 and x_2, and $x_3 P x_2$. Given the emptiness of $M(A)$ and the foundedness of P which implies the acyclicity of P, this sequence has to continue indefinitely. In this case, since A is infinite, we do not run into the difficulty of exhausting all the elements of A. However, if the sequence continues indefinitely, then we have an infinitely long descending chain

$$(\ldots \ \& \ x_4 P x_3 \ \& \ x_3 P x_2 \ \& \ x_2 P x_1).$$

But this violates the assumption that P is founded over A. Therefore, in this case also $M(A)$ must be non-empty.

Necessity. Suppose P is not founded over S. Then we have an infinitely long descending chain of the type

$$(\ldots \ \& \ x_3 P x_2 \ \& \ x_2 P x_1),$$

$x_1, x_2, x_3, \ldots$ all belonging to S. Consider any x_r involved in this chain, such that r is finite. If $x_r = x_j$ for some $j \leqslant r$, then the set $x_r, x_{r-1}, \ldots, x_j$ will clearly have an empty maximal set. If there does not exist a finite r such that for some j ($j \leqslant r$), $x_r = x_j$, then we have an infinitely long chain of the type $(\ldots \ \& \ x_3 P x_2 \ \& \ x_2 P x_1)$ where $x_1, x_2, x_3, \ldots$ are all distinct and belong to S. In this case, it is clear that S has an infinite subset with an empty maximal set. Thus in all cases, if P is not founded over S, then R fails to generate a non-empty maximal set for some subset of S.   Q.E.D.

THEOREM 1.2.   *R generates a choice function over S if and only if R is reflexive and connected, and P is founded over S.*

PROOF:

Sufficiency. Since P is founded, by Theorem 1.1 it generates a non-empty maximal set for every non-empty subset of S. Since R is also reflexive and connected, by Lemma 1.2 (ii), it follows that R generates a non-empty choice set for every non-empty subset of S. Hence R generates a choice function over S.

Necessity. We have already shown the necessity of the reflexivity and connectedness of R, for the existence of a social choice function over S. Therefore, we have only to show that if P is not founded, then R does not generate a choice function over S. If P is not founded, then by Theorem 1.1, the maximal set for some non-empty subset of S will be empty. By Lemma 1.2 (i) it follows

that if P is not founded, then R fails to generate a non-empty choice set for some non-empty subset of S. Hence it follows that if P is not founded over S, then no choice function is defined over S in terms of R.
                                                                    Q.E.D.

Theorem 1.2 is a generalized version of Lemma 1.1 of Sen [10], which shows that reflexivity and connectedness of R and acyclicity of P are together necessary and sufficient for R to generate a choice function over a finite set S. Two points should be noted here. Firstly, even when R does not generate a choice function over a particular set A, there may still be a non-empty choice set for A. This can be seen from the following examples. Let $A = \{x, y, z, w\}$ and let $[xRx \,\&\, xRy \,\&\, xRz \,\&\, xRw \,\&\, \sim (yRz) \,\&\, \sim (zRy)]$. R does not generate a choice function over A since $C(\{y, z\})$ is empty. Nevertheless, $x \in C(A)$. Similarly, if

$$[xRx \,\&\, xRy \,\&\, xRz \,\&\, xRw \,\&\, yPz \,\&\, zPw \,\&\, wPy],$$

then $C(\{x, y, z\})$ being empty, again R fails to generate a choice function over A. However $C(A)$ is non-empty since $x \in C(A)$. The motivation behind demanding a choice function over S is that no matter which subset of S is offered for choice, there should be a clear decision. In some real situations, however, we may be fairly confident that choice will be confined to some particular set of alternatives. In such a case so long as the particular set has a non-empty choice set, we may not be too depressed if there is no clear decision for some other subset of the set S which we may feel will never be offered as the set to choose from. Thus in certain situations we may be primarily interested in the choice set for a given subset A of S rather than in the social choice function defined over S or over A.

Secondly, it must be emphasized that R can generate a choice function over S even without satisfying transitivity or quasi-transitivity.[1] Since this is a point of considerable importance for our later discussion it may be elaborated a little further. Consider a reflexive R defined over $\{x, y, z\}$ such that $(xPy \,\&\, yPz \,\&\, xIz)$. R violates both transitivity and quasi-transitivity over $\{x, y, z\}$. However, it can be easily checked that every subset of $\{x, y, z\}$ has a non-empty choice set. Thus transitivity or quasi-transitivity of R is not a necessary condition for the existence of a choice

---

[1] See Sen [7].

function over S. Also it can be easily seen that even if R is a complete ordering over S still a social choice function may not be defined if S is an infinite set. Let S be an infinite set having for its elements $x_1, x_2, x_3, \ldots$. Let R be a complete ordering such that for all finite i, $x_{i+1}Px_i$. It is clear that we do not have a non-empty choice set for S since for each x_i belonging to S we can find an alternative in S which is socially preferred to x_i.

The following theorem, however, is true.

THEOREM 1.3. *If S is finite, then a sufficient condition for R to generate a choice function over S is that R should satisfy reflexivity, connectedness, and quasi-transitivity.*[1]

PROOF:

It will be shown that if R is quasi-transitive over S, then P must be founded over S. Suppose P is not founded over S. Since S is finite by Lemma 1.3 (ii) it follows that P is not acyclic over S. Then we must have a P-cycle of the type

$$(x_1Px_2 \ \& \ x_2Px_3 \ \& \ \ldots \ \& \ x_{n-1}Px_n \ \& \ x_nPx_1).$$

Since $x_1Px_2 \ \& \ x_2Px_3$ we have x_1Px_3 by the quasi-transitivity of R. Similarly from $(x_1Px_3 \ \& \ x_3Px_4)$ we have x_1Px_4. Proceeding thus we shall ultimately have $(x_1Px_{n-1} \ \& \ x_{n-1}Px_n \ \& \ x_nPx_1)$ which violates quasi-transitivity of R. Thus quasi-transitivity of R over S implies that P is founded over S. Therefore by Theorem 1.2 it follows that if R is reflexive, connected, and quasi-transitive, then R generates a choice function over the finite set S.

Q.E.D.

The following theorem follows immediately from Theorem 1.3 and Lemma 1.1 (i).

THEOREM 1.4. *If S is finite then a sufficient condition for R to generate a choice function over S is that R should be a complete ordering over S.*

It is thus clear that if S is finite, then a group decision Rule the range of which is a set of complete social orderings will necessarily be a SDF though the converse is not necessarily true. Such a group decision Rule will be called a social welfare function.

[1] See Sen [7]. See also Pattanaik [1].

Individual Preferences and Social Decision

DEFINITION 1.9. *A social welfare function (SWF) is a group decision Rule the range of which is a set of complete social orderings.*

If individual weak preference relations are complete orderings the definition of a SWF that is given above is equivalent to Arrow's [1] definition of a social welfare function. The term social welfare function was first introduced by Bergson ([1], [2]) who used it in a somewhat different sense from ours.[1] Since Bergson's social welfare function is closely related to the notion of a SWF as defined above, it may be useful to clarify the distinction between the two. In what follows I shall refer to the social welfare function as defined here simply as the social welfare function (SWF); the Bergson concept will be referred to as the Bergson social welfare function.

The Bergson social welfare function is a real valued function the arguments of which consist of magnitudes representing different aspects of a social state, and the values of which give the social welfare indices corresponding to different social states. It may be written as

$$W = W(\alpha_1, \alpha_2, ..., \alpha_n)$$

where $\alpha_1, \alpha_2, ..., \alpha_n$ stand for the different aspects of a social state (e.g., the amount of commodity C going to individual i, the amount of factor E employed by individual i in industry D, the foreign policy followed by the government and so on). Given a social state the values of $\alpha_1, ..., \alpha_n$ are known and then taking the individual preferences as given, the Bergson social welfare function assigns a real number as the welfare index of the social state. Presumably, for each configuration of individual preferences we shall have a set of Bergon welfare indices for the set of social states, and therefore a Bergson social welfare function. But it is obvious that each set of welfare indices will imply a complete social ordering. How is this complete ordering arrived at? It is here that the SWF enters the picture. For the *method* of deriving the complete ordering implied by a Bergson social welfare function is nothing other than a SWF. The converse, however, is not necessarily true; we cannot say that a SWF is necessarily implied by some Bergson social welfare function. This

[1] An extensive discussion of Bergson's concept of a social welfare function is also to be found in Samuelson.

16

is because the Bergson concept refers to a real valued function while a SWF gives us a complete social ordering of the social states. The existence of a complete social ordering, though a necessary condition for the existence of a real valued function of the Bergson type, is not a sufficient condition. We may, therefore, have situations where we have a complete social ordering, but no real valued function corresponding to the complete ordering.[1] We need not, however, be disturbed by such cases since the existence of a complete social ordering of the alternatives is enough for the purpose of social decision;[2] we do not need a real valued function in addition to the complete ordering. Even when a real valued function of the Bergson type exists, only its ordinal properties seem to be relevant for social choice.

[1] Lexicographic ordering of two-dimensional real space is a case in point. In this context see Sen [5]. For proof of the theorem that a lexicographic ordering of two-dimensional real space cannot be represented by a real valued function see Debreu, pp. 69–70.

[2] Strictly speaking, this is necessarily true only in the case of finite sets of alternatives. As we have seen, in the case of infinite sets of alternatives, even a complete social ordering may be inadequate for the existence of a social choice function.

2

VALUE JUDGMENTS AND THE
THEORY OF SOCIAL CHOICE

2.1. *Introduction*

In Chapter 1 a group decision Rule was defined as a functional relation between the set of individual weak preference relations and the social weak preference relation. No restriction has been imposed on the nature of this functional relation; the concept is perfectly general. For example, we can have a Rule under which, for all x and y, x is socially preferred to y if and only if every individual prefers y to x, or, we can have a Rule under which for all x and y, x is socially preferred to y whenever some particular individual prefers y to x. Absurd as these Rules seem to be, there is nothing in the concept of a Rule as such to rule out these possibilities. The crucial problem is, therefore, one of imposing 'reasonable' restrictions on the Rule. Should a Rule yield xPy whenever every individual prefers x to y? Should a Rule be non-dictatorial in the sense that R under the Rule does not always coincide with the preference pattern of some particular individual irrespective of the preference patterns of the rest of the individuals? Problems such as these are ethical in nature, and a basic function of any adequate theory of social choice is to investigate such problems. It is, therefore, surprising that in certain fields of study basically concerned with problems of group choice, there has been a marked reluctance to accept ethical judgments as part of the system. This is particularly true of Welfare Economics. The problem of aggregating individual preferences so as to arrive at social preference is central to Welfare Economics. Yet frequently attempts have been made to construct a value-free Welfare Economics on the ground that no rational argument is possible regarding value judgments. If this contention were correct, then it would have serious implications not only for Welfare Economics, but also for the theory of social choice in general. For, as it has been argued above, the problem

18

of social choice is essentially an ethical problem; if value judgments lie beyond the scope of rational argument then so will the theory of social choice. In view of the recent developments in ethics[1] I find it difficult to accept this position; I believe that in general, value judgments are subject to reasoning though the mode of reasoning is different from that in the case of empirical propositions. In this chapter I try to clarify these methodological problems regarding value judgments and their role in the theory of social choice.

2.2. *The Nature of Ethical Argument*

What exactly is a value judgment? The precise nature of value judgments has been the bone of contention among the different schools of Ethics. I shall, however, follow the highly persuasive account which has been advanced by Hare ([1], [2]) regarding the logic of value judgments. Hare's analysis explains the nature of value judgments by analysing what kind of speech one makes when one makes a value judgment. Consider the following statements:

(1) John has brown eyes.

(2) John is a good man.

(3) The decision of the majority should be enforced.

Propositions (2) and (3) are clearly different from proposition (1). Unlike proposition (1), they use prescriptive[2] language. The descriptive content, if any, does not exhaust their entire meaning; they have a prescriptive content as well. For example, when we say that John is a good man, we may or may not be describing a fact, but if we are using the words in their ordinary sense, then we are certainly commending John. Similarly statement (3) is prescribing the enforcement of the majority decision.

Statements (2) and (3), however, are similar to statement (1) in one fundamental respect. When we say that John's eyes are brown, there must be some reason for it. In other words, John's eyes must be having certain properties because of which we applied the descriptive term brown, and whenever some other

---

[1] For example, see Nowell-Smith, Hare ([1], [2]), and Sen[6].

[2] The term prescription is used in a broad sense to cover praise, commendation, exhortation, etc. To prescribe, if the prescription is sincere, involves what Nowell-Smith calls a pro-attitude.

2-2

object possesses the same properties, logically we are bound to say that that too is brown. It would be logically odd to say that *x* is brown but *y* which is similar to *x* in all relevant respects is not brown. Thus if *x* is brown, then *all* objects which are similar to *x* in all relevant respects are brown. Similarly when we say that John is a good man we cannot logically deny the proposition that all persons who resemble John in all relevant aspects are good. Again, if in a particular situation we say that the majority decision should be enforced, then the logic of the value terms compels us to say that in *all* situations which are similar to the given one in all relevant respects, the majority decision should be enforced. This is what Hare calls the 'universalizability' of a value judgment. The criteria because of which we prescribe something, and which provides the basis of universalizability, constitute what he calls the descriptive meaning of a prescriptive term.

Prescriptivity and universalizability constitute the essential features of a value judgment. Statements (2) and (3) both possess these features, and both are value judgments. Statement (1), however, is not a value judgment since it has no prescriptive content.[1] It is the prescriptive content of value judgments which has given rise to the frequently held view that unlike descriptive statements, value judgments cannot be rationally argued about. According to this view if John believes that majority decisions should be enforced and Steve believes that in the absence of unanimity a coin should be tossed to decide the issue, then all that they can do is to assert their respective beliefs; neither of them can possibly refute the position of the other. This is what seems to be implied by the classic statement of Robbins (p. 150): 'If we disagree about ends it is a case of thy blood or mine—or live and let live according to the importance of the difference, or the relative strength of the opponents.'

Since I believe that in general this position is not correct, I shall try to show how argument about value judgments need not be a case of 'thy blood or mine—or live and let live'. How do we argue about the value judgments involved in an ethical

---

[1] On the other hand, imperatives (e.g., commands), though prescriptive in nature, are not value judgments since they do not possess the feature of universalizability. On this point see Hare [1], pp. 175–9.

system?[1] It has been rightly pointed out that the methods of testing an empirical theory[2] are not applicable here. Nevertheless an analysis of the methods of testing an empirical theory is of relevance here since it sheds considerable light on the modes of reasoning about value judgments. Popper ([1], pp. 32–3) points out three different ways of testing an empirical theory. Firstly, we investigate the internal consistency of the system by logically comparing the conclusions among themselves. Secondly, we deduce conclusions from the theory and test them against experience. Thirdly, if the theory survives our first two tests, we consider whether it is an advancement over other competing theories which also satisfy the earlier tests. I shall argue below that methods of reasoning formally similar to these are applicable in the case of value judgments too.

Consider first the test of internal consistency. Obviously, we can test a system of value judgments for its internal consistency. We might have used a set of value premises which give us contradictory or contrary conclusions. In such a case the system is not internally consistent. Consider, for example, the famous compensation criterion of Kaldor in Welfare Economics. As demonstrated by Scitovsky[1], in certain situations it may lead to the conclusion that the social state a is better than b, and also that b is better than a.[3] These conclusions are obviously incompatible and therefore the analysis fails to satisfy the test of internal consistency.

Take another situation in which we use a set of value judgments which, taken together, are not logically compatible. The conditions 1' through 5 of Arrow[1] which I shall discuss in Chapter 3, provide the classic example of such a set. It is clear that such a system will fail to satisfy our test of internal consistency since from such a system we can draw *any* conclusion, including conclusions which contradict each other. The results of a test of

[1] Value judgments can be divided into two broad categories: ethical and non-ethical value judgments. The aesthetic judgment, 'This is a beautiful flower', may be cited as an example of the latter type. In what follows we shall be concerned with ethical value judgments only.

[2] Following Popper[1], I consider a strictly universal statement to be empirical if and only if it it falsifiable. In the case of strictly existential statements, however, the criterion adopted is that of verifiability.

[3] Scitovsky ([1], [2]) modifies Kaldor's criterion by introducing an additional condition. The modified criterion avoids the internal inconsistency referred to above.

internal consistency may sometimes be quite startling as in the case of Arrow[1]. For it may reveal that a set of values each of which highly appeals to us, lacks logical consistency; it will thus force us to reject or modify some of these values so as to render our value system logically consistent.

Popper's second test occupies a crucial place in the methodology of empirical sciences. Since I shall discuss a mode of argument over value judgments which has considerable formal similarity with this test, it may be useful to give a brief outline of the procedure involved. According to Popper a scientific hypothesis can never be verified though it may be falsified. This is because of the fact that a scientific hypothesis is a strictly universal proposition,[1] and we can never possibly examine all the cases covered by it. On the other hand, a single instance to the contrary can falsify it. We scrutinize these hypotheses with a view to falsifying them, and a hypothesis which survives such a scrutiny is confirmed, that is, accepted for the time being subject to possible falsification in the future. These attempts at falsification take the form of deducing conclusions from the hypothesis with the help of other accepted statements, and then finding out whether these conclusions are corroborated by experience or not. The empirical sciences thus appear to be constantly exploring for valid hypotheses, i.e., hypotheses which will survive our strongest efforts at falsification.

Is there any parallel form of argument with respect to value judgments? Consider the following illustrations:

(1) 'Real income is greater in situation A as compared with situation B if those who gain by the change from A to B can overcompensate those who lose'.
'Granted that the condition is fulfilled, would it still be correct to say that real income has increased, if the distribution became more unequal?'

(2) 'A more equal distribution of the existing collection of goods is always a social improvement.'

---

[1] 'Strictly universal' statements are those which cannot be expressed as the conjunction of a finite number of singular statements. 'All men are mortal' is such a statement. This can be contrasted with 'numerically universal' statements (e.g., 'All men living now are mortal') which, in principle, can be expressed as a conjunction of a finite number of singular statements.

Value Judgments

'Even if it involved one person's making as large a sacrifice as we can imagine so as to benefit another person by an infinitesimal amount?'

Both the illustrations have been taken from the literature of Welfare Economics. Illustration (1) refers to the compensation criterion of Kaldor and the criticism of it by Little[1]. Illustration (2) refers to the criterion proposed by Mishan[3] and the counterargument by Sen[1]. What Little and Sen are really trying to do is to deduce from the value judgments of Kaldor and Mishan other value judgments such that when confronted with the latter, Kaldor and Mishan would be unwilling to accept them, and, therefore, would be logically forced to abandon their original value judgments. Arguments about value judgments are typically of this type: Somebody advances a value judgment 'p'; we point out that 'p' entails 'q'; if he is unwilling to accept 'q' he is logically forced to abandon 'p' or to modify it. A slight variation is possible. It is possible that instead of the person being unwilling to accept 'q', 'q' conflicts with another value judgment 'r' which the person has explicitly introduced into his system. In such a case the person would be forced to abandon (or modify) either 'p' or 'r'.

But how do we derive 'q'? Consider again the examples given above. In both cases 'q' is derived by imposing a suitable factual restriction on the original value judgment. In Illustration (1) the factual restriction is introduced by visualizing a more specific situation where not only the original criterion is fulfilled but also there is an increase in inequality of distribution. In (2) the more specific judgment is derived by imposing a factual condition of different tastes in such a way that in the move towards equality one person suffers a great loss and the other gains but little. The process is similar to that of Popper, outlined above. In both cases we are deducing conclusions from the original hypotheses or value judgments. If these conclusions are not accepted, the hypotheses or the value judgments have to be abandoned, at least in their original forms.[1]

[1] The difference between the two procedures, which is important, should be noted. We reject a proposition deduced from an empirical hypothesis, on the basis of observation or experiment. But what makes a person reject a moral judgment is

Suppose, the man who advanced the original value judgment '*p*' was asked to justify it. He can do so by showing that '*p*' can be deduced from some more general value judgment '*m*'. In doing so he is actually adopting the same kind of procedure as outlined above. For

$$(m \to p) \to ((\sim p) \to (\sim m)).$$

Therefore a man who denies $\sim m$ (i.e., who accepts m) has also to deny $\sim p$ (i.e., to accept p). Thus an ethical argument is also an exploration, an exploration of value judgments with a view to assessing their acceptability by a thorough consideration of their consequences.

Two points should be noted here. First, let us assume that somebody holds a value judgment which he would not abandon or modify under *any* factual revision. This would be an instance of what Sen [6] calls a 'basic' value judgment. The method of argument outlined above does not apply to these 'basic' value judgments. Those who deny the arguability of value judgments are really referring to 'basic' value judgments, which, one can be sure, are extremely rare. Moreover, as Sen points out, it is impossible in practice to know if somebody has made a basic value judgment. For there is always the possibility that under some factual revision the person would abandon or modify the original value judgment. This is similar to the case of empirical sciences in which we can only conclusively falsify a strictly universal hypothesis but can never verify it conclusively since there is always the possibility of its being falsified in the future.

Secondly, how important for the validity of a theory involving value judgments is the fact that the author of the theory cannot accept a certain conclusion which we have deduced from his value premises by way of factual revision referred to above? The answer to this question will depend on the nature of the factual revision involved. If the specification proposed is extremely

his 'inclination'. If a man of normal sight and intellect, when faced with the phenomenon that a piece of stone left in the air falls to the ground, refuses to admit it, we can only say that either he is not telling what he believes or he does not know the use of some of the words involved. But the same cannot be said of Mishan, for example, if he persists in the value judgment that a more equal distribution of the existing goods will increase social welfare even if it involves very little additional benefit for one person at the cost of a huge sacrifice on the part of another.

improbable, the author may admit his value judgment to be non-basic with respect to the specification but may, at the same time, point out that it matters very little in practice since the situation visualized is extremely unlikely to occur to actual life.[1] Argument can then proceed on the factual level, regarding the likelihood of the situation suggested. Suppose, empirically there were reasons to believe that a situation which is better in terms of Kaldor's test than another situation, should be characterized by a more equal distribution. In such a case, the criticism mentioned, though it may demonstrate the original value judgment to be non-basic, would have little force in practice. The fact that we consider this to be a very pertinent criticism is partly due to the fact that we consider the question of distribution to be important in judgments of welfare and also partly due to the fact that the situation visualized by Little is, empirically viewed, not an improbable one.

We now come to the third test of Popper—that of judging the relative merits of two competing hypotheses. Here Popper's criterion is formulated in terms of the degree of falsifiability. A hypothesis which is falsifiable to a greater degree than a competing hypothesis is to that extent a better one. This is because a more falsifiable hypothesis possesses a greater empirical content than a less falsifiable one. From this it would follow that if the hypothesis h_1 entails the hypothesis h_2 but not vice versa and if both of them have been found internally consistent and corroborated by experience, then h_1 is preferred to h_2. In an ethical system, however, the position is, in some respects, just the reverse. Here we want to use as weak a value judgment as possible. If the value judgment 'p' entails the value judgment 'q', other things remaining the same, there is a presumption in favour of using the weaker value judgment 'q' rather than 'p' in the analysis. This is because 'q' can be more acceptable than 'p'. Any one who consents to 'p' will necessarily also consent to 'q' but the converse is not necessarily true. The same point can be put in a slightly different fashion. The set of all value judgments which

[1] Cf. Sen [6] who points out that 'admissible' factual revisions (i.e., factual revisions which prove to be unacceptable) need not necessarily be probable ones. Sen is concerned with the non-basicness as such of a value judgment while what I am considering here is the importance of such non-basicness, and for this the plausibility of the factual revision is relevant.

can be derived from 'q' will form a proper subset of all value judgments which can be derived from 'p'. It is therefore less likely that we shall find ourselves in disagreement with some consequence of 'q' than that we shall disagree with a consequence of 'p'.

2.3 *The Status of Value Judgments Regarding the Group Decision Rule*

Suppose an individual lays down certain value judgments which define a unique group decision Rule. Suppose that this individual's ordering of the alternative social states belongs to the set of individual orderings to be aggregated by the group decision Rule. What exactly is the status of the choice arrived at by the Rule, *vis-à-vis* the individual's ordering which together with other individual orderings constitutes the basis of such choice? If the decision reached by the Rule happens to be different from that implied by the ordering of the individual, why should the individual assent to the decision under the Rule?

In answering these questions it is useful to distinguish between two different senses in which one can speak of individual orderings of the social states. Consider the following two questions:

(1) Do you prefer x to y?

(2) Do you think that x is a better social state than y?

Will the answers to these two questions be identical? Not necessarily. For the standards of evaluation appealed to by the two questions are basically different. The answer to question (1) will express what may be called the subjective preferences[1] of individuals, i.e., their personal likings and dislikings; this is, in fact, what we ordinarily understand by the word 'preference'. The answer to question (2), however, will be a value judgment, and will express what may be called the ethical preference[2] of the individual. It is, of course, true that in answering question (1) the individual is free to employ whatever standards he likes. If he is a person who always prefers (in the usual sense of the word) what he thinks to be ethically right, then the distinction between the two orderings will be eliminated. But this does not always

---

[1] The term subjective preference has been taken from Harsanyi [2].

[2] The term ethical preference has been taken from Harsanyi [2]. Harsanyi uses the term in a somewhat different sense. For a discussion of Harsanyi's concept of ethical preference see Chapter 9.

happen: we do not always prefer what we consider to be ethically right. Otherwise, there would be no point in common statements of the type 'I should not do x instead of y although I prefer x to y'. The difference between subjective preference and ethical preference consists of the fact that ethical preference is characterized by universalizability whereas subjective preference does not possess this characteristic. If in a certain situation I say that I prefer x to y in the sense of wanting x rather than y, then I am *not* saying that everybody should want x rather than y in a similar situation. If, however, I say that x is a better social state than y, then I am laying down a universal, practical principle commending x rather than y to everybody faced with the problem of ranking the two alternatives.

Now consider an individual i who has accepted a certain set of value judgments V_i. Let V_i define a unique group decision Rule. If the individual's preference ordering is interpreted as referring to subjective preferences, then it is clear that there is no contradiction in the individual's accepting a decision in favour of x rather than y under the group decision Rule defined by V_i, even though R_i shows a preference for y over x. For, obviously there is no contradiction in saying that I like y rather than x, but for society it is x which should be chosen. But suppose the individual's ordering R_i is an ethical ordering and shows a preference for y over x while the Rule defined by V_i decides in favour of x. In this case also there is really no ethical contradiction when the individual accepts the decision of the Rule. All that it means is that R_i represents what has been called a 'non-compulsive' value judgment,[1] and that in a conflict between the values underlying R_i and V_i, V_i always wins. For example it is perfectly consistent for the individual to say:

x is better than y.	(1)
But the choice of x rather than y will go against the will of a majority of individuals.	(2)
Social choice should be made on the basis of majority decision.	(3)
Therefore y should be chosen rather than x.	(4)

[1] See Sen [6] for a detailed discussion of the distinction between compulsive and non-compulsive value judgment.

(1) corresponds to R_i. (3) represents a value judgment regarding the Rule. Given (2), (3) conflicts with (1). In this conflict the individual gives priority to (3) and thus arrives at the prescriptive judgment (4). There is, therefore, no real ethical contradiction of the type in which the individual may seem to be involved, at first sight.

2.4. *Value Judgments and Welfare Economics*

In the light of what I have said above I shall now consider certain methodological issues which have often been raised in Welfare Economics. We cannot, however, discuss the methodology of a particular branch of study unless we have defined it, at least tentatively. For our purpose, Welfare Economics will be considered to be that branch of Economics which is essentially concerned with policy recommendations. The policies it considers are presumably ' economic', though the distinction between economic and non-economic policies is by no means clear. If each policy is assumed to have a definite consequence in terms of social states,[1] this amounts to saying that the problem of choosing the best social state in different choice situations is crucial to Welfare Economics. This, of course, is a definition, and like any other definition, it is to be accepted or rejected by reference to its usefulness and current usage. Some writers (e.g., Archibald) have taken exception to it, and I shall presently discuss their objection. But it is necessary first to clarify certain implications of this definition.

Prescription, in a broad sense of the term, can be made in many ways. Commands, exhortation, requests, etc. all involve prescriptive elements. In Welfare Economics, however, we are not concerned with such imperatives; the policy prescription typically assumes the form of a value judgment. But how do Welfare Economists arrive at these prescriptions embodied in value judgments? Take, for example, the prescription that disparity in income distribution should be reduced. Suppose somebody described to us all the effects (if that is possible) of a

---

[1] This is a restrictive assumption. A particular policy, for example, may be associated with several possible consequences of known probabilities. Alternatively, there may be complete uncertainty regarding the consequences of a policy. These complications will, however, be ignored in the following discussion.

reduction in the disparity in income distribution. We are told that it will increase the longevity of certain sections of people, that it will reduce the number of strikes, and so on. But can we deduce from these factual premises the value judgment that inequality in income distribution should be reduced? We cannot do so unless we add the further premise that these effects are, in aggregate, good or desirable for society, just as we cannot deduce the proposition that John should study hard from the purely factual proposition that studying hard will fetch him higher grades in the examination unless we had the further premise that securing higher grades in the examination is a good thing. If value judgments in the set of premises are frequently suppressed in actual life, it is because we think them to be too obvious to need an explicit statement. But this fact should not make us forget that they are there, implicit in the background.

In fact, this only refers to the famous law of Hume—that an 'ought'-proposition cannot be deduced from a set of 'is'-propositions; to deduce an 'ought'-proposition we need at least one 'ought'-proposition in the set of premises.[1] Since Welfare Economics is, according to my definition, concerned with policy recommendations, and since policy recommendations belong to the class of value judgments, it follows that Welfare Economics, if it is to derive its conclusions legitimately, must make use of value judgments in its set of premises.

In other words, value judgments are essential for Welfare Economics since Welfare Economics seeks to explore the problem of what constitutes the best alternative for society in various situations, which is basically an ethical problem. We may now compare this with the stand taken by Little ([1], pp. 79–80):

> Welfare economics and ethics cannot, then, be separated. They are inseparable because the welfare terminology is a value terminology. It may be suggested that welfare economics could be purged by the strict use of a technical

[1] Sen [3] has demonstrated that Hume's Law is not consistent with the view that value judgments are universalizable prescriptive judgments—a view to which I have subscribed above. To be more precise, what Sen has proved is that if value judgments are universalizable prescriptive judgments, then there exists a value judgment which can be derived from purely factual premises. This logically important result may, however, be ignored for our purposes.

terminology, which, in ordinary speech, had no value implications. The answer is that it could be, but it would no longer be welfare economics. It would then consist of an uninterpreted system of logical deductions, which would not be about anything at all....

The second sentence of the passage quoted is rather misleading. It might appear that according to Little value judgments are indispensable in Welfare Economics because the terminology used in Welfare Economics is a value terminology. This way of putting the matter seems to confuse the issue. Surely the fact that Welfare Economics uses a particular terminology is not important in itself? The value terminology in our language performs a typical function—that of offering guidance in a situation involving choice. Thus normally one does not speak of good mistakes since in the ordinary sense of the terms the problem of choice in connection with mistakes does not arise. If in Welfare Economics we use the words, 'good', 'desirable', 'welfare', etc., it is because, given the purpose of Welfare Economics, we need to use them. The value terminology in Welfare Economics only reflects the basic concern of welfare economists—policy prescription, which cannot be done without value judgments being involved. Little, however, does clarify his position more acceptably:

> What, after all, is the object of welfare economics? Surely it is to find out what is the best thing to do in various situations.[1]

and more clearly again

> Yet people study economic welfare largely for the purpose of discovering the best thing to do, and for making recommendations. It was therefore not unnatural that welfare economists should, without realizing it, restore the ethical force which descriptive happiness judgments now seemed to lack.[2]

[1] Little[1], p. 81.
[2] Little[1], p. 79. Nevertheless the emphasis on the value terminology as such, at a crucial step in the argument was rather unfortunate since it is likely to confuse, as is clear from the interpretation put upon the passage by Archibald.

Value Judgments

If the basic reason for the use of value judgments is the fact that we want to prescribe, it will not do to replace the value terminology by a strictly technical terminology. The technical terminology cannot perform the task of giving guidance in a situation involving choice; it will thus fail to carry out the aims with which we started. The entire system will cease to be Welfare Economics (as defined by us); but this will be so not because, as Little says, it would be an uninterpreted system of logical deductions, but because the system, though admitting a positive interpretation, will fail to give conclusions with prescriptive force. Suppose, for example, instead of saying that welfare increases if at least one person is better off without anybody else being worse off we say that α increases if at least one person is better off without anybody being worse off, and then carry out an investigation into the policies that will increase α. The system which we shall have thus constructed will not be an uninterpreted one but the conclusion will definitely lack prescriptive force, for to say that a certain policy will increase α will not entail that the policy is desirable.

We would have the same result if instead of α, we used the term welfare but used the phrase 'increase in welfare' as a shorthand expression for indicating a situation where at least one person is better off without anybody else becoming worse off, i.e., if by definition we divested the term of its prescriptive content and identified its *meaning* with some criterion.[1] In this context any emphasis on the value terminology as such, as being responsible for the ethical character of Welfare Economics, is likely to be misleading since it tends to shift attention from the crucial issue. It is likely to suggest the line of thought that if value terminology in itself were the only obstacle in making Welfare Economics a positive science, then Welfare Economics could be converted into positive analysis by dispensing with the value terminology and providing what have been called 'nominalistic' definitions of the relevant terms.[2] In fact, this was the course

[1] See Hare ([1], Chapter 6) for a distinction between the meaning of a value term and the criterion for using it.

[2] A nominalistic definition arises where we start with a particular expression and find out a short and convenient substitute for it. Thus the word 'man' may be used as a mere shorthand expression for the longer expression 'rational animal'. In an essentialistic definition we start with the term 'man' itself and try to describe the intuitive meaning of the term through the definition of 'man' as a 'rational animal'. See Popper [2], Chaper 11, esp. pp. 13–14.

taken by Archibald.[1] This, of course, would create a gulf between economic analysis and policy prescription, a gulf to be bridged by the introduction of value judgments as to whether we should increase welfare thus defined.

If Archibald's purpose were only to divide up the business of Welfare Economics into two parts, one part being concerned with a positive analysis of the different policies which can be adopted to promote, say, α, β, etc. and the other part being concerned with the problem as to whether α or β should be maximized, then one would have little to quarrel with his analysis.[2] But in Archibald's Welfare Economics prescription is, by definition, ruled out. If anybody wants to prescribe he has to introduce his own value judgments; as welfare economists in Archibald's sense we need not bother about whether α should be maximized or β.

But what are the advantages in eschewing all policy prescriptions from Welfare Economics and in replacing the so-called essentialistic definitions by nominalistic ones?[3] The basic objection of Archibald to introduction of value judgments into economics and also to the use of essentialistic definitions seems to be based on the contention that it is not possible to argue rationally about value judgments. 'Given the starting point if the logic is correct the results is universal truth. And we can only question the starting point by saying 'That's not how I should define Welfare'. Reply: 'It suits me'. This is an argument of the 'It is: it isn't variety...'[4] Archibald is, of course, reiterating the classic Robbinsian view about the futility of arguing about ends. But this is precisely the view which we have found to be unacceptable.

It is, of course, possible to take the stand that irrespective of whether value judgments are rationally arguable or not, the economist *qua* economist should have nothing to do with value

---

[1] The reason why Archibald has been singled out for criticism here is that his paper gives one of the clearest and most cogent exposition of the views of the 'anti-value' school.

[2] It is, however, difficult to see what exactly will be gained by such circumlocution.

[3] The two positions are logically connected. If we want to avoid all prescriptions we must divest all our terms of their value content. This can be done by providing nominalistic definitions. On the other hand, if we define words like 'welfare' nominalistically, it is not possible to derive policy prescriptions from our analysis.   [4] Archibald, p. 319.

judgments. As 'welfare economists' we shall, of course, save ourselves a good deal of trouble associated with policy prescription, if we simply refuse to have anything to do with that sort of thing. But note that we are not solving the problem; we are only stowing it away by a trick of definition. There does not seem to be any reason for doing so, especially when the value judgments relate to matters typically dealt with by economists.

In actual practice value judgments have been used by welfare economists. The well known Pareto Criterion which constitutes the basis of so much of Welfare Economics is nothing but a value judgment, though a weak one. Together with the factual premises, the value judgments constitute the set of premises from which the conclusions of Welfare Economics are derived by the methods of logical inference. Facts, values and logic are thus the three elements which characterize the structure of any piece of welfare analysis, and there can be rational argument with respect to each of these three elements. But it is true that despite the formal similarity between the mode of argument regarding value premises, and that regarding factual premises, the two are basically different. It is, therefore, of utmost importance that the two sets of premises should be explicitly stated so as to avoid any possible confusion on this account. This has not always been done by welfare economists. Attempts have often been made to do away with value premises altogether, and to deduce conclusions about social welfare from factual propositions alone, which is clearly an impossible task. Sometimes again, value premises have been introduced but care has not been taken to keep them distinct from the factual premises, and this has resulted in misunderstanding and confusion. From this point of view, the social welfare function of Bergson ([1], [2]) was an important theoretical construction: it provided a general framework within which the implications of different sets of value judgments could be conveniently worked out.

In Chapter 1 I have already referred to Bergson's concept of a social welfare function. As seen there, the Bergson social welfare function is a real valued function which attaches a welfare index to each social state, given the different magnitudes representing different aspects of the social state under consideration, and given the individual preferences. The most important thing to be noted is that nothing whatsoever is specified as regards the form of the function: it is left to be determined by the value judgments which may be considered relevant. The Bergson social welfare function is thus a perfectly general tool into which one can feed any set of value judgments and get the results accordingly.

This concept of a social welfare function served to achieve conceptual clarification in so far as it brought out the basic importance of value judgments in the context of policy pre-scription, and at the same time isolated these value judgments by leaving the form of the function to be exclusively determined by them. But it raised certain fundamental questions. What are the value judgments which determine the shape of the Bergson social welfare function? How do we get these value judgments? These are the questions which would appear to be crucial in Bergson's framework. Yet no answer to these questions is pro-vided, for the starting point of the analysis consists of values given somehow or other to the welfare economist. Samuelson (p. 221) in his discussion of the Bergson concept, is particularly explicit on this point: 'Without enquiring into its origin, we take as a starting point for our discussion a function of all the economic magnitudes of a system which is supposed to characterize some ethical belief—that of a benevolent despot, or a complete egotist, or 'all men of good will', a misanthrope, the state, race, or group mind, God, etc. Any possible opinion is admissible...'. To take the relevant values as given, however, is to ignore the basic problem of social choice. Therefore, the Bergson approach, while important in clearing up an enormous amount of con-fusion in Welfare Economics, regarding the role of value judg-ments, seems to leave us in an ethical vaccuum.

Arrow's[1] seminal work may be regarded as an attempt to fill up this vaccuum. Arrow is concerned with the SWF. As we have seen, underlying every Bergson social welfare function there must be a SWF, but Arrow goes beyond the Bergson formulation when he explores the desirable properties that a SWF should satisfy. In the next chapter I shall discuss the properties that Arrow requires a SWF to satisfy, and the problem that arises from the restrictions that he imposes on SWFs.

3

THE SEARCH FOR A
SATISFACTORY GROUP DECISION
RULE: ARROW'S DILEMMA

3.1. *The Pareto Criterion*

One value judgment that has been extensively discussed in Welfare Economics concerns the pattern of social preference when individual preferences do not conflict. If everyone in the society prefers x to y it will be generally agreed that x should be socially chosen rather than y. Even a stronger value judgment seems to be universally acceptable; if every individual in the society considers x to be at least as good as y and at least one individual strictly prefers x to y, then probably everybody would agree that society should choose x rather than y. Similarly, if everyone is indifferent between two alternatives x and y, then it seems reasonable that society should be indifferent between x and y. Weak as these restrictions on the group decision Rule seem to be, a considerable volume of Welfare Economics has been built around them. I shall consider below these restrictions and certain related concepts.

DEFINITION 3.1.   *Let π be any set of weak preference relations*

$$\{\bar{R}_1, \bar{R}_2, ..., \bar{R}_n\}$$

defined over S. Let A be any subset of S.

(i) *For all x and y belonging to S, $xQ_\pi y$ if and only if $x\bar{R}_i y$ for all $\bar{R}_i$ belonging to π.*

(ii) *For all x and y belonging to S, $x\bar{Q}_\pi y$ if and only if*

$$[xQ_\pi y \ \& \sim (yQ_\pi x)].$$

(iii) *For all x and y belonging to S, $x\bar{\bar{Q}}_\pi y$ if and only if $x\bar{P}_i y$ for all $\bar{R}_i$ belonging to π.*

(iv) *For all x, $[x \in A_\pi^*]$ if and only if*

$$[(x \in A) \ \& \sim (\exists y)\{(y \in A) \ \& \ (y\bar{Q}_\pi x)\}].$$

Search for Group Decision Rule:

When π refers to the set of individual weak preference relations under consideration I shall omit the subscript π and simply write Q, $\bar{Q}$, $\bar{\bar{Q}}$, and A^*, rather than Q_π, $\bar{Q}_\pi$, $\bar{\bar{Q}}_\pi$, and A^*_π.

LEMMA 3.1. *Let π be any set of weak preference relations $\{\bar{R}_1, ..., \bar{R}_n\}$ defined over S.*

(i) *For all x and y belonging to S, $[x\bar{\bar{Q}}_\pi y \rightarrow x\bar{Q}_\pi y]$.*

(ii) *If every $\bar{R}_i$ belonging to π is quasi-transitive over S, then $\bar{\bar{Q}}_\pi$ is transitive over S.*

(iii) *If every $\bar{R}_i$ belonging to π is transitive over S, then $\bar{Q}_\pi$ is transitive over S.*

(iv) *If every $\bar{R}_i$ belonging to π is transitive over S, then for every finite subset A of S, A^*_π is non-empty.*

PROOF:

(i) The proof follows directly from the definitions of $\bar{\bar{Q}}_\pi$ and $\bar{Q}_\pi$.

(ii) Suppose $x\bar{\bar{Q}}_\pi y$ and $y\bar{\bar{Q}}_\pi z$. Then by definition $(\forall i)$ $(x\bar{P}_i y)$ and $(\forall i)$ $(y\bar{P}_i z)$. Since every $\bar{R}_i$ is quasi-transitive, every $\bar{P}_i$ is transitive. Hence it follows that $(\forall i)$ $(x\bar{P}_i z)$. Therefore, $x\bar{\bar{Q}}_\pi z$.

(iii) Suppose $x\bar{Q}_\pi y$ and $y\bar{Q}_\pi z$. By definition, $x\bar{Q}_\pi y$ implies $[xQ_\pi y \,\&\sim (yQ_\pi x)]$ which in turn implies

$$[(\forall i)\,(x\bar{R}_i y) \,\&\, (\exists j)\,(x\bar{P}_j y)].$$

Similarly $(y\bar{Q}_\pi z)$ implies $[(\forall i)\,(y\bar{R}_i z) \,\&\, (\exists j)\,(y\bar{P}_j z)]$. Since every $\bar{R}_i$ is transitive, from

$$[(\forall i)\,(x\bar{R}_i y) \,\&\, (\exists j)\,(x\bar{P}_j y)] \quad \text{and} \quad [(\forall i)\,(y\bar{R}_i z) \,\&\, (\exists j)\,(y\bar{P}_j z)]$$

it follows that $[(\forall i)\,(x\bar{R}_i z) \,\&\, (\exists j)\,(x\bar{P}_j z)]$. Hence

$$[xQ_\pi z \,\&\sim (zQ_\pi x)]$$

which implies $x\bar{Q}_\pi z$.

(iv) Let $x_1 \in A$. Either $x_1 \in A^*_\pi$ or $(\exists a)$ $(a \in A \,\& \, a\bar{Q}_\pi x_1)$. If $x_1 \in A^*_\pi$, then A^*_π is non-empty. Suppose $\sim (x_1 \in A^*_\pi)$. Then assume that $(x_2 \in A \,\& \, x_2\bar{Q}_\pi x_1)$. x_2 must be distinct from x_1 since from the definition of $\bar{Q}_\pi$ it is clear that $\bar{Q}_\pi$ is asymmetric over S. Either $x_2 \in A^*_\pi$ or $(\exists a)$ $(a \in A \,\& \, a\bar{Q}_\pi x_2)$. If $x_2 \in A^*_\pi$, then A^*_π is non-empty. Suppose $\sim (x_2 \in A^*_\pi)$. Then assume that $[x_3 \in A \,\& \, x_3\bar{Q}_\pi x_2]$. Since $[x_3\bar{Q}_\pi x_2 \,\& \, x_2\bar{Q}_\pi x_1]$, and since by Lemma 3.1 (iii) $\bar{Q}_\pi$ is transitive over S, we have $x_3\bar{Q}_\pi x_1$. Since $x_3\bar{Q}_\pi x_2$ and $x_3\bar{Q}_\pi x_1$, by the asymmetry of $\bar{Q}_\pi$ it follows that x_3 is distinct from x_1 and x_2. Now $x_3 \in A^*_\pi$

or $(\exists a)\, (a \in A \,\&\, a\bar{Q}_\pi x_3)$. Continuing like this, since A is finite, we shall ultimately arrive at $\tilde{x}$ such that $\tilde{x} \in A^*_\pi$.   Q.E.D.

DEFINITION 3.2.

   (i) *Weak Pareto Criterion:*

$$(\forall x)\, (\forall y)\, [(x\bar{\bar{Q}}y \to xPy) \,\&\, \{(xQy \,\&\, yQx) \to xIy\}]$$

  (ii) *Strict Pareto Criterion:*

$$(\forall x)\, (\forall y)\, [(x\bar{Q}y \to xPy) \,\&\, \{(xQy \,\&\, yQx) \to xIy\}]$$

 (iii) *Pareto Optimality:*
For any subset A of S, A^* is the set of Pareto optimal alternatives and $(A - A^*)$ is the set of Pareto inoptimal alternatives.

Thus the Strict Pareto Criterion amounts to saying that if everyone is indifferent between x and y, then so is society; and if everyone considers x to be at least as good as y and at least one individual strictly prefers x to y, then society strictly prefers x to y. Under the Weak Pareto Criterion, if everyone is indifferent between x and y, then society is also indifferent between x and y; and if everyone strictly prefers x to y, then society strictly prefers x to y.[1]

The following lemma follows immediately from Lemma 3.1 (i).

LEMMA 3.2.   *The Strict Pareto Criterion implies the Weak Pareto Criterion.*

The Strict Pareto Criterion[2] is a property of the group decision Rule and not a group decision Rule by itself. This is because it gives only a sufficient condition for social strict preference and for social indifference, rather than a necessary and sufficient condition for social weak preference. In fact, a large number of group decision Rules satisfy the Strict Pareto Criterion; whenever for some alternatives x and y one individual prefers x to y and another prefers y to x, the Strict Pareto Criterion becomes non-applicable for the comparison between x and y, and any social decision as between x and y becomes compatible with the Strict Pareto Criterion.

   [1] These criteria are associated with Pareto. Hence the names 'Strict Pareto Criterion' and 'Weak Pareto Criterion'.

   [2] In the rest of this section I shall discuss the Strict Pareto Criterion. It will, however, be clear that similar remarks apply to the Weak Pareto Criterion also.

This, in fact, is the basic difficulty with the Strict Pareto Criterion; it is too weak to take us very far. As noted above, it is universally acceptable, and as such it is useful in narrowing down the range of alternatives within which the socially best alternatives should be looked for. If A is the set from which choice is to be made, then under any group decision Rule satisfying the Strict Pareto Criterion, the choice set $C(A)$ must be a subset of A^* which in turn is a subset of A. No element of $(A - A^*)$ can belong to $C(A)$, since for all x belonging to $(A - A^*)$ there exists y such that $y\bar{Q}x$, and under a group decision Rule satisfying the Strict Pareto Criterion $y\bar{Q}x$ implies yPx. Thus as a preliminary criterion the Strict Pareto Criterion is useful. But at the same time it is clear that no adequate theory of social choice can be constructed on such a slender basis. In real life we would expect conflict of individual strict preferences to be fairly common and it is precisely in these situations of conflict that the Strict Pareto Criterion does not tell us anything; the greater the degree of conflict the wider becomes the range over which the Strict Pareto Criterion is non-applicable. In any given situation the usefulness of the Strict Pareto Criterion would depend on the size of A^* relative to the set A from which social choice is to be made. In the limiting case where A^* has only one element or several elements between which every individual is indifferent, the problem of social decision would be solved so far as that particular choice situation is concerned, without resorting to any value judgment other than the Strict Pareto Criterion. This however is unlikely; it would be a rare case indeed if in a specific choice situation, every individual in the society considers one of the alternatives in the given set to be at least as good as every other alternative in the same set.

3.2   *Arrow's General Possibility Theorem*

An adequate theory of social choice must go beyond the Pareto criteria, and must explore other desirable restrictions on the group decision Rule. The experience with the Pareto criteria, however, points to a possible difficulty. Restrictions on the group decision Rule that are widely acceptable may be so weak that a large number of group decision Rules may be compatible with them and as a result too little may be said about social decisions over certain ranges. Arrow[1], however, shows that formidable difficulties may arise from just the opposite direction; sometimes the problem may be not that too little can be said with generally acceptable value judgments regarding the group decision Rules, but that if we insist on the simultaneous fulfillment of certain widely acceptable value judgments as a necessary condition for a satisfactory group decision Rule, then we may end up without a single 'satisfactory' group decision Rule. In other words, certain highly appealing restrictions on group decision Rules may be logically inconsistent.

There are five conditions which Arrow[1] requires the group decision Rule[1] to fulfill:

CONDITION 1'. (i) *Every weak social preference relation in the range of a group decision Rule is a complete ordering.*

(ii) *Every logically possible set of individual orderings belongs to the domain of the group decision Rule.*[2]

Condition 1'(i) ensures that the group decision Rule is a SWF, while Condition 1'(ii) requires the domain of the SWF to be unrestricted in the sense that it should contain every conceivable set of individual orderings.

Suppose we have two different sets of individual orderings defined over S. For each set of individual orderings the group decision Rule yields a unique social preference relation. The next two conditions stipulate that if the sets of individual orderings are related in a particular fashion, then the corresponding social preference relations should also be related in a certain way.

CONDITION 2 (*Positive Association of Social and Individual Values*). *Let R and R' be the social weak preference relations corresponding respectively to the sets of individual orderings $\{R_1, ..., R_N\}$ and $\{R'_1, ..., R'_N\}$. Suppose that for all a and b distinct from a given alternative x,*

$$(aR_i b \leftrightarrow aR'_i b)$$

---

[1] Strictly speaking, Arrow[1] stated his conditions with reference to social welfare functions, i.e., group decision Rules the ranges of which are sets of complete orderings. For reasons that will be clear later I shall restate Arrow's conditions as conditions on group decision Rules, the restriction that the range of a group decision Rule should be a set of complete orderings being introduced explicitly as Condition 1'(i) below.

[2] Condition 1' was introduced in the second edition of Arrow[1]. Arrow[1] has a different condition called Condition 1. See the appendix to this chapter for a statement of Condition 1 of Arrow, and its relevance.

for each i; and for all a, $[(xP_i a \to xP'_i a)$ & $(xI_i a \to xR'_i a)]$ for each i. Then for all y, $[(xPy \to xP'y)$ & $(xIy \to xR'y)]$.

Condition 2 implies that if the individual orderings remain exactly the same except for the fact that x rises in some persons' orderings, then x does not fall *vis-à-vis* any alternative in the social preference pattern in the new situation.

CONDITION 3 (*Independence of Irrelevant Alternatives*). *Let R and R' be the social weak preference relations corresponding respectively to the sets of individual orderings $\{R_1, ..., R_N\}$ and $\{R'_1, ..., R'_N\}$. Let A be any subset of S and let $C(A)$ and $C'(A)$ be the choice sets generated by R and R' respectively. If for all x and y belonging to A and for all i, $(xR_i y \leftrightarrow xR'_i y)$, then $C(A) = C'(A)$.*

Condition 3 implies that if individual orderings over any subset of S remain the same, then the choice set assigned by the group decision Rule for that subset of S also remains the same.

The following two conditions complete the set of value judgments Arrow seeks to impose on the group decision Rule.

CONDITION 4 (*Citizens' Sovereignty*). *For all distinct x and y belonging to S, there exists a set of individual orderings for which xPy.*

CONDITION 5 (*Nondictatorship*). *There does not exist any individual such that for all x and y belonging to S, the group decision Rule yields the result xPy whenever he prefers x to y, irrespective of the orderings of all other individuals.*

Arrow's General Possibility Theorem tells us that if S has at least three distinct elements, then there does not exist any group decision Rule that satisfies the conditions stated above. Henceforth it will be assumed that S has at least three distinct elements —an assumption which seems to be very reasonable in most situations. Given this assumption, it follows from Arrow's theorem that if we find a group decision Rule which satisfies any four of his five value judgments, it must violate the remaining one. The result is perfectly general: the impossibility of fulfilling all the five value judgments holds for any and every Rule that we can devise. The sting of Arrow's theorem lies here: even the 'best' group decision Rule that one can suggest is not good enough in terms of Arrow's criteria. It may be noted that the value judgments advanced by Arrow are not meant to be an exhaustive list of all value judgments which the group decision Rule should satisfy; they are meant to be only a subset of the set of all value judgments which a reasonable group decision Rule should satisfy. For example, we would certainly wish the group decision Rule to satisfy the Strict Pareto Criterion. The Strict Pareto Criterion does not belong to the set of value judgments stated above nor does it follow from any consistent subset of this set.[1] Since, however, Arrow's General Possibility Theorem is mainly destructive in its impact in so far as it demonstrates that certain value judgments are logically incompatible, there does not seem to be much point in adding any more conditions to the set or in strengthening one of the existing conditions unless the incompatibility is first removed by rejecting one of the existing conditions or by suitably weakening one of them.

As I pointed out in Chapter 2, one of the ways of judging a set of value judgments is to test for their internal consistency. If they are found to be mutually incompatible, then a modification is in order. Arrow's General Possibility Theorem is just such an exercise in consistency. The significance of this exercise would depend on how persuasive his value judgments are thought to be. Since the theorem applies to every possible group decision Rule, the consequence will be serious indeed if we think that all these conditions are highly appealing. If, however, we find that some of the conditions make an unnecessary or an undesirable demand on the group decision Rule we can reject or modify the conditions suitably, and thereby escape the impasse to which Arrow's theorem leads us. It must once again be emphasized that the argument in which we are involved is basically ethical in character, and will follow the pattern outlined in Chapter 2. It is, therefore, necessary to examine precisely the value content of each condition, by bringing out their implications as well as the implications of denying them.

Of the five value judgments enumerated above, 4 and 5 are

---

[1] Since the five conditions given above are logically inconsistent, *any* conclusion including the Strict Pareto Criterion can be derived from them. Therefore, the relevant question is whether we can derive a specific conclusion from those of Arrow's conditions which, taken together, are logically compatible.

generally acceptable. Condition 5 (i.e., Nondictatorship) will appear to be eminently reasonable, particularly in a democratic set-up. To deny Condition 5 would amount to saying that there may be an individual (e.g., the priest, the philosopher king, or the benevolent despot) whose will should prevail in the choice from every pair of alternatives under consideration, regardless of the orderings of other individuals. This is a position which few of us would like to take in choosing a satisfactory group decision Rule. Similarly, Condition 4 would appear to be a very weak and generally acceptable value judgment. For surely we would want the group decision Rule to decide in favour of x rather than y whenever there is a unanimous preference for x. To reject Condition 4 would be to accept the position that the choice of certain alternatives should be taboo irrespective of the pattern of individual preferences.

Unlike Conditions 4 and 5, Condition 3 has been the target of considerable criticism. Condition 3 imposes the restriction that for any subset A of S, $C(A)$ remains the same so long as individual orderings over A remain the same. This may be further elaborated as follows. Let $\{R_1, ..., R_N\}$ and $\{R'_1, ..., R'_N\}$ be two sets of individual orderings defined over S. Let R and R' respectively be the corresponding social weak preference relations. Let A be any subset of S. Assume that for all x and y belonging to A and for all i, $[xR_iy \leftrightarrow xR'_iy]$. Let $C(A)$ be the choice set generated by R and $C'(A)$ be the choice set generated by R'. Condition 3 has the following implications:

(i) If for all x and y belonging to A and for all i, $(xR_iy \leftrightarrow xR'_iy)$, then $C(A) = C'(A)$ even if individual orderings over S as a whole might have changed.

In other words, if the position of the alternatives in A *relative to each other*, in the individual orderings, remain the same, then no matter how the individual orderings defined over S change, the choice set corresponding to A remains unaltered. To take a specific example, let us assume that $S = \{x, y_1, y_2, ..., y_n, z\}$. Suppose, in situation I

$$xP_izP_iy_1P_iy_2P_i...P_iy_n$$

or

$$zP_iy_1P_iy_2P_i...P_iy_nP_ix$$

is the preference ordering for every i. Let us assume the group decision Rule gives the result zPx in situation I. In situation II let $xP_iy_1P_iy_2P_i...P_iy_nP_iz$ be the preference pattern for every i who preferred x to z in situation I, and $zP_ixP_iy_1P_iy_2P_i...P_iy_n$ be the preference ordering for every i who preferred z to x in situation I. Since for every individual the relative position of x and z is the the same in both situations, and since in situation I $C(\{z, x\}) = \{z\}$, Condition 3 would require the group decision Rule necessarily to yield the result $C(\{z, x\}) = \{z\}$ in situation II also.

(ii) It may seem that Condition 3, in addition to ruling out the influence of 'irrelevant alternatives' on social choice out of any subset A of S, also rules out the possibility of any change in the choice set for A in response to changes in the intensities of individual preferences, so long as individual *orderings* over A remain unchanged.[1] It may, however, be pointed out that the insensitivity of R to changes in individual preference intensities as distinguished from changes in individual orderings is a property that has been built into the definition of a group decision Rule, and, therefore Condition 3 does not impose any additional constraint in this respect. To see this clearly let us rule out the irrelevant-alternative case discussed above by assuming that for all i, R_i and R'_i as defined over S are exactly identical. Let us now assume that there is a change in individual preference intensities.[2] To take the most relevant case, it may be assumed that there is a change in the intensities of individual preferences as between some alternatives in A. In this case R as defined over S by the group decision Rule will remain unchanged, and consequently $C(A)$ will also remain unchanged. But this will be so irrespective of whether we introduce Condition 3 or not since by definition, a group decision Rule is a functional relation which specifies only one social weak preference relation for each set of individual weak preference relations (defined over S) in its domain. It is, however possible to redefine a group decision

---

[1] See Rothenberg, p. 132 and also pp. 134–5.

[2] The question as to how we come to know about changes in the intensities of individual preferences need not detain us here. All that we need assume here is that it is meaningful to speak of preference intensities as distinguished from preference orderings and that preference intensities can change even if the orderings remain the same.

Rule so as to allow R to be influenced not only by changes in the set of individual orderings but also by changes in individual preference intensities even though the individual orderings might have remained the same. In that case the implication of Condition 3 with respect to preference intensities becomes an independent restriction.

The problem of allowing changes in individual orderings of 'irrelevant' alternatives to affect social choice and that of incorporating individual preference intensities as a determinant of social choice, though logically distinct, are, in fact, closely related, and will be discussed further in Chapter 9. The following point should, however, be noted here. Since the set A referred to in the statement of Condition 3 may be interpreted as any two-element set of S, Condition 3 ensures that social decision between any two alternatives depends on, and only on, the individual orderings of *those two alternatives*. In fact, Condition 3 is really equivalent to saying that the group decision Rule should be binary, binariness being defined as follows:

DEFINITION 3.3.   *Let* $\{R_1, ..., R_N\}$ *and* $\{R'_1, ..., R'_N\}$ *be any two sets of individual orderings defined over S. Let a group decision Rule map these two respectively into social weak preference relations R and R'. The group decision Rule is binary if and only if for all x and y belonging to S,* $[(\forall i)\,(xR_i y \leftrightarrow xR'_i y \ \& \ yR_i x \leftrightarrow yR'_i x) \rightarrow (xRy \leftrightarrow xR'y \ \& \ yRx \leftrightarrow yR'x)]$.

So far as Condition 2 is concerned, its acceptability depends, to a large extent, on whether we consider preference intensities to be relevant or not. The individual orderings remaining the same otherwise, x might have moved up in the preference orderings of some individuals. But preference intensities of other individuals, as between x and y, might have undergone a change. If we think that preference intensities are relevant in social choice, then we may not require the group decision Rule to declare x to be necessarily better than y in the changed situation, even though it declared x to be socially better than y before the change. However, given that somebody does not object to R being determined by only the set of individual orderings, it is difficult to find some reasonable objection which he can advance against Condition 2.

Like Condition 3, Condition 1' is also open to criticism.

44

Condition 1′(i) imposes the restriction that R should be a complete ordering while Condition 1′(ii) requires all logically possible sets of individual orderings to be in the domain of the group decision Rule. In trying to modify Condition 1′ one may question 1′(i) alone or 1′(ii) alone or both 1′(i) and 1′(ii).

Consider first 1′(i). A complete social ordering implies that R should satisfy reflexivity, connectedness and transitivity. Reflexivity of R does not impose any serious restriction; to say that x is socially at least as good as x is so reasonable that it almost appears to be trivial. To say that social decision should be connected is no more than to impose the condition that faced with any two alternatives x and y, society should be able to choose between the two. Suppose x and y are the only alternatives available to society and the social decision process cannot tell us whether x is socially better than, indifferent to, or worse than y. What is to be done in such a case? One possible answer might be that society should not make any choice when such non-comparability occurs. But 'no choice' is not a feasible alternative since the society, if it is to exist at all, must be in some state or other. It may be thought that faced with such situations of non-comparability, the status quo may be maintained or some procedure of random choice such as tossing a coin may be adopted. But in such a case what we are really doing is to restore connectedness by supplementing the original group decision Rule by an additional principle governing choice where the original Rule fails to compare the alternatives under consideration.

It is true that a given set of alternatives can have a non-empty choice set even if R violates connectedness over some pairs of alternatives belonging to the set; this we have seen in Chapter 1. In some real situations we may be sure that choice will be confined to a given set A and that no proper subset of A will ever be offered as the set of alternatives to choose from. In such a case even if R violates connectedness over some pairs of alternatives belonging to A, we may not feel particularly disturbed if $C(A)$ is non-empty. In general, however, connectedness of R would seem to be a highly desirable property.

All this is generally recognized, and the desirability of connectedness has rarely been challenged. Such is not the case with transitivity. The necessity of this property has been questioned by several writers including Bergson[3], Graaff, and Kemp. The arguments advanced in favour of rejecting transitivity run as follows. It is held that unlike transitivity of individual preferences, transitivity of social preferences cannot be justified as a value in itself; the only justification of it can, therefore, be made in terms of its consequences. So far as the consequences are concerned, it is argued that the harm done by intransitivity of social decisions is negligible. Bergson ([3], p. 237), for example writes: 'An occasional inconsistency might give rise to circularity in the collective choices, but in view of ever-occurring changes in data there is no danger that the system would whirl about forever at any such point.' Graaff would go even further, and maintain that intransitivity of the majority decisions may prove to be a positive virtue in a democracy since the occasional inconsistency of majority decisions makes democratic rule more palatable to the minority.

Just how much weight can be attached to these objections? The fact that intransitivity and reversibility of majority decisions may sometimes protect minority interest is true. But protection of minority interests represents a type of values which can hardly be satisfactorily reconciled with those embedded in the majority decision procedure. In any case, if we want to protect minority interests at all, surely we should rely on some more effective device than the intransitivity of majority decisions? Bergson's [3] argument also does not seem very convincing. Consider the case where the set of alternatives under consideration is $\{x, y, z\}$, and we have xPy & yPz & zPx. The basic problem remains here as to what decision society should take. For, whatever alternative may be selected, there exists another alternative which, on the basis of the values implied by the decision process, is superior to the selected alternative. In such a situation it may be little consolation to be told that a change of data may occur, which will release us from this deadlock.

On the other hand, it is arguable that the whole problem is spurious. For, if we take policy decision by pairwise comparison and an alternative which is defeated in any pairwise comparison is not allowed to enter the sequence again, then we are bound to arrive at some decision. In the example given above, a pairwise comparison of x and y will result in the elimination of y, and then if we compare x with z, z will defeat x. If we stop at this point and do not undertake the further comparison between z and y, z will be the final outcome.[1] All this is true: we shall arrive at *some* decision by this method. But if we are taking decisions by a sequence of pairwise comparisons, then unless transitivity is fulfilled the final outcome *may* depend on the nature of the sequence itself. For example, if we had compared y and z first, and then compared the winner with x, x would have been the ultimate outcome to be chosen. Thus, unless the condition of transitivity is satisfied, social decision through pairwise comparisons may become a matter of chance. Probably this in itself will seem distasteful to some. But what is more important, and what has already been emphasized, through such a method we may arrive at a decision which directly conflicts with the values implicit in the decision process. It will be useful at this point to give an example in terms of some specific method of social decision.

DEFINITION 3.4. *The Majority Decision Rule (MD-Rule). For all x and y belonging to S, xRy if and only if $[N(xR_iy) \geqslant N(yR_ix)]$.*

If we have three individual orderings xP_1yP_1z, yP_2zP_2x, and zP_3xP_3y over $\{x, y, z\}$, then the MD-Rule gives us

$$(xPy \text{ \& } yPz \text{ \& } zPx).$$

Here if we take up the pair $[x, y]$ first, x becomes the winner. Then in the comparison between x and z, z wins. If we stop here, and do not compare z and y, then z emerges as the final choice. But two things should be noted. Firstly, if we had taken up the pair $[y, z]$ first rather than the pair $[x, y]$, and compared the winner with x, then x would have emerged as the final choice. Secondly, the choice of z is a direct violation of the values underlying the MD-Rule since a majority of individuals strictly prefers

---

[1] In this case intransitivity of social decisions will not be revealed at all. In certain other situations intransitivity may be revealed even when a defeated alternative is not allowed to enter the sequence again. For example, this is the case where we have $(cPa \text{ \& } aIb \text{ \& } bIc)$ and we start with the pairwise comparison between a and b, followed by comparisons between a and c, and between b and c. However, in this case also we arrive at a decision: b and c emerge as the final outcomes. In fact, irrespective of whether intransitivity is revealed or not we shall always reach a decision so long as an alternative once defeated in a pairwise comparison is not allowed to enter the sequence again.

y to z. In fact, the choice of z while y is available, will represent a minority choice in the sense that only a minority of individuals considers z to be at least as good as y which has not been selected.[1] The choice of any alternative will be a minority choice in this sense since for every alternative there exists another alternative which is considered strictly better, by a majority of individuals.

If R is a complete ordering, then given the assumption that S is a finite set, we avoid all the difficulties discussed above in connection with the violation of connectedness and transitivity. For, in that case whatever subset of S may be offered, the group decision Rule will define a non-empty choice set.[2] Also the choice made out of any subset A of S will be independent of the sequence of pair-wise comparisons followed, since whatever be the sequence of pairwise comparisons, once an element of $C(A)$ enters the sequence, it survives till the end without being defeated. In the rest of this book it will be assumed that S is a finite set of alternatives. Given this assumption a complete social ordering is sufficient to eliminate difficulties of the type mentioned above.

But is a complete social ordering necessary to remove these difficulties? It seems that all that we need is that R should be reflexive and connected, and P should be acyclic. Given the assumption that S is a finite set of alternatives a reflexive and connected R, such that P is acyclic, defines a choice function over S. Also, the choice from any subset A of S will be independent of the sequence of pairwise comparisons followed since $C(A)$ will be non-empty and every element of $C(A)$ will remain undefeated till the end in any sequence of pairwise comparisons. In so far as reflexivity and connectedness of R, and acyclicity of P, together constitute a considerably weaker condition than that R should be a complete ordering, Condition $1'$ (i) would seem to impose an unneccessarily strong restriction on the group decision Rule. To state the point in a slightly different fashion, what we really need is a SDF; we need not make a stronger demand on the group decision Rule by requiring it to be a SWF too.

[1] Cf. Riker, who taking a specific case shows how intransitive majority decisions may result in minority choice in the presence of procedural rules which conceal the intransitivity.

[2] See Theorem 1.4. As noted earlier, if S is not finite, then difficulties may arise even if R is a complete ordering since we can have an infinitely long descending chain of the type $(\ldots \& \, x_3 P x_2 \, \& \, x_2 P x_1)$ where $x_1, x_2, x_3, \ldots$ are all distinct elements.

Arrow's Dilemma

The existence of a social choice function solves the basic problem of rational social choice. But we might wish that the choice function should satisfy certain additional conditions of rationality. One such condition is given by Arrow[2].[1]

DEFINITION 3.5. *Arrow's Condition of Rationality: For all subsets A and B of S, if $A \subset B$ and $C(B) \cap A$ is non-null, then*

$$C(A) = C(B) \cap A.$$

This condition requires that 'if some elements are chosen out of B and then the range of alternatives is narrowed to A but still contains some previously chosen elements, no previously unchosen element becomes chosen and no previously chosen element becomes unchosen'.[2] Arrow [2] shows that the choice function generated by a binary relation R satisfies the condition given above if and only if R is a complete ordering. Therefore, if we not only want a social choice function but also require the choice function to fulfill Arrow's condition of rationality, then we shall have Condition 1′ (i). There does not, however, seem to be any intuitively compelling reason why we should require the social choice function to fulfill Arrow's condition of rationality.

Independently of whether we require the group decision Rule to be a SWF or only a SDF, Condition 1′ (ii) would seem to be stronger than is necessary. Suppose we accept Condition 1′ (i) and require the group decision Rule to be a SWF.[3] Condition 1′ (ii) then imposes the restriction that the SWF should have an unrestricted domain. But why should we require an unrestricted domain? Assume that some set of individual orderings do not belong to the domain of the SWF. But if we know that these sets of individual orderings are unlikely to be found in real life then we need not be very much disturbed by the fact that they do not belong to the domain of the SWF. I shall return to this argument later on. But at this stage it may be noted that Condition 1′ (ii) is overly demanding if we have reason to believe that certain configurations of individual preferences never arise in actual life.

---

[1] For a similar condition see Sen[7].

[2] See Arrow[2], p. 123. In the quotation given I have replaced Arrow's notations X and Y by A and B respectively.

[3] The argument that follows applies to social decision functions also.

3.3. *Some Group Decision Rules*

To conclude this chapter I shall consider certain group decision Rules in the light of Arrow's General Possibility Theorem. In the course of my discussion of these group decision Rules I shall refer to certain properties in addition to those mentioned in the context of the General Possibility Theorem. I define these properties below.

DEFINITION 3.6. *Decisiveness.* *A group decision Rule is decisive if and only if for every logically possible set of individual orderings it defines a social weak reference relation satisfying reflexivity and connectedness.*

A group decision Rule satisfying Arrow's Condition 1′ will necessarily be decisive, though clearly the converse is not necessarily true.

DEFINITION 3.7. *Let $\{R_1, ..., R_N\}$ and $\{R'_1, ...,R'_N\}$ be any two sets of individual orderings belonging to the domain of a group decision Rule. Let the group decision Rule map these two sets respectively into social weak preference relations R and R'.*

(i) *Anonymity: If for any pair of individuals j and k, $R_j = R'_k$ and $R_k = R'_j$, and for all i other than j and k, $R_i = R'_i$, then $R = R'$.*

(ii) *Neutrality: Let $[x, y]$ and $[z, w]$ be any two ordered pairs of alternatives. Suppose that for all a and b distinct from x, y, z, and w, we have $(aR_i b \leftrightarrow aR'_i b)$ for each i; for all a distinct from x, y, z, and w, we have*

$$[(xR_i a \leftrightarrow zR'_i a) \; \& \; (aR_i x \leftrightarrow aR'_i z) \; \& \; (yR_i a \leftrightarrow wR'_i a)$$
$$\& \; (aR_i y \leftrightarrow aR'_i w)]$$

for each i; and for all i we have

$$[(xR_i y \leftrightarrow zR'_i w) \; \& \; (yR_i x \leftrightarrow wR'_i z)].$$

Then $(xRy \leftrightarrow zR'w)$.

(iii) *Positive Responsiveness: Let $[x,y]$ be any ordered pair of alternatives. Suppose that for all a and b distinct from x, $(aR_i b \leftrightarrow aR'_i b)$ for each i; for all a, $[(xP_i a \rightarrow xP'_i a) \; \& \; (xI_i a \rightarrow xR'_i a)]$; and for some i, either $(xI_i y \; \& \; xP'_i y)$ or $(yP_i x \; \& \; xR'_i y)$. Then $(xRy \rightarrow xP'y)$.*

(iv) *Non-negative Responsiveness: Let x be any given alternative. Suppose that for all a and b distinct from x, $(aR_i b \leftrightarrow aR'_i b)$ for* each i; and for all a, $[(xP_i a \to xP_i' a)$ & $(xI_i a \to xR_i' a)]$ for each i. Then for all y, $[(xPy \to xP'y)$ & $(xIy \to xR'y)]$.

The first three properties were first introduced by May[1]. May[1], however, defined these properties only for the case of two alternatives since he was essentially concerned with pairwise comparisons. The definitions of anonymity, neutrality, and positive responsiveness, as given here, are extensions of May's[1] definitions to the case where we have more than two alternatives.[1] Anonymity requires that a permutation of individual orderings leaves R unchanged, assuming that the sets of individual orderings before and after the permutation belong to the domain of the group decision Rule. As an example of a group decision Rule that violates anonymity we may cite a voting system under which society considers x to be at least as good as y if and only if the number of ballots cast in favour of x is at least as great as the number of ballots cast in favour of y, but under which some, and not all, individuals can cast more than one ballot. Anonymity rules out all possible 'discrimination' between individuals and, as such, has a strong ethical appeal. Neutrality requires that a permutation of the alternatives in everyone's preference should produce the same permutation in social preference. Neutrality thus rules out possible 'discrimination' between alternatives. For example, a decision procedure under which the status quo can be changed if and only if two-thirds of the total number of individuals strictly prefer the change, violates neutrality. Non-negative responsiveness implies that if the set of individual orderings remains exactly the same except for the fact that x rises in some persons' orderings, then x does not fall in the social ordering. The condition of non-negative responsiveness is slightly stronger than Arrow's Condition 2 in so far as Arrow's Condition 2 is concerned only with social strict preference whereas the property of non-negative responsiveness concerns social strict preference as well as social indifference. One would not, however, expect any objection to the property of non-negative responsiveness if Arrow's Condition 2 is accepted. The property of positive

---

[1] The definitions of anonymity and neutrality given here are essentially the same as the definitions given by Arrow ([1], second edition). Positive responsiveness and non-negative responsiveness are respectively equivalent to strong monotonicity and monotonicity of Murakami[4] in the case of more than two alternatives

responsiveness requires that if the set of individual orderings remain the same except that x rises *vis-à-vis* certain alternatives in some individual's orderings then if x was originally socially at least as good as any of those alternatives, now x must be socially preferred to it.

The following results are immediate, and are noted here without proof:[1]

LEMMA 3.3
    (i) *Anonymity implies Arrow's Condition 5.*
    (ii) *Positive responsiveness implies non-negative responsiveness.*
    (iii) *Non-negative responsiveness implies Arrow's Condition 2.*
    (iv) *For any binary, decisive, and neutral group decision Rule*

$$(\forall x)\ (\forall y)\ [(\forall i)\ (xI_i y)\ \rightarrow xIy].$$

    (v) *For a binary group decision Rule, decisiveness, neutrality, and non-negative responsiveness together imply that either the Weak Pareto Criterion is fulfilled or social indifference holds for every pair of alternatives.*

    (vi) *For a binary group decision Rule, decisiveness, neutrality, and positive responsiveness together imply the Strict Pareto Criterion.*

I shall now consider several group decision Rules in terms of the various properties of a group decision Rule that have been defined so far. The first two group decision Rules that I take up are closely related to the Pareto criteria considered in Section 1 of this chapter.

DEFINITION 3.8
    (i) *Extended Weak Pareto Criterion:*

$$(\forall x)\ (\forall y)\ [xRy \leftrightarrow\ \sim (y\bar{\bar{Q}}x)].$$

    (ii) *Extended Strict Pareto Criterion:*

$$(\forall x)\ (\forall y)\ [xRy \leftrightarrow\ \sim (y\bar{Q}x)].$$

The Extended Weak Pareto Criterion is consistent with the Weak Pareto Criterion, but it goes further in so far as it generates a group decision Rule out of the Weak Pareto Criterion by declaring all x and y non-comparable under the Weak Pareto Criterion to be socially indifferent. Similarly, the Extended

---

[1] (iv), (v), and (vi) in Lemma **3.3** are due to Murakami [4]. For a discussion of many other interesting properties of a group decision Rule see Murakami ([2], [4]).

Strict Pareto Criterion generates a group decision Rule out of the Strict Pareto Criterion by declaring all x and y non-comparable under the Strict Pareto Criterion to be socially indifferent.

It is clear that both these group decision Rules are binary, i.e., both the Rules satisfy Arrow's Condition 3. Also both the Rules satisfy neutrality, non-negative responsiveness and anonymity. Since, by Lemma 3.3, non-negative responsiveness and anonymity imply respectively Arrow's Conditions 2 and 5, the two group decision Rules satisfy these conditions. They satisfy Condition 4 since $x\bar{Q}y$ implies xPy under the Extended Weak Pareto Criterion and $x\bar{\bar{Q}}y$ implies xPy under the Extended Strict Pareto Criterion. Thus the two Rules defined above satisfy all of Arrow's conditions excepting Condition 1'. As regards Condition 1', it can be easily seen that they yield reflexive and connected R for every logically possible set of reflexive and connected individual weak preference relations. Also, since

$$(x\bar{Q}y \leftrightarrow xPy)$$

under the Extended Weak Pareto Criterion, $(x\bar{\bar{Q}}y \leftrightarrow xPy)$ under the Extended Pareto Criterion, and by Lemma 3.1, $\bar{\bar{Q}}$ and $\bar{Q}$ are transitive for every logically possible set of individual orderings, it follows that the two Rules yield quasi-transitive results for every logically possible set of individual orderings.[1] They, however, fail to satisfy Arrow's Condition 1' in so far as they do not necessarily give us a transitive R. Consider two individuals having the orderings zP_1xP_1y and xP_2yP_2z. Both the Rules give us the intransitive results $(xPy \ \& \ yIz \ \& \ zIx)$. But we have seen that reflexivity, connectedness, and quasi-transitivity of R are together sufficient for R to generate a choice function over any finite set of alternatives. Therefore the failure to satisfy transitivity of R for every logically possible set of individual orderings does not constitute an overwhelming defect of these Rules. The real defect lies elsewhere. In spite of the fact that they satisfy most of Arrow's conditions they are extremely unsatisfactory since they give a veto power to every individual in the sense that an individual can always bring about social indifference

---

[1] See Sen [7]. Sen shows that the Extended Strict Pareto Criterion is a SDF with unrestricted domain, that satisfies Arrow's Conditions 2, 3, 4, and 5.

between x and y even if the rest of the society strictly prefer x to y. It is this feature which accounts for the unsatisfactory nature of these Rules rather than the failure to satisfy the transitivity of R.

We consider next a class of group decision Rules which in the absence of a convenient terminology will be called the class of M-Rules.

DEFINITION 3.9. *M-Rule.*

$$(\forall x)\ (\forall y)\ [xRy \leftrightarrow \{N(yP_ix)/[pN + (1-p)\ N^*] \leqslant \tfrac{1}{2}\}]$$

for some p chosen from the closed interval $[0, 1]$, where N is the total number of individuals and N^* is the number of individuals preferring x to y or y to x.

With each different p we get a different M-Rule. All M-Rules are binary, decisive, neutral, and non-negatively responsive. Also all M-Rules satisfy anonymity and the Weak Pareto Criterion. It is thus obvious that all M-Rules satisfy Arrow's Conditions 2, 3, 4, and 5. By the General Possibility Theorem, therefore, they must violate Condition 1'. In fact this violation takes a particularly disturbing form in so far as for some sets of individual ordering the M-Rules not only fail to define a complete social ordering but also fail to define a social choice function.

LEMMA 3.4 *Every M-Rule violates acyclicity of P and, therefore, fails to generate a choice function, for some set of individual orderings.*

PROOF:

The proof consists of an example. Let there be three individual orderings as follows over the subset $\{x, y, z\}$ of S:

$$xP_1yP_1z \qquad yP_2zP_2x \qquad zP_3xP_3y.$$

Since for every pair of alternatives $N^* \leqslant N$, it is clear that for all a and b belonging to $\{x, y, z\}$

$$[N(aP_ib)/N > \tfrac{1}{2}] \to [N(aP_ib)/pN + (1-p)\ N^* > \tfrac{1}{2}]. \quad (1)$$

In the given example we have

$$[N(xP_iy)/N = N(yP_iz)/N = N(zP_ix)/N > \tfrac{1}{2}]. \quad (2)$$

From (1) and (2) it follows that $(xPy\ \&\ yPz\ \&\ zPx)$ for every M-Rule, which implies a non-empty choice set for $\{x, y, z\}$ under every M-Rule.   Q.E.D.

The M-Rules constitute a continuum of group decision Rules. The two extremes of this continuum, corresponding to $p = 1$ and $p = 0$, are of particular interest. When $p = 0$, we have the MD-Rule defined earlier. When $p = 1$, the M-Rule will be called *the method of non-minority decision*.

In some ways, the method of non-minority decision reflects an essential feature of our intuitive notion of democracy. Although there are likely to be wide differences of opinion as to what we mean by democracy it will probably be agreed that the concept of democratic choice implies at least this much: we should not choose an alternative x from a set A, when there is another alternative y in A such that a majority of individuals strictly prefers y to x.[1] If this value judgment is accepted, then the choice set $C(A)$ for a given set A under the method of non-minority decision assumes a special significance: we can satisfy this value judgment only by choosing an element of $C(A)$ since by definition, for every x belonging to $[A - C(A)]$ there exists y in A such that a majority of individuals strictly prefers y to x.

Choice out of $C(A)$ defined in terms of the method of non-minority decision, however, satisfies only a minimal requirement of democratic choice. The term democracy as we ordinarily understand it has innumerable shades of meaning, and it is practically impossible for any particular logical criterion to capture all the different aspects of the concept. All that we can do is to formulate our criterion so as to bring as much of the democratic values as possible under its coverage. How much of these values escapes our method of non-minority decision can be best seen from the following examples:

Let $N = 100$, and $A = \{x, y, z\}$. Let

$$N(zP_ixI_iy) = 30, \quad N(yP_ixP_iz) = 45 \quad \text{and} \quad N(xP_izP_iy) = 25.$$

Under the method of non-minority decision $C(A) = \{x\}$ and x will, therefore be chosen. But the number of persons who strictly prefer y to x is greater than the number of persons who strictly prefer x to y.

What is more disturbing than the possibility mentioned above is that the method of non-minority decision may violate the

---

[1] This is what is referred to as non-minority rule in Leibenstein, and in Pattanaik [2].

Strict Pareto Criterion which is generally acceptable. Let $N = 100$, and $A = \{x, y\}$. Let $N(xI_iy) = 50$, and $N(xP_iy) = 50$. We have $x\bar{Q}y$, but xIy under the method of non-minority decision.

This second difficulty can be removed by suitably modifying the method of non-minority decision so as to take into account the Strict Pareto Criterion.

DEFINITION 3.10. *The Pareto-inclusive Method of Non-minority Decision.*

$$(\forall x)\,(\forall y)\,[xRy \leftrightarrow (\sim (y\bar{Q}x)\ \&\ \{N(yP_ix)/N \leqslant \tfrac{1}{2}\})].$$

The following lemma will be used later.

LEMMA 3.5. *For any set of individual orderings defined over a finite set of alternatives S, the method of non-minority decision generates a choice function over S if and only if the Pareto-inclusive method of non-minority decision generates a choice function over S.*

PROOF:

Suppose the method of non-minority decision defines a choice function over S. It will be shown that the Pareto-inclusive method of non-minority decision also defines a choice function over S. To avoid confusion the social weak preference relation under the method of non-minority decision will be indicated by R, and that under the Pareto-inclusive version by R'. Similarly the choice sets will be indicated by $C(A)$ and $C'(A)$ respectively for any subset A of S. Let A be any subset of S. By hypothesis $C(A)$ is non-empty. Hence

$$(\exists x)\,[x \in A\ \&\ (\forall y)\,\{(y \in A) \to (N(yP_ix) \leqslant N/2)\}].$$

Hence either $x \in C'(A)$ or $(\exists y')\,(y'\bar{Q}x)$. If $y'\bar{Q}x$, then it is clear that $(\forall z)\,\{(z \in A) \to (N(zP_iy) \leqslant N/2)\}$. Hence either $y' \in C'(A)$ or $(\exists y'')\,(y''\bar{Q}y')$. Proceeding like this, since A is finite, we shall ultimately reach y such that $y \in C'(A)$. $C'(A)$ will therefore be non-empty. Since this is true of every subset A of S, the Pareto-inclusive method of non-minority decision defines a choice function over S.

Suppose the Pareto-inclusive method of non-minority decision defines a choice function over S. It is clear that

$$(\forall x)\,(\forall y)\,(xR'y \to xRy).$$

56

Hence for any subset A of S, if $x \in C'(A)$, then $x \in C(A)$. Since by hypothesis $C'(A)$ is non-empty for every non-empty subset A of S, it follows that the method of non-minority decision defines a non-empty choice set $C(A)$ for every non-empty subset A of S, i.e., it defines a choice function over S. This completes the proof. Q.E.D.

The MD-Rule which constitutes the other extreme case of a M-Rule is one of the most widely discussed group decision Rules. Interest in the analytical problems of the MD-Rule goes back at least two centuries to Borda and Condorcet. The reason for this sustained interest is not difficult to see. Besides having the virtue of considerable simplicity, the MD-Rule possesses several attractive properties. By the theorem of May [1] it satisfies decisiveness, neutrality, positive responsiveness, and anonymity and is the only binary group decision Rule to do so. Since positive responsiveness implies Arrow's Condition 2, and anonymity implies Arrow's Condition 5, the MD-Rule satisfies these conditions. Binariness is of course equivalent to satisfying Arrow's Condition 3. Since decisiveness, neutrality, and positive responsiveness together imply the Strict Pareto Criterion, for a binary group decision Rule, the MD-Rule satisfies the Strict Pareto Criterion and hence Arrow's Condition 4. However, the MD-Rule does not satisfy Arrow's Condition 1' though it is decisive. Like every other M-Rule the MD-Rule is a SDF and also a SWF (for the sake of brevity the MD-Rule will be called MD–SDF when it is viewed as SDF, and MD–SWF when it is viewed as SWF). However like every other M-Rule the MD-Rule has a restricted domain both as SDF and as SWF since for certain sets of individual orderings the MD-Rule violates acyclicity of P. This can be seen from the example given in the proof of Lemma 3.4, which constitutes the famous voting paradox.[1]

The method of majority decision corresponds to our notion of direct democracy. In actual practice, however, many other more complicated methods of social decision are used, involving what may be called the principle of indirect or representative democracy. Murakami ([3], [4]) extensively discusses a class of such group decision Rules. I take a slightly different version of the class of group decision Rules discussed by Murakami and call these Rules *multi-stage majority decision Rules* (MMD-Rules).

---

[1] See Arrow [1].

In explaining the structure of MMD-Rules the notion of a majority voting operation will be useful.

Definition 3.11. *Majority Voting Operation. Let $\{\bar{R}_1, ..., \bar{R}_n\}$ be any set of binary weak preference relations defined over S. Majority voting operation is a Rule f such that for all x and y belonging to S*

$$x\bar{R}y \leftrightarrow [N(x\bar{R}_j y) \geqslant N(y\bar{R}_j x)] \quad \text{where} \quad \bar{R} = f(\bar{R}_1, ..., \bar{R}_n).$$

For the sake of convenience we shall indicate $f(\bar{R}_1, ..., \bar{R}_n)$ by $((\bar{R}_1, ..., \bar{R}_n))$ where f is the majority voting operation.

The MD-Rule as defined earlier is clearly a majority voting operation viewed as a group decision Rule. Under the MD-Rule the aggregation of individual preferences into social preferences takes place at one stage through a single majority voting operation. Under a MMD-Rule, however, the aggregation of individual preferences between any two alternatives may be effected by several stages of majority voting operation, the result of one majority voting operation often figuring as an entry in another majority voting operation. Not only a MMD-Rule may involve several majority voting operations but also the ordering of one individual may enter into more than one majority voting operation and more than once into the same majority voting operation. The ordering of each individual, however, figures in at least one majority voting operation. The concept may be explained by a specific example. Suppose $S = \{x, y, z\}$, and we have four individuals having the orderings xP_1yP_1z, yP_2xP_2z, xP_3zP_3y, and zP_4yP_4x. The following is an example of a MMD-Rule involving this set of individual orderings:

$$((R_1, ((R_2, R_4)), R_2, R_2, R_3))$$
$$= ((xP_1yP_1z, ((yP_2xP_2z, zP_4yP_4x)), yP_2xP_2z, yP_2xP_2z, xP_3zP_3y)).$$

The majority voting operation $((yP_2xP_2z, zP_4yP_4x))$ gives $(y\bar{I}z \,\&\, z\bar{I}x \,\&\, y\bar{P}x)$ as a result, and this figures as an entry in another majority voting operation, namely

$$((xP_1yP_1z, y\bar{I}z \,\&\, z\bar{I}x \,\&\, y\bar{P}x, yP_2xP_2z, yP_2xP_2z, xP_3zP_3y)).$$

The final result is $(yPx \,\&\, yPz \,\&\, xPz)$. The ordering of individual 2 enters into more than one majority voting operation. Also it enters more than once into one majority voting operation.

A MMD-Rule is thus a binary group decision Rule made up of one or more majority voting operations in each of which the entries consist of individual orderings or the results of some other majority voting operation.[1] The majority decision Rule defined earlier is a special type of MMD-Rule, namely, one which involves one and only one majority voting operation in which the ordering of each individual figures only once.

A few points may be noted here. Given a set of individual orderings, we can have different MMD-Rules. For example, with the same set of individual orderings R_1, R_2, and R_3, we can have many different MMD-Rules such as

$$((R_1, ((R_2, R_3))\,)); \quad ((\,((R_1, R_2)), R_3, R_1)); \quad ((R_1, R_2, R_3, R_3))$$

and so on. Also the same MMD-Rule can be represented in different ways. For example,

$$((R_1, R_1, R_2)) \quad \text{and} \quad ((\,((R_1, R_2)), R_1, R_1))$$

are different representations of the same MMD-Rule involving two individual orderings R_1 and R_2. This is because for all possible patterns that R_1 and R_2 may take, the social weak preference relation R is the same under both representations. But for any particular MMD-Rule, the set of different possible structures of majority voting operations by which we can represent the MMD-Rule is the same for all pairs of alternatives. For example, if a certain MMD-Rule can be represented by $((R_1, ((R_2, R_3)), R_2))$ for any given pair of alternatives, then for every other pair of alternatives it can be represented by $((R_1, ((R_2, R_3)), R_2))$. In what follows I shall ignore the complications that arise from the possibility of representing the same MMD-Rule in different ways and proceed as if a given MMD-Rule has one unique representation in terms of hierarchy of majority voting operations. This, however, will not involve any loss of generality for the subsequent discussion of these Rules.

In the context of multi-stage majority decisions $G_j^{(0)}$ will indicate the jth group of preference patterns to be aggregated by the majority voting operation, such that each preference pattern

---

[1] Note that this definition does not exclude the possibility of a dictator in Arrow's sense. Suppose we have three individuals with orderings R_1, R_2, and R_3. The MMD-Rule $((R_1, R_1, R_1, R_2, R_3))$ involving these orderings violates Arrow's Condition of Non-dictatorship. In this respect MMD-Rules are not always democratic in Murakami's [4] sense.

in the group is an individual ordering. The preference patterns in $G_j^{(0)}$ will be indicated by $R_{ij}^{(0)}$ and the preference pattern arrived at by aggregating the preference patterns in $G_j^{(0)}$ by the majority voting operation will be indicated by $R_j^{(0)}$. $G_j^{(1)}$ will indicate the jth group of preference patterns to be aggregated by the majority voting operation, such that each preference pattern in the group is either an individual ordering or $R_l^{(0)}$ for some l, and at least one preference pattern in the group is $R_l^{(0)}$ for some l. The elements of $G_j^{(1)}$ will be indicated by $R_{ij}^{(1)}$ and the preference pattern arrived at by aggregating the preference patterns in $G_j^{(1)}$ by the majority voting operation will be indicated by $R_j^{(1)}$. $G_j^{(2)}$ will indicate the jth group of preference patterns [to be aggregated by the majority voting operation, such that each preference pattern in the group is either an individual ordering or $R_l^{(0)}$ for some l or $R_m^{(1)}$ for some m, and at least one preference pattern in the group is $R_m^{(1)}$ for some m. Continuing like this we can define $G_j^{(k)}$ for any k. R is reached after a finite number of such aggregations.

These notations may be illustrated with an example. Suppose we have four individuals and the following MMD-Rule.

$$((((R_1, R_2)), R_2, R_2, R_3, R_4)).$$

Here R_1 and R_2 constitute the set of $R_{i1}^{(0)}$. $R_1^{(0)}$ is the result arrived at by aggregating R_1 and R_2 by the majority voting operation. $R_1^{(0)}$, the two R_2's, R_3, and R_4 constitute the set of $R_{i1}^{(1)}$. R is nothing but $R_1^{(1)}$—the result of aggregating the set of $R_{i1}^{(1)}$ by the majority voting operation.

Every MMD-Rule is binary and neutral; since every MMD-Rule is built up of a series of majority voting operations, it is also decisive. Since each majority voting operation involved in a MMD-Rule has for its entries only individual orderings or results of a lower-stage majority-voting operation it is clear that every MMD-Rule is non-negatively responsive[1] and satisfies the

---

[1] Though all MMD-Rules are binary, decisive, neutral, and non-negatively responsive, a binary, decisive, neutral, and non-negatively responsive group decision Rule is not necessarily a MMD-Rule. For example, the Extended Weak Pareto Criterion is a binary, decisive, neutral, and non-negatively responsive Rule, but it is not a MMD-Rule as is clear from the fact that it does not satisfy the Strict Pareto Criterion which is satisfied by every MMD-Rule. However, by a theorem due to Murakami ([4], Chapter 3) a binary, decisive, neutral, and positively responsive Rule will necessarily be a MMD-Rule.

Strict Pareto Criterion. It follows that every MMD-Rule satisfies Arrow's Conditions 2, 3, and 4. However as noted in footnote on p. 59, every MMD-Rule does not satisfy Arrow's Condition 5. If we require a MMD-Rule to satisfy Condition 5, by the General Possibility Theorem it must violate Condition 1'. Since a MMD-Rule is always decisive, it follows that every MMD-Rule that is non-dictatorial in Arrow's sense must violate transitivity of R for some sets of individual orderings. In other words every non-dictatorial MMD-Rule viewed as SWF has a restricted domain.

A MMD-Rule when viewed as SWF will be called a MMD–SWF, and when viewed as SDF it will be called MMD–SDF. Not only every non-dictatorial MMD–SWF has a restricted domain but also some non-dictatorial MMD–SDFs have restricted domains. This is clear from the fact that the MD-Rule is a non-dictatorial MMD-Rule and that the MD–SDF has a restricted domain.

Appendix to Chapter 3

There have been several versions of the General Possibility Theorem, some of them advanced by Arrow and some by other writers. In an earlier version of the theorem Arrow ([1], Chapters 3 and 5) required the group decision Rule to satisfy Conditions 2, 3, 4 and 5 as given above, but instead of Condition 1' a weaker condition (to be called Condition 1) was imposed. Under Condition 1' R is a complete ordering for all logically possible sets of individual orderings. In other words, the individuals may order the alternatives in any way they like, but the group decision Rule always yields a complete social ordering. Under Condition 1 also R has to be a complete ordering, but Condition 1 only requires that among all the alternatives there should be at least three such that the individuals can order them in any way they like. More formally, Condition 1 may be stated as follows:

Condition 1

    (i) *The range of the group decision Rule is a set of complete orderings defined over S.*

    (ii) *In the set S there exists at least one subset $\bar{S}$ of three alternatives* *fulfilling the following condition: for every logically possible set of individual orderings $\{R_1, R_2, ..., R_N\}$ defined over $\bar{S}$, there exists a set of individual orderings $\{R_1', ..., R_N'\}$ over S such that $\{R_1', ..., R_N'\}$ belongs to the domain of the group decision Rule, and for all a and b belonging to $\bar{S}$, and for all i, $aR_i b$ if and only if $aR_i' b$.*

Thus, while under Condition 1' (ii) all triples are 'free', the existence of only one 'free' triple will meet the requirement of Condition 1 (ii). It was claimed in Arrow ([1], Chapter 5) that Conditions 1, 2, 3, 4 and 5 were incompatible. But the proof of this result contained an error, and in an ingenious counter-example Blau demonstrated that it *was* possible to construct a group decision Rule which satisfies Conditions 1, 2, 3, 4 and 5. The secret of the counterexample lies in the fact that while Condition 1 is satisfied if there is only one free triple, the Condition of Non-dictatorship is stated in terms of *all* the alternatives. If a dictator with respect to a set of alternatives, is defined as an individual whose strict preference prevails in every pairwise comparison of the alternatives in that set, regardless of the preferences of others, Condition 5 forbids the existence of a dictator with respect to the entire set of alternatives under consideration. But it does not rule out the possibility of an individual becoming a dictator over a proper subset of that set. It is thus clear that under Conditions 1, 2, 3, 4 and 5 there may be only one free triple and there may exist an individual who is a dictator with respect to that triple. It is this feature of the set of conditions 1, 2, 3, 4, and 5, which was successfully utilized by Blau in producing a counterexample to the earlier version of the General Possibility Theorem.

Blau's counterexample, though it served to demonstrate the logical flaw in the original version, hardly changed the destructive impact of Arrow's theorem. This is because the group decision Rule implied by Blau's counterexample is highly arbitrary and almost dictatorial in nature, and also because the original set of conditions being really very weak, it is possible to remove the logical difficulty by a reasonable strengthening of the conditions. One way of removing the error will be to replace Condition 1 by Condition 1' which makes every triple 'free'. Conditions 1', 2, 3, 4 and 5 can then be shown to be incompatible. Another highly appealing method has been suggested by

Murakami[1], and is based on a strengthening of Conditions 2 and 5 into 2' and 5' respectively.

CONDITION 2'. *If the group decision Rule yields the result xPy for some x and y, and for some set of individual orderings, and if subsequently x rises (relative to y), in the orderings of some individuals without falling (relative to y) in the orderings of others, then the group decision Rule yields the result xPy for the set of individual orderings after this change.*[1]

CONDITION 5'. *Among the triples of alternatives, which satisfy the restriction referred to in Condition 1 (ii) there exists at least one triple such that no individual is a dictator with respect to that triple.*

Condition 2' may be compared with Condition 2. Under Condition 2 the individual orderings are assumed to remain exactly the same except for the fact that x rises in the preference orderings of some individuals. Under Condition 2', however, the individual orderings may vary in any fashion, but if x rises *relative to y* in some preference orderings without falling *relative to y* in any, then the position of x relative to y in the social ordering does not worsen as compared to the initial situation. To take a simple example, let us assume that x, y and z constitute the total set of alternatives and that the group decision Rule in the initial situation gives the result xPy. Now let us assume that the preference orderings for all other individuals remaining the same, the ordering of individual 1 changes from xI_1yP_1z to xP_1zP_1y. Condition 2' will prescribe xPy in the new situation since, by hypothesis, x has risen relative to y in the preference ordering of individual 1 without falling (relative to y) in the preference ordering of any other individual. But in this case Condition 2 will not be applicable at all, since the ordering of individual 1 as between z and y has changed.

Condition 2', though stronger than Condition 2, is not likely to be objected to, by anyone who accepts Condition 2. The replacement of Condition 5 by the stronger Condition 5' will also seem to be very reasonable. All that Condition 5' requires is that among the free triples there should be at least one with respect to which no one is a dictator. Rejection of Condition 5' would, therefore, mean that we are prepared to accept dicta-

---

[1] This condition was first introduced by Blau.

63

torial decision for every triple of alternatives, with respect to which the individuals really have freedom of ordering. Thus, Murakami's theorem that Conditions 1, 2′, 3, 4 and 5′ are incompatible removes the logical error in the original version without strengthening the conditions substantially.

Arrow ([1], second edition; [3]) gives yet another version of the General Possibility Theorem under which Conditions 2 and 4 are replaced by the Weak Pareto Criterion. It is demonstrated that Conditions 1′, 3, 5, and the Weak Pareto Criterion are incompatible. Since Conditions 2′, 3 and 4 together imply the Weak Pareto Criterion[1] and since Conditions 1′, 2 and 3 together imply condition 2′, it follows that Conditions 1′, 2′, 3, 4 and 5 are incompatible and also that Conditions 1′, 2, 3, 4 and 5 are incompatible. Arrow ([1], second edition) also pointed out that, in the theorem of Murakami [1] quoted above, Conditions 2′ and 4 can be replaced by the Weak Pareto Criterion, and Conditions 1, 3, and 5′ and the Weak Pareto Criterion can be shown to be inconsistent.

Recently, Hansson has proved another 'impossibility' theorem which is closely related to some of the results discussed above. Consider the following condition:

Absence of Universal Indifference. The range of the group decision Rule is not a one-element set such that the single social weak preference relation belonging to it shows indifference for every pair of alternatives belonging to S.

What Hansson demonstrates is that a group decision Rule that satisfies neutrality, anonymity, and Arrow's Conditions 1′ and 3 must violate the condition of Absence of Universal Indifference. In other words, neutrality, anonymity, Absence of Universal Indifference, and Arrow's Conditions 1′, and 3 are incompatible. This may be compared with Arrow's theorem that Conditions 1′, 3, 5 and the Weak Pareto Criterion are incompatible. Hansson includes Conditions 1′, and 3. Anonymity, as we have seen, is a much stronger condition than Arrow's Condition 5. The Weak Pareto Criterion in Arrow's version has been replaced by neutrality and the Absence of Universal Indifference. Since, however, the Weak Pareto Criterion has rarely been disputed, and since the acceptance of the Weak Pareto

---

[1] See Arrow [1].

Criterion is likely to be one of the main reasons why anybody
would object to violating the Condition of Absence of Universal
Indifference, there does not seem to be much gain in terms of
ethical acceptability in replacing the Weak Pareto Criterion by
neutrality and the Absence of Universal Indifference. In view of
this, the incompatibility unearthed by Hansson may be considered to be *almost* a special case of the incompatibility of
Conditions 1′, 3, 5, and the Weak Pareto Criterion, proved by
Arrow.[1]

The different versions of the General Possibility Theorem
referred to above may be summed up as follows:[2]

(*a*) Arrow [1]: Conditions 1, 2, 3, 4 and 5 are incompatible.
(Invalid.)

(*b*) Murakami [1]: Conditions 1, 2′, 3, 4 and 5′ are incompatible.

(*c*) Arrow ([1], second edition; [3]): Conditions 1′, 3, 5 and
the Weak Pareto Criterion are incompatible.

(*d*) Arrow ([1], second edition): Conditions 1, 3, 5′, and the
Weak Pareto Criterion are incompatible.

(*e*) Arrow ([1], second edition): Conditions 1′, 2′, 3, 4 and 5
are incompatible.

(*f*) Arrow ([1], second edition): Conditions 1′, 2, 3, 4 and 5
are incompatible.

(*g*) Hansson: Neutrality, anonymity, Absence of Universal
Indifference, and Conditions 1′ and 3 of Arrow are incompatible.
In Chapter 3 we selected the version (*f*) for discussion.

[1] Hansson interpreted his theorem as showing the unreasonable nature of
Arrow's Condition 3. This interpretation, of course, assumes that the other conditions, i.e., neutrality, anonymity, Absence of Universal Indifference, and Arrow's
Condition 1′, are all reasonable. This, however, is far from being clear. In particular, as we have seen above, there does not seem to be any compelling reason for
accepting Condition 1′.

[2] Besides these, other formulations of the General Possibility Theorem have been
given by Vickrey, Inada [1], Murakami [4], and Sen [9]. As shown by Blau,
Inada's [1] formulation involves the same type of error as the original formulation
of Arrow. Murakami [4] contains an extensive discussion of several different
versions of the General Possibility Theorem. Sen [9] poses an interesting problem
arising out of the conflict between certain liberal values and the Weak Pareto
Criterion.

4

RESTRICTIONS ON SETS OF INDIVIDUAL PREFERENCE PATTERNS

4.1. *Introduction*

In the last chapter it was argued that there is no reason why we should require a social decision function[1] f to have for its domain the class of all possible sets of individual orderings. If the sets of individual orderings in real life always exhibit certain specific properties, then for all practical purposes it will be enough if all sets of individual orderings possessing the properties in question belong to the domain of f. There may be other logically possible sets of individual orderings outside this domain but this should not worry us so far as the problem of actual social choice is concerned. This line of approach was first suggested by Black ([1], [2]) and Arrow [1] in the context of the majority decision Rule. However, the point is perfectly general, and applies to any f with a restricted domain.

If the above contention is accepted, then the task would seem to be twofold. First, given a particular f, we have to provide a systematic characterization of the sets of individual orderings that belong to the domain of f. Second, we have to test empirically whether these characteristics hold in actual practice. The first problem is a purely logical one whereas the second is essentially a factual problem and is more difficult to tackle. In this book I shall be mainly concerned with the first problem and ignore the second with the hope that it will be taken up by interested scholars in future.

4.2. *Definition of a Sufficient Condition*

Suppose we have an otherwise acceptable f which has a restricted domain, and we are interested in systematically specifying the sets of individual orderings which belong to its domain. One can

---

[1] The discussion that follows applies to social welfare functions also. I shall, therefore, simply speak of f, which may be interpreted either as a SDF or as a SWF.

think of a large number of alternative definitions of a sufficient condition (in terms of restrictions on sets of individual orderings) for a set of individual orderings to belong to the domain of f. I discuss below the two alternative definitions that seem to be most relevant to us. I label them as Type I and Type II sufficient conditions.

DEFINITION 4.1. *A set of individual orderings and a set of possible preference orderings correspond to each other if and only if the preference ordering implied by every individual ordering in the former set belongs to the latter set and every preference pattern belonging to the latter set is implied by some individual ordering in the former.*

For example, the set of individual orderings $\{xP_1y, xP_2y, xI_3y\}$ defined over $\{x, y\}$ corresponds to the set of possible orderings $\{x\bar{P}_jy, x\bar{I}_jy\}$ but does not correspond to $\{x\bar{P}_jy, x\bar{I}_jy, y\bar{P}_jx\}$. This is because there does not exist any individual ordering corresponding to the possible ordering $y\bar{P}_jx$ belonging to

$$\{x\bar{P}_jy, x\bar{I}_jy, y\bar{P}_jx\}.$$

DEFINITION 4.2. *A sufficient condition of Type I for a set of individual orderings to be in the domain of f specifies a class Ω^I of permissible sets of orderings such that any set of individual orderings corresponding to any set in Ω^I is in the domain of f.*

A sufficient condition of Type I thus specifies certain permissible sets of orderings. A set of individual orderings which corresponds to any of these permissible sets of orderings belongs to the domain of f, irrespective of the distribution of the individuals over the different orderings in the permissible set. Since, however, the set of individual orderings *corresponds* to the permissible set of orderings, the implicit restriction on the distribution of individuals over the different orderings in the permissible set is that there must be at least one individual for each of these orderings.

DEFINITION 4.3. *A sufficient condition of Type II for a set of individual orderings to be in the domain of f specifies a class Ω^{II} of permissible sets of orderings such that any set of individual orderings corresponding to a subset of any set in Ω^{II} is in the domain of f.*

Like a sufficient condition of Type I, a sufficient condition of Type II also specifies certain permissible sets of orderings. But here we have no restriction regarding the distribution of individuals over the different orderings in the permissible set. There may be more than one individual for the same ordering in the permissible set, or none at all.

The difference between the two definitions of a sufficient condition can be further explained as follows. If a permissible set of orderings A belongs to Ω^{II}, then any subset of A also belongs to Ω^{II}. Ω^{I}, however, does not necessarily possess this characteristic: a permissible set of orderings A may belong to Ω^{I} without every subset of A belonging to Ω^{I}. It is clear that a sufficient condition of Type II is also a sufficient condition of Type I but the converse is not necessarily true.

Which definition of a sufficient condition should one adopt? I shall consider sufficient conditions of both the types mentioned above. From one standpoint, however, it seems appropriate to use sufficient conditions of Type I. For our interest in the sufficient conditions in terms of restrictions on permissible sets of orderings arises from their significance for actual policy prescription. For the purpose of policy prescription it seems to be enough if the set of individual orderings in actual life always corresponds to some set A belonging to Ω^{I}. It would be irrelevant in this context to point out that if the set of individual orderings corresponded to a subset of A, then it might not have belonged to the domain of f.

4.3. *Definition of a Necessary Condition*

Can we formulate a necessary condition for a set of individual orderings to be in the domain of f? If we define a necessary condition as one which must be satisfied by every set of individual orderings in the domain of f, then it is clear that for many f no significant necessary condition can be formulated in terms of restrictions on permissible sets of orderings. For example, it will be impossible to formulate any necessary condition of this type for a set of individual orderings to be in the domain of the majority decision Rule either as a SWF or as a SDF. This can be easily seen with the help of the following result.

Restrictions on Preference Patterns

DEFINITION 4.4. *A preference pattern $\bar{R}_i$ connected over a set of alternatives, A, is said to be* concerned *with respect to A if and only if it does not show indifference between all the alternatives in A.*[1] Similarly we also speak of a concerned individual.

LEMMA 4.1. *The MD-Rule yields transitive results if for every triple of alternatives (a, b, c) more than half of the total number of individuals concerned with respect to (a, b, c) have identical preference orderings.*[2]

PROOF:

Let (x, y, z) be a given triple of alternatives. It is clear that a necessary and sufficient condition for R to be intransitive over (x, y, z) is that one and only one of the two 'cycles'

$$(xRy \ \& \ yRz \ \& \ zRx) \quad \text{and} \quad (yRx \ \& \ xRz \ \& \ zRy)$$

holds.

Let the total number of individuals concerned with respect to (x, y, z) be N^*. Without loss of generality we can assume that more than $N^*/2$ individuals have one of the following preference patterns in common:

$$(1) \ xP_iyP_iz, \quad (2) \ xI_iyP_iz \quad \text{and} \quad (3) \ xP_iyI_iz.$$

If (1) or (3) is the common preference pattern then we have $N(xP_iy) > N^*/2$ and $N(xP_iz) > N^*/2$. The MD-Rule will, therefore, yield the result $(xPy \ \& \ xPz)$ in which case neither of the cycles holds. R will therefore be transitive.

If (2) is the common preference pattern then we have $N(xP_iz) > N^*/2$ and $N(yP_iz) > N^*/2$. The MD-Rule will yield

---

[1] See Sen [4].

[2] It is not, however, necessarily true that if more than half of the total number of concerned individuals have identical orderings over a triple, then the results of the MD-Rule over that triple will coincide with that common ordering. If we have three individual orderings xI_1yP_1z, xI_2yP_2z, and zP_3xP_3y, then a majority of concerned individuals have the ordering xI_iyP_iz but the MD-Rule yields

$$(xPy \ \& \ yPz \ \& \ xPz).$$

The same example shows that even if a majority of all individuals, concerned as well as unconcerned, have identical preference orderings, the results of the MD-Rule may not coincide with this common ordering. The following statement of Arrow ([1], p. 74) has therefore to be interpreted as referring to a situation where a majority of the individuals have the same *linear* ordering of social alternatives:

> Suppose it is assumed in advance that a majority of the individuals will have the same ordering of social alternatives. . . . Then the method of majority decision . . . will pick out this agreed-on ordering and make it the social ordering.

the result *(xPz & yPz)* in which case again neither of the cycles holds. *R* will, therefore, be transitive in this case also.   Q.E.D.

Now assume that a majority of individuals concerned with respect to the entire set have identical linear orderings. In this case it is obvious that a majority of individuals concerned with respect to any triple have identical preference orderings. By Lemma 4.1, the MD-Rule will yield transitive results. The set of individual orderings will, therefore be in the domain of MD–SWF. If the set of alternatives is finite, then the set of individual orderings will also be in the domain of MD–SDF. The orderings of individuals other than the given majority can, however, be allowed to vary so as to violate any form of restriction, without affecting transitivity of the results under the MD-Rule.

Thus from one point of view we cannot really hope to formulate a necessary condition in terms of restricted individual preferences for a set of individual orderings to be in the domain of certain social decision functions. There are, however, other more fruitful approaches to the problem of formulating a necessary condition. In particular, I shall distinguish two different definitions of a necessary condition and call them necessary conditions of Type I and Type II respectively.[1]

DEFINITION 4.5.   *A necessary condition of Type I for a set of individual orderings to be in the domain of f specifies a class Ω_I of permissible sets of orderings such that for every permissible set of orderings, A, not belonging to Ω_I there exists a set of individual orderings which corresponds to A and which does not belong to the domain of f.*

DEFINITION 4.6.   *A necessary condition of Type II for a set of individual orderings to be in the domain of f specifies a class Ω_{II} of permissible sets of orderings such that for every permissible set of orderings, A, not belonging to Ω_{II} there exists a set of individual orderings which corresponds to a subset of A and which does not belong to the domain of f.*

From the definitions it is clear that a necessary condition of Type I will also be a necessary condition of Type II though the converse is not necessarily true.

[1] A necessary condition of Type II was first proposed by Inada [3] in the context of the MD-Rule.

Restrictions on Preference Patterns

4.4   The Concept of a Necessary and Sufficient Condition

A condition which is sufficient in Type I sense and also necessary in Type I sense will be called a necessary and sufficient condition of Type I. A condition which is sufficient in Type II sense and also necessary in Type II sense will be called a necessary and sufficient condition of Type II.

The significance of these two types of necessary and sufficient conditions may be explained a little further. Consider a case where S contains only three alternatives.[1] There are altogether 13 possible types of preference orderings over these three alternatives. Therefore the number of permissible sets of orderings is 2^{13} ($= 8,192$). Among these there are some sets with the characteristic that *whenever* a set of individual orderings corresponds to one of them, it belongs to the domain of f regardless of the distribution of individual orderings over the different orderings in the permissible set. In the three-alternative case, the task of formulating a necessary and sufficient condition of Type I is one of systematically specifying from among the 8,192 possible sets of individual preference patterns *all* the sets possessing this characteristic. Similarly the problem of formulating a necessary and sufficient condition of Type II is one of systematically specifying *all* the permissible sets of orderings having the characteristic that whenever a set of individual preference orderings corresponds to a subset of a permissible set, the set of individual orderings belongs to the domain of f regardless of the distribution of individual orderings. The class which will be specified under a necessary and sufficient condition of Type II will clearly be a subclass of the class that will be specified under a necessary and sufficient condition of Type I.

In the following four chapters I shall be concerned with the problem of formulating necessary and sufficient conditions for a set of individual orderings to belong to the domain of different types of social decision functions and social welfare functions.

---

[1] The specific case of three alternatives is chosen for two reasons. Firstly, we can readily generalize the discussion to take into account any number of alternatives. Secondly, all the restrictions on permissible sets of orderings that I shall consider subsequently are formulated in terms of triples of alternatives.

5

THE EXISTENCE OF A SOCIALLY
BEST ALTERNATIVE UNDER THE
MAJORITY DECISION RULE

5.1. *Introduction*

In Chapter 3 we saw that the MD-Rule has several desirable properties. Not only does it satisfy Arrow's conditions of Positive Association, Independence of Irrelevant Alternatives, Citizens' Sovereignty, and Non-dictatorship, but also it satisfies decisiveness, neutrality, positive responsiveness, and anonymity— properties that have a strong ethical appeal for many people. However, the MD-Rule has a restricted domain as a SDF. As was argued in the last chapter, this need not constitute an overwhelming defect, since the domain, though restricted, may still contain all the sets of individual orderings likely to be found in actual life. This consideration lends considerable interest to the study of the conditions under which a set of individual orderings belongs to the domain of MD–SDF. In this chapter I shall establish necessary and sufficient conditions for a set of individual orderings to be in the domain of MD–SDF, i.e., necessary and sufficient conditions under which the MD-Rule defines a non-empty choice set for every non-empty subset of S. Also, I shall consider the conditions under which a given set of alternatives has a non-empty choice set under the MD-Rule.

5.2. *Some Conditions on Sets of Orderings*

I shall define several restrictions on a given set of preference orderings. All the restrictions have the following general form: if a preference pattern of the type p belongs to the given set, then a preference pattern of the type q does not belong to that set. Let Π be any set of preference orderings $\{\bar{R}_1, ..., \bar{R}_n\}$. The restrictions defined below are all conditions on Π and all of them refer to a given ordered triple of alternatives (x, y, z). $a, b,$ and c are three *distinct* variables each of which can assume one of the values x, y, and z.

DEFINITION 5.1. *For a given $\bar{R}_i$, x is said to be given the* worst value *in the triple (x, y, z) if and only if $(y\bar{R}_i x \,\&\, z\bar{R}_i x)$; it is given the* best value *if and only if $(x\bar{R}_i y \,\&\, x\bar{R}_i z)$; it is given the* medium value *if and only if $[(y\bar{R}_i x \,\&\, x\bar{R}_i z) \vee (z\bar{R}_i x \,\&\, x\bar{R}_i y)]$.* Similarly for the worst, best and medium values of y and z.

DEFINITION 5.2. *Value Restriction (VR): In the triple there is an alternative such that it is not given the worst value in any concerned $\bar{R}_i$, or it is not given the best value in any concerned $\bar{R}_i$, or it is not given the medium value in any concerned $\bar{R}_i$.* More formally,

$$(\exists a)\,(\exists b)\,(\exists c)\,(\forall i)\,[\sim (x\bar{I}_i y \,\&\, y\bar{I}_i z \,\&\, z\bar{I}_i x)$$
$$\rightarrow (a\bar{P}_i b \vee a\bar{P}_i c)]$$
$$\vee\,(\exists a)\,(\exists b)\,(\exists c)\,(\forall i)\,[\sim (x\bar{I}_i y \,\&\, y\bar{I}_i z \,\&\, z\bar{I}_i x)$$
$$\rightarrow (b\bar{P}_i a \vee c\bar{P}_i a)]$$
$$\vee\,(\exists a)\,(\exists b)\,(\exists c)\,(\forall i)\,[\sim (x\bar{I}_i y \,\&\, y\bar{I}_i z \,\&\, z\bar{I}_i x)$$
$$\rightarrow \{(a\bar{P}_i b \,\&\, a\bar{P}_i c) \vee (b\bar{P}_i a \,\&\, c\bar{P}_i a)\}].$$

The condition of Value Restriction was first proposed by Sen[4]. It subsumes several conditions proposed earlier by Black ([1], [2]), Arrow[1], Inada[2], Vickrey, and Ward, and is equivalent to the union of all these conditions.[1] As is clear from the definition, VR ean take three forms: not-worst (NW), not-best (NB), and not-medium (NM).

DEFINITION 5.3. *Limited Agreement (LA): In the triple (x, y, z), there exists an ordered pair of distinct alternatives such that in all $\bar{R}_i$, the first alternative in the ordered pair is considered to be at least as good as the second, i.e.,*

$$(\exists a)\,(\exists b)\,(\forall i)\,(a\bar{R}_i b).$$

The condition of Limited Agreement is a weaker version of the restriction of Taboo Preference of Inada[3]. Inada rules out the

---

[1] For a discussion of some of these conditions see the appendix to this chapter.

possibility of indifference between all the alternatives in the triple, and requires that for all $\bar{R}_i$, $\sim (x\bar{I}_i y\bar{I}_i z)$ and that

$$(\exists a)\,(\exists b)\,(\forall i)\,[\sim (b\bar{P}_i a)].{}^{1}$$

We shall not require the restriction that $(\forall i)\,[\sim (x\bar{I}_i y\bar{I}_i z)]$.

We now introduce three restrictions—'Dichotomous Preferences', 'Echoic Preferences', and 'Antagonistic Preferences' —proposed by Inada[3].

DEFINITION 5.4.   *Dichotomous Preferences (DP): No $\bar{R}_i$ is antisymmetric over $\{x, y, z\}$, i.e.,*

$$\sim (\exists a)\,(\exists b)\,(\exists c)\,(\exists i)\,(a\bar{P}_i b \,\&\, b\bar{P}_i c \,\&\, a\bar{P}_i c).$$

DEFINITION 5.5.   *Echoic Preferences (EP): If there is an $\bar{R}_i$ which is antisymmetric over $\{x, y, z\}$, then the worst alternative for that $\bar{R}_i$ in the triple is never preferred to the best alternative in the triple for that $\bar{R}_i$, in any $\bar{R}_j$ belonging to Π. More formally,*

$$(\forall a)\,(\forall b)\,(\forall c)\,[(\exists i)\,(a\bar{P}_i b \,\&\, b\,\bar{P}_i c \,\&\, a\bar{P}_i c) \rightarrow (\forall j)\,\{\sim (c\bar{P}_j a)\}].$$

DEFINITION 5.6.   *Antagonistic Preferences (AP): If there is an $\bar{R}_i$, say, $(x\bar{P}_i y \,\&\, y\bar{P}_i z \,\&\, x\bar{P}_i z)$, which is antisymmetric over $\{x, y, z\}$, then for every $\bar{R}_j\ (j \neq i)$ belonging to Π either $(z\bar{P}_j y \,\&\, y\bar{P}_j x \,\&\, z\bar{P}_j x)$ or $x\bar{I}_j z$. More formally,*

$$(\forall a)\,(\forall b)\,(\forall c)\,[(\exists i)\,(a\bar{P}_i b \,\&\, b\bar{P}_i c \,\&\, a\bar{P}_i c)$$
$$\rightarrow (\forall j)\,\{(a\bar{I}_j c) \vee (c\bar{P}_j b \,\&\, b\bar{P}_j a \,\&\, c\bar{P}_j a)\}].$$

The conditions DP, EP, and AP of Inada [3] can be conveniently combined into a single condition—'Extremal Restriction'— which we shall show to be equivalent to the union of the three conditions. The condition of Extremal Restriction was first introduced by Sen and Pattanaik[1].

DEFINITION 5.7.   *Extremal Restriction (ER): If there is an $\bar{R}_i$, say $(x\bar{P}_i y \,\&\, y\bar{P}_i z \,\&\, x\bar{P}_i z)$, which is antisymmetric over (x, y, z), then for every $\bar{R}_j\ (j \neq i)$ belonging to Π, z is uniquely best if and only if x is uniquely worst, i.e.,*

$$(\forall a)\,\forall b)\,(\forall c)\,[(\exists i)\,(a\bar{P}_i b \,\&\, b\bar{P}_i c \,\&\, a\bar{P}_i c)$$
$$\rightarrow (\forall j)\,(\{c\bar{P}_j a \,\&\, c\bar{P}_j b\} \leftrightarrow \{c\bar{P}_j a \,\&\, b\bar{P}_j a\})].$$

---

[1] Since every $\bar{R}_i$ satisfies connectedness $(\exists a)\,(\exists b)\,(\forall i)\,[\sim (b\bar{P}_i a)]$ implies $(\exists a)\,(\exists b)\,(\forall i)\,(a\bar{R}_i b)$.

It can be checked that this is equivalent to saying that if for some $\bar{R}_i$, a is preferred to b, and b is preferred to c, then for all $\bar{R}_j$ such that c is preferred to a, c is also preferred to b and b is preferred to a, i.e.,

$$(\forall a)\,(\forall b)\,(\forall c)\,[(\exists i)\,(a\bar{P}_i b \;\&\; b\bar{P}_i c \;\&\; a\bar{P}_i c)$$
$$\rightarrow (\forall j)\,(c\bar{P}_j a \rightarrow \{c\bar{P}_j b \;\&\; b\bar{P}_j a\})].$$

5.3. *Some Preliminary Results*

I now prove certain preliminary lemmas concerning the conditions defined above.

LEMMA 5.1.   *ER is equivalent to the union of DP, EP and AP.*

PROOF:

Suppose a set of preference orderings Π satisfies ER over a triple (x, y, z). If there does not exist an $\bar{R}_i$ which is a linear ordering over (x, y, z), then ER is trivially satisfied. In this case DP is satisfied. Suppose there exists $\bar{R}_i$ which is a linear ordering over (x, y, z). Without loss of generality we can assume that $(x\bar{P}_i y\bar{P}_i z)$ belongs to Π. By the definition of ER it follows that $(\forall i)\,[z\bar{P}_i x \rightarrow (z\bar{P}_i y\bar{P}_i x)]$. There are now two possibilities: (1) $\sim (\exists i)\,(z\bar{P}_i x)$ and (2) $(\exists i)\,(z\bar{P}_i x)$. If (2) holds, then $(\exists i)\,(z\bar{P}_i y\bar{P}_i x)$ in which case $(\forall i)\,[x\bar{P}_i z \rightarrow x\bar{P}_i y\bar{P}_i z]$. It follows that if (2) holds then $(\forall i)\,[x\bar{P}_i y\bar{P}_i z \vee z\bar{P}_i y\bar{P}_i x \vee x\bar{I}_i z]$. AP is satisfied in this case. Thus for all a, b, and c belonging to $\{x, y, z\}$, if Π includes $a\bar{P}_i b\bar{P}_i c$, then $(\forall j)\,[\sim (c\bar{P}_j a)]$ or AP holds. This implies that AP or EP is fulfilled when Π includes a linear ordering. Thus in all cases ER implies DP or EP or AP.

Now suppose ER is violated. Then without loss of generality we can assume that

$$(\exists i)\,(x\bar{P}_i y\bar{P}_i z) \quad \text{and} \quad (\exists j)\,[z\bar{P}_j x \;\&\; \sim (z\bar{P}_j y \;\&\; y\bar{P}_j x)].$$

Then either (1) Π contains $x\bar{P}_i y\bar{P}_i z$ and $y\bar{R}_j z\bar{P}_j x$ or (2) Π contains $x\bar{P}_i y\bar{P}_i z$ and $z\bar{P}_j x\bar{R}_j y$. In each of these cases all the three conditions —DP, EP and AP—are violated.   Q.E.D.

LEMMA 5.2.   *ER, VR and LA are completely independent of each other*, i.e., any pair of these three could be satisfied without the third, and any one of these could be satisfied without the remaining pair.

PROOF:

The following set of six examples suffices for the proof.

(1) $x\bar{P}_1 y\bar{P}_1 z$ $z\bar{P}_2 y\bar{P}_2 x$ $y\bar{P}_3 x\bar{I}_3 z$ $x\bar{I}_4 z\bar{P}_4 y$

ER is satisfied by this set of orderings but VR and LA are violated.

(2) $x\bar{P}_1 y\bar{P}_1 z$ $z\bar{P}_2 x\bar{P}_2 y$

ER is violated but VR and LA are satisfied.

(3) $x\bar{P}_1 y\bar{P}_1 z$ $z\bar{P}_2 y\bar{P}_2 x$ $y\bar{P}_3 z\bar{P}_3 x$

VR is satisfied but ER and LA are violated.

(4) $x\bar{P}_1 y\bar{P}_1 z$ $y\bar{P}_2 z\bar{I}_2 x$ $z\bar{I}_3 x\bar{P}_3 y$

VR is violated but ER and LA are both satisfied.

(5) $x\bar{P}_1 y\bar{P}_1 z$ $y\bar{P}_2 z\bar{P}_2 x$ $x\bar{P}_3 y\bar{I}_3 z$ $x\bar{I}_4 y\bar{P}_4 z$ $y\bar{I}_5 z\bar{P}_5 x$

LA is satisfied but ER and VR are violated.

(6) $x\bar{P}_1 y\bar{P}_1 z$ $z\bar{P}_2 y\bar{P}_2 x$

LA is violated but ER and VR are both satisfied.

The next lemma concerns the joint denial of VR, ER, and LA.

LEMMA 5.3.   *If a set of orderings over a triple violates VR, ER and LA, then there is a subset of three orderings in that set which itself violates VR, ER and LA over that triple.*

PROOF:

Over a triple x, y, z, there are thirteen logically possible orderings, and there are $8{,}192$ $(= 2^{13})$ different subsets of the set of these thirteen orderings. Orderings are labelled in a special manner for convenience.

(1.1) $x\bar{P}_i y\bar{P}_i z$	(1.2) $x\bar{P}_i y\bar{I}_i z$	(1.3) $x\bar{I}_i y\bar{P}_i z$
(2.1) $y\bar{P}_i z\bar{P}_i x$	(2.2) $y\bar{P}_i z\bar{I}_i x$	(2.3) $y\bar{I}_i z\bar{P}_i x$
(3.1) $z\bar{P}_i x\bar{P}_i y$	(3.2) $z\bar{P}_i x\bar{I}_i y$	(3.3) $z\bar{I}_i x\bar{P}_i y$
(4) $x\bar{P}_i z\bar{P}_i y$	(5) $z\bar{P}_i y\bar{P}_i x$	(6) $y\bar{P}_i x\bar{P}_i z$
(7) $x\bar{I}_i y\bar{I}_i z$.		

If ER is to be violated, at least one of the orderings must be linear, i.e., satisfy anti-symmetry. Without loss of generality, let us choose ordering 1.1, i.e., $x\bar{P}_i y\bar{P}_i z$. We may first note that there is no other ordering which combined with 1.1 will form a pair that violates VR and LA. Hence the smallest set of orderings that violates VR, ER and LA, must have at least three elements.

It is easy to check that the only three-ordering sets inclusive of 1.1 that violate VR are given by: [1.1, 2.1 *or* 2.2 *or* 2.3, 3.1 *or* 3.2 *or* 3.3]. There are nine such sets. One of these satisfies ER and LA, viz., [1.1, 2.2, 3.3]. Each of the rest violates ER as well as LA. There are, thus, eight three-ordering sets that violate VR, ER and LA, and this class of eight sets we call *K*.

Consider next sets inclusive of 1.1 but having more than three orderings that violate VR, ER and LA. If these sets include any member of *K*, then the result follows immediately. It is easily checked that in order to violate VR without including any member of *K* a set of orderings inclusive of 1.1 must include at least one of the following four-ordering sets.[1]

(I) 1.1, 1.2, 1.3, 2.3;   (II) 1.1, 1.2, 1.3, 3.2;

(III) 1.1, 1.2, 2.2, 2.3;   (IV) 1.1, 1.3, 3.2, 3.3.

Do these four-ordering sets violate LA? None of them do. For example, $y\bar{R}_i z$ holds in every ordering in (I). To include an ordering with $z\bar{P}_i y$, either (*a*) we must include 3.1, or 3.2, or 3.3, in which case the set will then include some member of *K*, or (*b*) we must include ordering 4 or 5, in which case again the set can be seen to include some member of *K* except for formal interchange of *y* and *z*, and of *x* and *z*, respectively. Similarly (II) lacks $y\bar{P}_i z$, (III) lacks $z\bar{P}_i y$, and (IV) lacks $y\bar{P}_i x$, and in each case the inclusion of any ordering filling this gap brings in some member of *K*. This establishes the Lemma.

5.4. *VR and LA: Sufficiency for Quasi-transitivity under the MD-Rule*

The following theorems establish certain sufficient conditions for quasi-transitivity under the MD-Rule. Each of the sufficient conditions specifies a class of permissible sets of orderings such that the MD-Rule yields quasi-transitive results, whenever the set of individual orderings corresponds to a subset of a permissible set of orderings. The sufficient conditions established in these

---

[1] This might appear to be not so if we include ordering 4 or 5 or 6, e.g., [1.1, 4, 5 *or* 3.2 *or* 2.3, 6 *or* 2.2 *or* 1.3]. But the last three elements of each of these possibilities do form a member of *K* except for the substitution of *x* and *y*, or *y* and *z*, or *z* and *x*.

theorems are thus sufficient conditions of Type II mentioned in Chapter 4.[1]

THEOREM 5.1. *A sufficient condition of Type II for the MD-Rule to yield quasi-transitive results over any triple* (x, y, z) *is that every permissible set of orderings satisfies VR over* (x, y, z).

PROOF:

To prove the quasi-transitivity of R it will be enough to show that given VR, $[(xPy \,\&\, yPz) \to xPz]$.[2] Let $\{R_1, ..., R_N\}$ correspond to a subset of a permissible set of orderings satisfying VR. Clearly $\{R_1, ..., R_N\}$ will satisfy VR.

$$(\forall i) \, [\sim (xI_i y I_i z) \to \sim (yR_i z \,\&\, zR_i x)]$$

$$\to (\forall i) \, [\sim (xI_i y I_i z) \to (zP_i y \vee xP_i z)]$$

$$\to \{[N(zP_i y) \geq N^*/2] \vee [N(xP_i z) > N^*/2]\} \text{ where } N^* \text{ is the number of individuals concerned with respect to } \{x, y, z\}.$$

$$\to [\sim (yPz) \vee xPz]$$

$$\to [(xPy \,\&\, yPz) \to xPz] \tag{1}$$

Again,
$$(\forall i) \, [\sim (xI_i y I_i z) \to \sim (zR_i x \,\&\, xR_i y)]$$

$$\to (\forall i) \, [\sim (xI_i y I_i z) \to (xP_i z \vee yP_i x)]$$

$$\to \{[N(xP_i z) > N^*/2] \vee [N(yP_i x) \geq N^*/2]\}$$

$$\to [xPz \vee \sim (xPy)]$$

$$\to [(xPy \,\&\, yPz) \to xPz]. \tag{2}$$

Also,
$$(\forall i) \, [\sim (xI_i y I_i z) \to \sim (xR_i y \,\&\, yR_i z)]$$

$$\to (\forall i) \, [\sim (xI_i y I_i z) \to (yP_i x \vee zP_i y)]$$

$$\to \{[N(yP_i x) \geq N^*/2] \vee [N(zP_i y) \geq N^*/2]\}$$

$$\to [\sim (xPy) \vee \sim (yPz)]$$

$$\to [(xPy \,\&\, yPz) \to xPz]. \tag{3}$$

---

[1] Since a sufficient condition of Type II is also a sufficient condition of Type I, it follows that the sufficient conditions established by these theorems are also sufficient conditions of Type I.

[2] This is because by suitably interchanging x, y, and z, we can obtain
$$[(yPz \,\&\, zPx) \to yPx], \quad [(zPx \,\&\, xPy) \to zPy],$$
and so on, from $[(xPy \,\&\, yPz) \to xPz]$.

From (1), (2), and (3) it follows that each of the following is a sufficient condition for $[(xPy \ \& \ yPz) \to xPz]$:

$$(\forall i) \ [\sim (xI_iyI_iz) \to \sim (yR_iz \ \& \ zR_ix)] \qquad \text{(i)}$$

$$(\forall i) \ [\sim (xI_iyI_iz) \to \sim (zR_ix \ \& \ xR_iy)] \qquad \text{(ii)}$$

$$(\forall i) \ [\sim (xI_iyI_iz) \to \sim (xR_iy \ \& \ yR_iz)]. \qquad \text{(iii)}$$

It can be easily checked that any form of Value Restriction implies (i) or (ii) or (iii). Suppose the set of individual orderings is subject to *NW* value restriction with respect to x. Then (i) is satisfied. For if (i) is violated then

$$(\exists i) \ [\sim (xI_iyI_iz) \ \& \ (yR_iz \ \& \ zR_ix)]$$

which implies $(\exists i) \ [\sim (xI_iyI_iz) \ \& \ (yR_ix \ \& \ zR_ix)]$. But this is not possible if we have *NW* value restriction with respect to x. Similarly *NM* and *NB* value restrictions with respect to x imply (ii) and (iii) respectively. *NW*, *NM* and *NB* value restrictions with respect to y imply (ii), (iii) and (i) respectively. *NW*, *NM* and *NB* value restrictions with respect to z imply (iii), (i) and (ii) respectively. Hence fulfillment of VR implies

$$[(xPy \ \& \ yPz) \to xPz].$$

This completes the proof. $\qquad$ Q.E.D.
The following lemma is useful in proving the next theorem.

LEMMA 5.4. *For any triple* (x, y, z), *the following is true under the MD-Rule*

$$(a) \ \ [(xRy \ \& \ yQz) \to xRz]$$

$$(b) \ \ [(xQy \ \& \ yRz) \to xRz]^1.$$

PROOF:

(a) Assume that $(xRy \ \& \ yQz)$ but $\sim (xRz)$. It will be shown that this leads to a contradiction.

Since yQz, $xR_iy \to xR_iz$, by transitivity of R_i.

Therefore $\qquad\qquad N(xR_iz) \geqslant N(xR_iy).$ $\qquad\qquad$ (1)

Since xRy, $\qquad\qquad N(xR_iy) \geqslant N(yR_ix).$ $\qquad\qquad$ (2)

Since yQz, $zR_ix \to yR_ix$, by transitivity of R_i.

Therefore $\qquad\qquad N(yR_ix) \geqslant N(zR_ix).$ $\qquad\qquad$ (3)

Since by assumption $\sim (xRz)$,

$$N(zR_ix) > N(xR_iz). \qquad\qquad (4)$$

---

[1] As noted earlier, for all x and y, $xQy \leftrightarrow (\forall i) \ (xR_iy)$.

From (1), (2), (3), and (4) we have

$$N(xR_iz) \geqslant N(xR_iy) \geqslant N(yR_ix) \geqslant N(zR_ix) > N(xR_iz)$$

which is a contradiction.

Therefore $\qquad (xRy \And yQz) \rightarrow xRz.$

(*b*) Suppose $(xQy \And yRz)$ but $\sim (xRz)$. It will be shown that this leads to a contradiction.

Since xQy, $yR_iz \rightarrow xR_iz$, by the transitivity of R_i.

Therefore $\qquad N(xR_iz) \geqslant N(yR_iz).$ (5)

Since yRz, $\qquad N(yR_iz) \geqslant N(zR_iy).$ (6)

Since xQy, $zR_ix \rightarrow zR_iy$, by the transitivity of R_i.

Therefore $\qquad N(zR_iy) \geqslant N(zR_ix).$ (7)

Since $\qquad \sim (xRz), \quad N(zR_ix) > N(xR_iz).$ (8)

From (5), (6), (7) and (8) we have

$$N(xR_iz) \geqslant N(yR_iz) \geqslant N(zR_iy) \geqslant N(zR_ix) > N(xR_iz),$$

which is a contradiction.

Therefore $\qquad (xQy \And yRz) \rightarrow xRz.$ $\qquad$ Q.E.D.

THEOREM 5.2. *A sufficient condition of Type II for the MD-Rule to yield quasi-transitive results over any triple (x, y, z) is that every permissible set of orderings satisfies LA over (x, y, z).*

PROOF:

As in the proof of Theorem 5.1 it will be enough if we prove that $\qquad [(xPy \And yPz) \rightarrow xPz)].$

Let there be a set of individual orderings $\{R_1, ..., R_N\}$ corresponding to a subset of a permissible set of orderings. It is clear that $\{R_1, ..., R_N\}$ satisfies LA over (x, y, z).

Therefore $\quad [xQy \lor yQx \lor yQz \lor zQy \lor zQx \lor xQz].$

$xQy \rightarrow [zRx \rightarrow zRy]$ by Lemma 5.4

$\qquad \rightarrow [\sim (zRy) \rightarrow \sim (zRx)]$

$\qquad \rightarrow [yPz \rightarrow xPz]$

$\qquad \rightarrow [(xPy \And yPz) \rightarrow xPz].$ (1)

$yQx \rightarrow yRx$

$\qquad \rightarrow [(xPy \And yPz) \rightarrow xPz],$ trivially. (2)

$yQz \rightarrow [zRx \rightarrow yRx]$, by Lemma 5.4

$\qquad \rightarrow [xPy \rightarrow xPz]$

$\qquad \rightarrow [(xPy \ \& \ yPz) \rightarrow xPz].$ \hfill (3)

$zQy \rightarrow zRy$

$\qquad \rightarrow [(xPy \ \& \ yPz) \rightarrow xPz]$, trivially. \hfill (4)

$zQx \rightarrow [xPy \rightarrow zRy]$, by Lemma 5.4

$\qquad \rightarrow [xPy \rightarrow \ \sim (yPz)]$

$\qquad \rightarrow [(xPy \ \& \ yPz) \rightarrow xPz]$, trivially. \hfill (5)

$xQz \rightarrow [\{(\forall i) \ (xR_i z) \ \& \ (\exists i) \ (xP_i z)\} \lor (\forall i) \ (xI_i z)]$

$\qquad \rightarrow [xPz \lor zQx]$

$\qquad \rightarrow [(xPy \ \& \ yPz) \rightarrow xPz],$ \hfill (6)

since as seen above

$$zQx \rightarrow [(xPy \ \& \ yPz) \rightarrow xPz].$$

From (1), (2), (3), (4), (5) and (6) it follows that if LA is satisfied

$$[(xPy \ \& \ yPz) \rightarrow xPz]. \qquad \text{Q.E.D.}$$

5.5. *ER: Sufficiency for transitivity under the MD-Rule*

The following theorem which is equivalent to Inada's[3] Theorems 1, 2 and 3 taken together establishes the sufficiency of ER for transitivity under the MD-Rule.

THEOREM 5.3. *A sufficient condition of Type II for the MD-Rule to yield transitive results over a triple* (x, y, z) *is that every permissible set of orderings satisfies ER over that triple.*

PROOF:

Let there be a set of individual orderings corresponding to a subset of a permissible set. It can be easily checked that the set of individual orderings will also satisfy ER over (x, y, z).

If every individual is indifferent between at least two alternatives in the triple (x, y, z), then the set of individual orderings satisfies ER trivially over (x, y, z), and the transitivity of majority decisions in this case follows from Theorem 2' in Inada[3]. We need be concerned, therefore, only with non-trivial fulfillment of ER. Without loss of generality let xP_iyP_iz for some i.

Suppose that contrary to the theorem ER holds over (x, y, z), but majority decisions are still intransitive. We know then that *exactly* one of the following must be true: (i) $[xRy \ \& \ yRz \ \& \ zRx]$, and (ii) $[yRx \ \& \ xRz \ \& \ zRy]$. Suppose (i) holds. Since there is an individual such that xP_iyP_iz, we have:

$$zRx \rightarrow [N(zP_ix) \geqslant N(xP_iz)] \rightarrow [N(zP_ix) \geqslant 1]$$
$$\rightarrow (\exists i) \ (zP_iy \ \& \ yP_ix),$$

by ER. The last is a linear ordering over this triple, and applying ER once again, we are left only with a set of four possible orderings that satisfy ER, which are:

(1) $x\bar{P}_iy\bar{P}_iz$; (2) $z\bar{P}_iy\bar{P}_ix$; (3) $y\bar{P}_iz\bar{I}_ix$; and (4) $x\bar{I}_iz\bar{P}_iy$.

Referring to the number of persons holding each of these orderings as N_1, N_2, N_3 and N_4, respectively, we obtain:

$$(xRy \ \& \ yRz \ \& \ zRx) \rightarrow \{[N_1 + N_4 \geqslant N_2 + N_3]$$
$$\& \ [N_1 + N_3 \geqslant N_2 + N_4] \ \& \ [N_2 \geqslant N_1]\}.$$
$$\rightarrow \{[N_1 = N_2] \ \& \ [N_3 = N_4]\}$$
$$\rightarrow (yRx \ \& \ xRz \ \& \ zRy).$$

Thus (i) implies (ii), and intransitivity is impossible.

The only remaining possibility is that (ii) holds alone.

$$(zRy \ \& \ yRx) \rightarrow (\{[N(zP_iy) - N(xP_iy)]$$
$$+ [N(yP_ix) - N(yP_iz)]\} \geqslant 0)$$
$$\rightarrow [N(zP_iyR_ix) + N(zR_iyP_ix) \geqslant 0].$$

If $(\exists i) \ (zP_iyP_ix)$, then we proceed as in the earlier case, and show the impossibility of intransitivity. If not, then thanks to ER, we must have: $N(zP_iyR_ix) = N(zR_iyP_ix) = 0$.

In that case $[N(zP_iy) - N(xP_iy)] + [N(yP_ix) - N(yP_iz)] = 0$. Therefore $(zRy \ \& \ yRx)$ will imply $(zIy \ \& \ yIx)$.

Now, $(\forall i) \ (zP_iy \rightarrow xR_iy)$, since $\sim (\exists i) \ (zP_iyP_ix)$.

Therefore

$$(\forall i) \ (zP_iy \rightarrow xP_iy), \quad \text{since } N(zP_iyR_ix) = 0.$$

Hence $N(xP_iy) \geqslant N(zP_iy)$. Exactly similarly we can show that $N(yP_iz) \geqslant N(yP_ix)$. Since we also have $zIy \ \& \ yIx$, we must have:

$N(yP_ix) = N(xP_iy) \geqslant N(zP_iy) = N(yP_iz) \geqslant N(yP_ix)$, so that $N(xP_iy) = N(zP_iy)$. But we also know from the fact that $(\forall i)\,(zP_iy \rightarrow xP_iy)$, and $(\exists i)\,(xP_iyP_iz)$, that $N(xP_iy) > N(zP_iy)$. This contradiction completes the proof of the theorem. Q.E.D.

5.6. *Necessary and Sufficient Conditions for the Existence of A Social Choice Function*

We now derive a necessary and sufficient condition of Type II for the existence of a SCF under the MD-Rule, for a finite set of alternatives.

THEOREM 5.4. *A necessary and sufficient condition of Type II for a set of individual orderings defined over a finite set of alternatives S to be in the domain of MD–SDF is that every permissible set of orderings must satisfy at least one of the conditions VR, ER and LA over every triple of alternatives belonging to S.*[1]

PROOF:

It is clear from the proofs of Theorems 5.1, 5.2 and 5.3 that if VR or LA or ER is satisfied over every triple of alternatives, then the social weak preference relation must be quasi-transitive over every triple. Hence by the decisiveness of the MD-Rule and by Theorem 1.3, the sufficiency of VR, LA and ER follows immediately. We need concern ourselves only with necessity.

From Lemma 5.3 we know that if a set of orderings violates VR, ER and LA, then that set must include a three-ordering subset which also violates those three restrictions. Further, from the proof we know that there are eight three-ordering subsets[2] that violate VR, ER and LA, viz. [1.1, 2.1 *or* 2.2 *or* 2.3, 3.1 *or* 3.2 *or* 3.3], excluding [1.1, 2.2, 3.3], where:

(1.1) $x\bar{P}_iy\bar{P}_iz$

(2.1) $y\bar{P}_iz\bar{P}_ix$ (2.2) $y\bar{P}_iz\bar{I}_ix$ (2.3) $y\bar{I}_iz\bar{P}_ix$

(3.1) $z\bar{P}_ix\bar{P}_iy$ (3.2) $z\bar{P}_ix\bar{I}_iy$ (3.3) $z\bar{I}_ix\bar{P}_iy$.

---

[1] The nature of restriction is allowed to vary from triple to triple. For example a permissible set of orderings may satisfy only *VR* over one triple, only *ER* over another triple and so on.

[2] There are in fact forty-eight such subsets if we treat x, y and z as constants. But the remaining ones are all exactly like the one described below but for the substitution of x for y; or y for z; or z for x; or y for x and z for y and x for z; or z for x and x for y and y for z. Exactly the same analysis applies in each case.

Existence of Socially Best Alternative

We have to show that in each of these eight cases some assignment of these orderings over some number of individuals will produce a majority preference relation that does not yield a choice function.

First consider the cases represented by [1.1, 2.1 *or* 2.3, 3.1 *or* 3.2]. Let N_1 be the number of persons holding 1.1, N_2 the number holding 2.1 or 2.3, and N_3 the number holding 3.1 or 3.2. If we assume $N_1 > N_2$, $N_1 > N_3$, and $(N_2 + N_3) > N_1$, then we must have xPy, yPz and zPx. A simple example is $N_1 = 3$, $N_2 = N_3 = 2$.

This leaves four cases. Consider next the following two sets, viz. [1.1, 2.1 *or* 2.3, 3.3]. With the same convention on numbering, if we take $N_2 > N_1 > N_3$, and $N_1 + N_3 > N_2$, we have again xPy, yPz and zPx. A simple example is $N_1 = 3$, $N_2 = 4$, and $N_3 = 2$. Finally, we take the cases given by [1.1, 2.2, 3.1 *or* 3.2]. Taking $N_3 > N_1 > N_2$, and $N_1 + N_2 > N_3$, we get xPy, yPz and zPx, as for example with $N_1 = 3$, $N_2 = 2$, and $N_3 = 4$. This completes the proof of necessity, which establishes the theorem.   Q.E.D.

It is thus clear that whenever VR, ER, or LA is satisfied over each triple, there must be for every non-empty subset of S a non-empty choice set irrespective of the number of individuals and their distribution over the orderings in the permissible set. On the other hand, whenever VR, ER and LA are violated for any triple, then a non-empty choice set will fail to exist for some subset of S (in particular, that triple), for some number of individuals distributed in some manner over the orderings in the permissible set.

Theorem 5.4 establishes a necessary and sufficient condition of Type II for a set of individual orderings to be in the domain of MD–SDF. However, I have not been able to derive a necessary and sufficient condition of Type I. My conjecture is that fulfillment of VR or LA or ER over every triple by every permissible set of orderings will prove to be a necessary and sufficient condition of Type I also.

5.7   *The Case of Antisymmetric Individual Preferences*

In the special case in which individual weak preference relations are antisymmetric,[1] i.e., individuals are never indifferent between

---

[1] Borda and Condorcet were mainly concerned with this case. This is true of quite a bit of modern work as well.

any pair of alternatives, the necessary and sufficient conditions for the existence of a choice function become somewhat simpler. This is mainly because ER and LA both imply VR when individual orderings are antisymmetric.

LEMMA 5.5. *A set of antisymmetric orderings satisfies ER or LA over a triple of alternatives only if it satisfies VR over that triple.*

PROOF:

Suppose a set of antisymmetric orderings $\{\bar{R}_1, ..., \bar{R}_n\}$ satisfies ER over a triple (x, y, z). Since indifference is impossible the case of trivial fulfillment of ER does not arise. Let us assume $x\bar{P}_i y\bar{P}_i z$ for some i. We know from ER that $(\forall i)\,[z\bar{P}_i x \rightarrow (z\bar{P}_i y\ \&\ y\bar{P}_i x)]$. If there is no ordering $\bar{R}_i$ such that $z\bar{P}_i x$, then z is not best in any ordering, since $\sim (z\bar{P}_i x) \rightarrow x\bar{P}_i z$, in the case of antisymmetric orderings. In this case VR holds. If, on the other hand, there is some $\bar{R}_i$ for which $z\bar{P}_i x$, and therefore $z\bar{P}_i y\bar{P}_i x$, then by ER $x\bar{P}_i y\bar{P}_i z$ must be true for any $\bar{R}_i$ for which $x\bar{P}_i z$ is true. Since

$$(\forall i)\,(x\bar{P}_i z \lor z\bar{P}_i z),$$

it follows that in this case $(\forall i)\,(x\bar{P}_i y\bar{P}_i z \lor z\bar{P}_i y\bar{P}_i x)$. Once again VR is satisfied since y is not best (nor indeed worst) in any ordering. Hence ER $\rightarrow$ VR.

Suppose LA is satisfied over some triple. Without loss of generality, let $x\bar{R}_i y$ hold for all i, which in this case means $(\forall i)\,(x\bar{P}_i y)$. Hence x is not worst (nor indeed is y best) in any ordering. Thus VR holds. Q.E.D.

It may be noted that the converse does not hold. VR does not imply either ER or LA. This is readily checked by looking at the following set of orderings: $\{x\bar{P}_1 y\bar{P}_1 z, z\bar{P}_2 y\bar{P}_2 x, y\bar{P}_3 z\bar{P}_3 x\}$. ER and LA are both violated, but y is not worst in any ordering, and hence VR holds. The following theorem can now be derived for the case of linear individual orderings.

THEOREM 5.5. *If individual preference orderings are antisymmetric, then a necessary and sufficient condition of Type II for a set of individual orderings defined over a finite set S to be in the domain of MD–SDF is that every permissible set of orderings must satisfy VR over every triple of alternatives belonging to S.*

PROOF:

Since ER, VR and LA are sufficient conditions of Type II irrespective of whether individual orderings are antisymmetric or not, VR is clearly sufficient in the case of antisymmetric individual orderings. By Theorem 5.4 fulfillment of VR or ER or LA over every triple is a necessary condition of Type II, and by Lemma 5.5, if ER or LA holds, then so must VR, in the case of antisymmetric orderings. Hence VR is both a sufficient and a necessary condition of Type II. 　　　　　　Q.E.D.

5.8. *The Existence of a Choice Set in a Given Set of Alternatives*

So far we have been concerned with the existence of a social choice function under the MD-Rule, i.e., the existence of a best alternative under the MD-Rule for every non-empty subset of S. We shall now consider the existence of a best alternative under the MD-Rule for any given subset of S. As explained in Chapter 1, the existence of a best alternative for a given subset A of S is a weaker requirement than the existence of a social choice function over S or A. It would be fair to expect that the restrictions can be relaxed for this more limited demand on the majority decision Rule.

LEMMA 5.6. *Let* Π *be any set of preference orderings defined over a finite set of alternatives* S. *For all* A ($A \subset S$), *and for all* x, *if* $x \in (A - A_\Pi^*)$,[1] *then there exists* y *such that* $y \in A_\Pi^*$ *and* $y\bar{Q}_\Pi x$.[2]

PROOF:

By definition

$$(\forall x)\,[\{x \in (A - A_\Pi^*)\} \to (\exists y)\,(y \in A \;\&\; y\bar{Q}_\Pi x)] \tag{1}$$

$(y \in A \;\&\; y\bar{Q}_\Pi x)$

$$\to [\{(y \in A_\Pi^*) \vee (\exists y')\,(y' \in A \;\&\; y'\bar{Q}_\Pi y)\} \;\&\; y\bar{Q}_\Pi x]$$

$$\to [\{y \in A_\Pi^* \;\&\; y\bar{Q}_\Pi x\} \vee \{(\exists y')\,(y' \in A \;\&\; y'\bar{Q}_\Pi y) \;\&\; y\bar{Q}_\Pi x\}]$$

$$\to [(y \in A_\Pi^* \;\&\; y\bar{Q}_\Pi x) \vee (\exists y')\,(y' \in A \;\&\; y'\bar{Q}_\Pi x)]$$

$$\text{by transitivity of } \bar{Q}_\Pi. \tag{2}$$

[1] For the definition of A_Π^*, see Chapter 3.
[2] See Lemma 1 in Pattanaik[1].

From (1) and (2),

$$(\forall x) [\{x \in (A - A_\Pi^*)\} \to \{(\exists y) \, (y \in A_\Pi^* \; \& \; y\bar{Q}_\Pi x)$$
$$\vee \, (\exists y') \, (y' \in A \; \& \; y'\bar{Q}_\Pi x)\}].$$

Proceeding in this fashion, since A is finite, we must get to a $\tilde{y}$ such that $\tilde{y} \in A_\Pi^*$ and $\tilde{y}\bar{Q}_\Pi x$. Q.E.D.

LEMMA 5.7. *Under the MD-Rule, a finite set of alternatives A has a non-empty choice set if and only if the subset A^* of Pareto-optimal alternatives has a non-empty choice set.[1]*

PROOF:

Sufficiency. Let $x \in C(A^*)$. It will be shown that $x \in C(A)$. Let $y \in A$. By definition $\{[y \in A^*] \vee [y \in (A - A^*)]\}$. If $y \in A^*$, then xRy since $x \in C(A^*)$. If $y \in (A - A^*)$, then by Lemma 5.6,

$$(\exists \tilde{y}) \, (\tilde{y} \in A^* \; \& \; \tilde{y}\bar{Q}y).$$

But $(\tilde{y} \in A^*) \to xR\tilde{y}$. Hence if $y \in (A - A^*)$, then $(\exists \tilde{y}) \, (xR\tilde{y} \; \& \; \tilde{y}\bar{Q}y)$. Hence by Lemma 5.4, it follows that if $y \in (A - A^*)$, then xRy.

Thus $(\forall y) \, (y \in A \to xRy)$. Also $x \in A$ since $x \in C(A^*)$.

Therefore $x \in C(A)$, and $C(A)$ is non-empty.

Necessity. Let $C(A^*)$ be empty. It will be shown that $C(A)$ is also empty. Since $C(A^*)$ is empty,

$$(\forall x) [(x \in A^*) \to (\exists y) \, (y \in A^* \; \& \; \sim (xRy))].$$

Therefore $(\forall x) [(x \in A^*) \to (\exists y) \, (y \in A \; \& \; \sim (xRy))].$ \hfill (1)

By definition

$$(\forall x) [\{x \in (A - A^*)\} \to (\exists y) \, (y \in A \; \& \; y\bar{Q}x)].$$

Therefore

$$(\forall x) [\{x \in (A - A^*)\} \to (\exists y) \, (y \in A \; \& \; \sim (xRy))]. \tag{2}$$

From (1) and (2), it follows that

$$(\forall x) [(x \in A) \to (\exists y) \, (y \in A \; \& \; \sim (xRy))].$$

Therefore $C(A)$ is empty. \hfill Q.E.D.

THEOREM 5.6. *A sufficient condition of Type II for a finite set of alternatives A to have a non-empty choice set under the MD-Rule is that*

---

[1] This is a generalization of Lemma 1 in Pattanaik [1].

every permissible set of orderings Π *should satisfy ER or VR over every triple of alternatives belonging to* A_Π^*.[1]

PROOF:

Let there be a set of individual orderings $\{R_1, ..., R_N\}$ corresponding to a subset of Π. Since $\{R_1, ..., R_N\}$ corresponds to a subset of Π and not necessarily to Π, A_Π^* and A^* need not be identical. By Lemma 3.1, however, both A_Π^* and A^* are non-empty.

A^* can be partitioned into two subsets $(A^* \cap A_\Pi^*)$ and $(A^* - A_\Pi^*)$. Let $x \in (A^* - A_\Pi^*)$. Clearly $x \in (A - A_\Pi^*)$. Therefore by Lemma 5.6 there exists y belonging to A_Π^* such that $y\bar{Q}_\Pi x$. Since $[y\bar{Q}_\Pi x \to yQx]$ it follows that $(\exists y)$ $(y \in A_\Pi^* \,\&\, yQx)$. But by hypothesis $x \in (A^* - A_\Pi^*)$. Therefore $x \in A^*$. Hence

$$\sim (\exists z)\ (z \in A\ \&\ z\bar{Q}x).$$

Since $[(\exists y)\ (y \in A_\Pi^*\ \&\ yQx)\ \&\ \sim (\exists z)\ (z \in A\ \&\ z\bar{Q}x)]$, it follows that $(\exists y)\ \{(y \in A_\Pi^*)\ \&\ (\forall i)\ (xI_i y)\}$.

Now let x, y, and z be any triple of alternatives belonging to A^*. It will be shown that there exist x', y' and z' belonging to A_Π^* such that $[(\forall i)\ (xI_i x')\ \&\ (\forall i)\ (yI_i y')\ \&\ (\forall i)\ (zI_i z')]$. For if $x \in (A^* - A_\Pi^*)$ then we have seen above that

$$(\exists x')\ \{(x' \in A_\Pi^*)\ \&\ (\forall i)\ (xI_i x')\}.\ \text{If}\ x \in (A^* \cap A_\Pi^*),$$

then clearly $\quad [x' \in A_\Pi^*\ \&\ (\forall i)\ (xI_i x')]$ where $x' = x$.

Thus in all cases

$$(\exists x')\ [x' \in A_\Pi^*\ \&\ (\forall i)\ (xI_i x')].$$

Similarly,

$$(\exists y')\ (\exists z')\ [(y' \in A_\Pi^*)\ \&\ (z' \in A_\Pi^*)\ \&\ (\forall i)\ (y'I_i y\ \&\ z'I_i z)].$$

Now consider the triple (x, y, z). $\{R_1, ..., R_N\}$ cannot violate both VR and ER over (x, y, z). For if $\{R_1, ..., R_N\}$ violates both VR and ER over (x, y, z), then it will violate both VR and ER over (x', y', z'), in which case Π will also violate both VR and ER

---

[1] This is a generalization of Theorem VI of Sen and Pattanaik. What Theorem VI of Sen and Pattanaik really proves is the following:

A sufficient condition of Type I for a finite set of alternatives to have a non-empty choice set under the MD-Rule is that every permissible set of orderings Π should satisfy ER or VR over every triple of alternatives belonging to A_Π^*.

Theorem 5.6 is a generalization of this since a sufficient condition of Type II is necessarily a sufficient condition of Type I though the converse is not always true.

over (x', y', z'). But this is impossible since x', y' and z' all belong to A_{Π}^*. $\{R_1, ..., R_N\}$ must therefore satisfy VR or ER over (x, y, z).

Thus $\{R_1, ..., R_N\}$ satisfies VR or ER over every triple of alternatives belonging to A^*. From the proofs of Theorems 5.1 and 5.3, it is clear that R must be quasi-transitive over every triple of alternatives belonging to A^*. Hence by the decisiveness of the MD-Rule and by Theorem 1.3 it follows that $C(A^*)$ must be non-empty. Therefore by Lemma 5.7, $C(A)$ must be non-empty.

Q.E.D.

Two points should be noted about Theorem 5.6. Firstly, the condition LA does not figure in the theorem. This is because fulfillment of LA over a triple of alternatives belonging to A_{Π}^* implies that there are at least two alternatives x and y in the triple such that for all $\bar{R}_i$ belonging to the permissible set of orderings Π, $(x\bar{I}_i y)$. But in this case ER is trivially satisfied. Secondly, Theorem 5.6 gives only a sufficient condition and not a necessary and sufficient condition. In fact, it is clear that the condition given in Theorem 5.6 cannot be a necessary condition for A to have a non-empty choice set. For if a permissible set of orderings Π violates both ER and VR over a triple of alternatives in A_{Π}^*, then for some set of individual orderings corresponding to a subset of Π, the choice set for that triple will be empty. But this does not prevent A_{Π}^* from having a non-empty choice set. Consider the following example where $A = A_{\Pi}^* = \{x, y, z, w\}$ and Π has for its elements the orderings $x\bar{P}_1 y\bar{P}_1 z\bar{P}_1 w$, $w\bar{P}_2 y\bar{P}_2 z\bar{P}_2 x$, and $w\bar{P}_3 z\bar{P}_3 x\bar{P}_3 y$. ER and VR are both violated over (x, y, z). However for any set of orderings corresponding to a subset of Π, either $[x \in C(A)]$ or $[w \in C(A)]$.

The difficulty arises from the fact that a given set of alternatives can have a non-empty choice set though a proper subset of the given set has none. This difficulty does not arise in the context of a choice function since if the choice function is not defined over a proper subset of any set of alternatives, then it is also not defined over the entire set of alternatives. Indeed no necessary condition of either type for the existence of a choice set could be defined in terms of restriction over every triple of alternatives in A_{Π}^*. To see this, take again $A = A_{\Pi}^* = \{x, y, z, w\}$. Let Π be a permissible set of orderings. Let the position in these orderings be determined according to the following rule. If none of the orderings in Π is concerned with respect to (x, y, z), then in all orderings excepting one w is strictly preferred to x, y and z, and in one ordering x, y and z are all strictly preferred to w;[1] if some orderings in Π are concerned with respect to (x, y, z), then in one of the orderings concerned with respect to (x, y, z), x, y and z are all strictly preferred to w, and in all the other orderings in Π, w is strictly preferred to x, y and z. So long as this rule regarding the position of w is satisfied, the orderings over (x, y, z) can be allowed to vary so as to violate any restriction, and yet we shall have a non-empty $C(\{x, y, z, w\})$ under the MD-Rule for any set of individual orderings corresponding to any subset of Π. This can be proved as follows. Take any set of individual orderings corresponding to a subset of Π. Given the rule regarding the position of w, at least one of the following must be true:

(1) All the individuals have identical orderings.

(2) For some individuals $x\bar{I}_i y\bar{I}_i z\bar{P}_i w$ is true and for the rest of the individuals $w\bar{P}_i x\bar{I}_i y\bar{I}_i z$ is true.

(3) For all individuals $w\bar{P}_i x$ & $w\bar{P}_i y$ & $w\bar{P}_i z$ is true.

(4) For some individuals $(w\bar{P}_i x$ & $w\bar{P}_i y$ & $w\bar{P}_i z)$ is true and the rest of the individuals have an identical ordering $\bar{R}_j$ such that

$$[\sim (x\bar{I}_j y\bar{I}_j z) \ \& \ x\bar{P}_j w \ \& \ y\bar{P}_j w \ \& \ z\bar{P}_j w].$$

In each of these cases it can be easily checked that $C(A)$ will be non-empty.

Appendix to Chapter 5

In Chapter 5 it was noted that Value Restriction introduced by Sen [4] is equivalent to the union of several conditions proposed earlier by Black ([1], [2]), Arrow [1], Inada [2], Vickrey and Ward. A separate discussion of some of these conditions is of interest in so far as it sheds further light on the intuitive significance of VR.

Consider first NW value restriction. Suppose the permissible sets of orderings satisfy NW value restriction over (x, y, z) with respect to x. Adopting the same convention of numbering the different possible orderings over (x, y, z) as in Lemma 5.3 we can say that any permissible set must be a subset of the following set of orderings: [1.1, 1.2, 1.3, 3.1, 3.3, 4, 6, 7]. This implies that no

---

[1] The existence of this ordering ensures that $\sim [w\bar{Q}_\Pi x \lor w\bar{Q}_\Pi y \lor w\bar{Q}_\Pi z]$.

permissible set of orderings can contain any of the following possible orderings: [2.1, 2.2, 2.3, 3.2, 5]. Consider the following diagrams. Along the horizontal axes we represent a linear ordering T of the alternatives x, y and z such that x comes between y and z. Let this linear ordering be $yTxTz$.[1] Along the vertical axes we represent order of preferences. Each possible preference ordering is thus represented by a preference curve

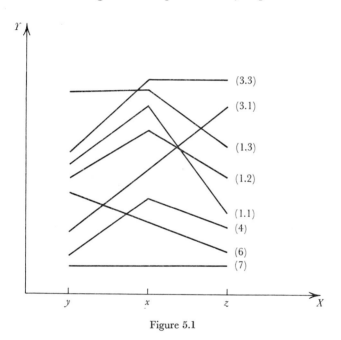

Figure 5.1

such that if, say, x is preferred to y, then the point on the preference curve corresponding to x will have a larger ordinate than the point on the same preference curve that corresponds to y, and if x is indifferent to y then the points on the curve corresponding to x and y have the same ordinates. We represent the set of orderings [1.1, 1.2, 1.3, 3.1, 3.3, 4, 6, 7] by the preference curves in Figure 5.1, and the set of orderings [2.1, 2.2, 2.3, 3.2, 5] by the preference curves in Figure 5.2. The curves in Figure 5.1 have a common characteristic: each curve has only one peak. The

[1] It is immaterial whether we take the linear ordering to be $yTxTz$ or $zTxTy$.

peak may consist of a single point [1.1, 1.2, 3.1, 4, 6] or it may be a horizontal plateau [1.3, 3.3, 7]. Also, the peak may be reached at different alternatives by different curves; but on each side of its peak, a curve, if it extends any further at all, slopes downwards. In contrast, no curve in Figure 5.2 possesses this feature.

In general, it can be easily seen that whenever a permissible set of orderings satisfies NW value restriction, the orderings in

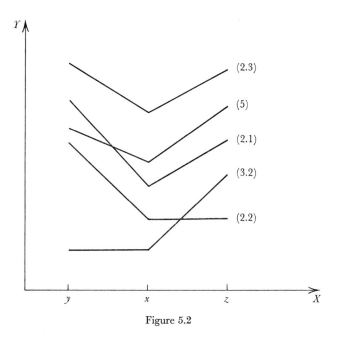

Figure 5.2

the permissible set will be single-peaked, i.e., there will exist a linear ordering T of x, y and z such that the curves representing the permissible set of orderings, and drawn with reference to the linear ordering T, will be all single-peaked. The converse is also true: if there exists a linear ordering T of x, y and z such that the set of curves representing a permissible set of orderings and drawn with reference to T are all single-peaked, then the permissible set is subject NW to value restriction over (x, y, z).

The condition of single-peakedness was first introduced by

Appendix to Chapter 5

Black ([1], [2]), and Arrow [1].[1] Closely akin to this condition is the condition of 'single cavedness' which was introduced by Inada [2] and which can be shown to be equivalent to NB value restriction. The concept of single-cavedness is, in a sense, complementary to that of single-peakedness. In the case of single-peakedness there exists a linear ordering T of x, y, z such that the curves representing a permissible set of orderings and drawn with reference to T, are all single-peaked. In the case of single-cavedness, there exists a linear ordering T of x, y and z such that the curves representing the orderings in the permissible set and drawn with reference to T are all 'singel-caved'. The cave may consist of a single point or a horizontal valley. Also, the different curves may reach their respective 'caves' at different alternatives. However, on each side of its cave, a curve, if it extends any further, slopes upwards. It can be easily shown that the condition of single-cavedness is equivalent to NB value restriction. If a permissible set of orderings satisfies NB value restriction, say, with respect to x, then it can be represented by a subset of the set of single-caved curves drawn in Figure 5.3 with reference to the linear ordering $yTxTz$. Conversely, if there exists a linear ordering $yTxTz$ such that the set of curves representing a permissible set of orderings, and drawn with reference to $yTxTz$, are single-caved, then the permissible set of orderings is subject to NB value restriction with respect to x.

Now consider NM value restriction which is equivalent to the condition of 'separability into two groups' proposed by Inada [2].

[1] Two points should be noted here. Firstly, both Black and Arrow assumed single-peakedness of preference orderings with respect to the entire set of alternatives. In other words, they assume the existence of a linear ordering of *all* the alternatives such that if we take any three alternatives x, y and z, ordered in the same way as they are in the linear ordering of all alternatives, referred to, then all the preference curves drawn for x, y and z are found to be single-peaked in the sense explained earlier. As Inada [2] points out, single-peakedness with respect to the entire set of alternatives is not necessary; it is enough if we have single-peakedness with respect to every triple of alternatives, which is a weaker condition. Secondly, it should be noted that the concept of single-peakedness of Black is different from that of Arrow. Black's concept admits a preference curve which is horizontal over a segment covering three or more alternatives, i.e., an individual can be indifferent as between three or more alternatives. Under Arrow's concept, however, a preference curve cannot show indifference between more than two alternatives. Single-peakedness, as defined in the text, corresponds to Black's concept in the three-alternative cases.

Suppose the permissible set of orderings satisfies *NM* value restriction over (x, y, z) with respect to x. Then the permissible set orderings must be a subset of [1.1, 1.2, 2.1, 2.3, 4, 5, 7]. The set [1.1, 1.2, 2.1, 2.3, 4, 5, 7] is represented in Figure 5.4 drawn with reference to the linear ordering $y\,Tx\,Tz$. It is clear that x is strictly worst or x is strictly best in every permissible preference ordering concerned with respect to (x, y, z). In other words the

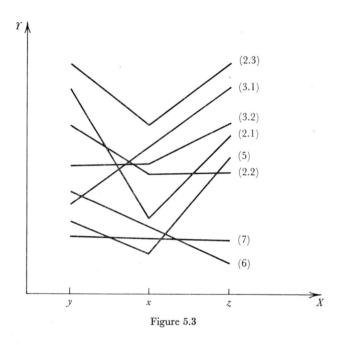

Figure 5.3

triple (x, y, z) can be separated into two groups $\{x\}$ and $\{y, z\}$—such that in every concerned preference ordering belonging to a permissible set, each alternative in one of the groups is strictly preferred to each alternative in the other.

These diagrammatic representations of different types of value restriction suggest several plausible circumstances where these restrictions are likely to be fulfilled. There may, sometimes, exist an agreed-on objective ordering of the alternatives, based on the extent to which they possess a certain attribute. In such a case, if this attribute constitutes the criterion of individual evaluation, then single-peakedness (i.e., NW value restriction) is likely to be satisfied. Such is the case, cited by Arrow, of voting among political parties ordered on the basis of 'left-or-right' criterion. In this case there is an agreed-on ordering of the alternatives involved, on the basis of the objective criterion of the degree of rightism or leftism. A concerned individual will have some best alternative in the set but as he moves further on either side of this

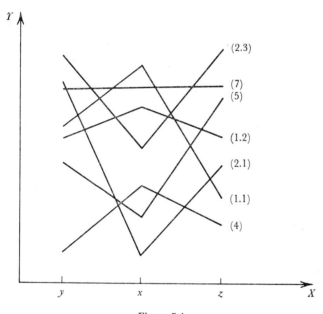

Figure 5.4

most preferred alternative, in the agreed-on objective ordering, he is likely to reach less and less preferred alternatives.[1]

In certain cases involving single criteria of evaluation, NB value restriction may be satisfied. Suppose there are three alternatives regarding the organization of a particular industry: complete nationalization, a mixed form of organization with public and private enterprises operating side by side, and pro-

---

[1] In such cases single-peakedness with respect to the entire set is likely to be fulfilled. This, as noted above, is a stronger requirement than single-peakedness for every triple.

duction through private enterprises only. It is possible that every individual gives the 'best' value to one of the extremes—complete nationalization or complete private ownership—and nobody gives the 'best' value to the mixed form of organization. This implies a purist attitude for all concerned individuals since by moving on either side of his least preferred alternative, in the agreed-on objective ordering, every concerned individual reaches more and more preferred alternatives.

NM value restriction will reflect a sharp division of opinion in the society regarding the position of one of the alternatives in the triple *vis-à-vis* the other two alternatives. A simple case of this arises where the society is divided into two groups whose conflicting interest and/or values make their ordering just the reverse[1] of each other (while individual orderings are identical within each group).[2]

[1] Two orderings $\bar{R}_i$ and $\bar{R}_j$ are said to be the reverse of each other if and only if for all x and y, $x\bar{R}_i y \leftrightarrow y\bar{R}_j x$.

[2] It is, however, doubtful whether in the case of such a sharp division the very social structure can be sustained. In fact, except in a crisis it is rare to find a society with two (and only two) groups with exactly opposite preference orderings. See Dahl (Chapter 3) for a discussion of the relationship between democratic structures and diversity of preferences.

6

THE EXISTENCE OF A SOCIALLY
BEST ALTERNATIVE UNDER SOME
OTHER GROUP DECISION RULES[1]

6.1. *Introduction*

Though the majority decision Rule has been most extensively discussed in the literature, in actual practice a wide range of other group decision Rules are frequently used. I now consider the problem of the existence of a choice function and also that of the existence of a non-empty choice set for a given set of alternatives, under some of these other group decision Rules. I continue to confine myself to binary Rules only; but I shall now consider the class of all binary group decision Rules which satisfy decisiveness, neutrality and non-negative responsiveness,[2] and several subclasses of this general class. This class of binary group decision Rules is of considerable interest since many people would regard neutrality and non-negative responsiveness as some of the minimal properties that a democratic group decision Rule should satisfy.[3] In the course of our investigation into the conditions for the existence of a best alternative under different Rules belonging to this class we shall find that some of the theorems proved in the last chapter can be generalized so as to apply to more general group decision Rules than the majority decision Rule.

6.2. *The Existence of A Choice Function under Binary, Decisive, Neutral, and Non-Negatively Responsive Rules*

In this section I prove a sufficient condition for the existence of a choice function under binary group decision Rules which satisfy decisiveness, neutrality, and non-negative responsiveness.

---

[1] This chapter is mainly based on Sen and Pattanaik, and Pattanaik [3].

[2] The majority decision Rule is clearly an element of this class since it satisfies positive responsiveness and anonymity in addition to decisiveness, neutrality, and non-negative responsiveness.

[3] As for the property of decisiveness, no choice function can exist in its absence (see Chapter 1).

In the theorem that follows I make use of the following lemma due to Murakami[4].

LEMMA 6.1 (*Murakami's Lemma*).   *For any binary, decisive, neutral, and non-negatively responsive Rule, and for all x, y, z and w belonging to S:*

$$\{(\forall i)\,[(xP_iy \rightarrow zP_iw) \,\&\, (xI_iy \rightarrow zR_iw)]$$
$$\rightarrow [(xPy \rightarrow zPw) \,\&\, (xIy \rightarrow zRw)]\}.$$

PROOF:

Since the Rule is binary, decisive and neutral

$$\{(\forall i)\,[(xR_iy \leftrightarrow zR_iw) \,\&\, (yR_ix \leftrightarrow wR_iz)] \rightarrow (xRy \leftrightarrow zRw)\}.$$

Lemma 6.1 follows immediately from this, given the properties of decisiveness and non-negative responsiveness.   Q.E.D.

THEOREM 6.1.   *A sufficient condition of Type II for a binary, decisive, neutral, and non-negatively responsive Rule to yield quasi-transitive results over a triple is that every permissible set of preference orderings should satisfy VR over that triple.*[1]

PROOF:

A necessary condition for R to violate quasi-transitivity over any triple (x, y, z) is that one of the following conditions should hold with at least two of the three Rs being Ps:

$$(xRy \,\&\, yRz \,\&\, zRx) \tag{i}$$
$$(yRx \,\&\, xRz \,\&\, zRy) \tag{ii}$$

$(\forall i)\,[\sim (xI_iyI_iz) \rightarrow \sim (yR_iz \,\&\, zR_ix)]$
$\quad \rightarrow (\forall i)\,[\sim (xI_iyI_iz) \rightarrow \{(yR_iz \rightarrow xP_iz) \,\&\, (zR_ix \rightarrow zP_iy)\}]$
$\quad \rightarrow (\forall i)\,[\{(yP_iz \rightarrow xP_iz) \,\&\, (yI_iz \rightarrow xR_iz)\}$
$\qquad\qquad\qquad\qquad \&\, \{(zP_ix \rightarrow zP_iy) \,\&\, (zI_ix \rightarrow zR_iy)\}]$
$\quad \rightarrow [(yRz \rightarrow xRz) \,\&\, (zRx \rightarrow zRy)]$, by Lemma 6.1
$\quad \rightarrow [(xRy \,\&\, yRz \,\&\, zRx) \rightarrow (xRy \,\&\, yIz \,\&\, zIx)]$.

Thus a sufficient condition for ruling out the possibility of (i) holding good with at least two of the Rs being Ps is

$$(\forall i)\,[\sim (xI_iyI_iz) \rightarrow \sim (yR_iz \,\&\, zR_ix)]. \tag{1}$$

Similarly it can be shown that each of (2) and (3) rules out the possibility of (i) holding with at least two of the Rs being Ps, and

---

[1] Theorem 6.1 is clearly a generalization of Theorem 5.1.

each of (4), (5) and (6) rules out the possibility of (ii) holding with at least two of the Rs being Ps.

$$(\forall i)\,[\sim (xI_iyI_iz) \rightarrow \sim (zR_ix\ \&\ xR_iy)] \qquad (2)$$

$$(\forall i)\,[\sim (xI_iyI_iz) \rightarrow \sim (xR_iy\ \&\ yR_iz)] \qquad (3)$$

$$(\forall i)\,[\sim (xI_iyI_iz) \rightarrow \sim (yR_ix\ \&\ xR_iz)] \qquad (4)$$

$$(\forall i)\,[\sim (xI_iyI_iz) \rightarrow \sim (xR_iz\ \&\ zR_iy)] \qquad (5)$$

$$(\forall i)\,[\sim (xI_iyI_iz) \rightarrow \sim (zR_iy\ \&\ yR_ix)]. \qquad (6)$$

Let the set $\{R_1, ..., R_N\}$ correspond to a subset of a permissible set of orderings satisfying VR. Clearly $\{R_1, ..., R_N\}$ will satisfy VR. Suppose it satisfies NW value restriction with respect to x. Then both (1) and (6) must be true. For, if (1) is false then

$$(\exists i)\,[\sim (xI_iyI_iz)\ \&\ (yR_iz\ \&\ zR_ix)].$$

This implies $\quad (\exists i)\,[\sim (xI_iyI_iz)\ \&\ (yR_ix\ \&\ zR_ix)]$

which is ruled out by NW value restriction with respect to x. Similarly if (6) is false, then

$$(\exists i)\,[\sim (xI_iyI_iz)\ \&\ (yR_ix\ \&\ zR_ix)]$$

which is again ruled out by NW value restriction with respect to x. Thus NW value restriction with respect to x implies both (1) and (6). Similarly it can be checked up that any form of VR implies at least one of (1), (2) and (3), and also at least one of (4), (5) and (6). Therefore neither (i) nor (ii) can be true with two of the Rs being Ps. This completes the proof. Q.E.D.

Given Theorem 1.3, the following theorem follows immediately from Theorem 6.1.

THEOREM 6.2. *If S is finite, then a sufficient condition of Type II for a set of individual orderings to be in the domain of a binary, decisive, neutral, and non-negatively responsive Rule viewed as SDF is that every permissible set of orderings should satisfy VR over every triple of alternatives belonging to S.*

Of the three main restrictions, VR, ER and LA, introduced in the last chapter, VR has been shown to be a sufficient condition of Type II for quasi-transitivity under binary, decisive, neutral, and non-negatively responsive Rules. In the next section we shall see that ER is not sufficient for quasi-transitivity even under binary group decision Rules which satisfy anonymity and the Strict Pareto Criterion in addition to decisiveness, neutrality, and non-negative responsiveness. The following example shows that LA is not a sufficient condition of Type I or Type II for quasi-transitivity under all binary group decision Rules satisfying decisiveness, neutrality, and non-negative responsiveness. Consider the set of three individual orderings xP_1yP_1z, yP_2zI_2x, zI_3xP_3y. LA is satisfied over the triple (x, y, z) since $(\forall i)\,(xR_iz)$. But the method of non-minority decision, which is a binary, decisive, neutral, and non-negatively responsive Rule, yields $(xPy \,\&\, yPz \,\&\, xIz)$, thus violating quasi-transitivity.

6.3. *The Existence of a Choice Function Under Binary, Decisive, Neutral, and Non-negatively Responsive Rules Satisfying the Strict Pareto Criterion*

I now consider the class of binary Rules which satisfy the Strict Pareto Criterion in addition to decisiveness, neutrality, and non-negative responsiveness.[1] In the following theorem it is shown that LA, which proved to be insufficient for quasi-transitivity of binary Rules satisfying decisiveness, neutrality, and non-negative responsiveness, turns out to be a sufficient condition of Type II when we additionally impose the Strict Pareto Criterion.

THEOREM 6.3. *A sufficient condition of Type II for a binary, decisive, neutral, and non-negatively responsive Rule satisfying the Strict Pareto Criterion, to yield quasi-transitive results over a triple (x, y, z) is that every permissible set of orderings should satisfy LA over it.*[2]

PROOF:

Let the set $\{R_1, ..., R_N\}$ correspond to a subset of a permissible set satisfying LA. Then $\{R_1, ..., R_N\}$ also satisfies LA. Without loss of generality we can assume that $(\forall i)\,(xR_iy)$.

---

[1] This is a proper subclass of the class of binary group decision Rules satisfying decisiveness, neutrality, and non-negative responsiveness. The method of non-minority decision is an example of a binary Rule which satisfies decisiveness, neutrality, and non-negative responsiveness, but which does not satisfy the Strict Pareto Criterion (see Chapter 3).

[2] Since the majority decision Rule satisfies the Strict Pareto Criterion besides satisfying binariness, decisiveness, neutrality, and non-negative responsiveness, Theorem 6.3 is a generalization of Theorem 5.2.

Hence $(\forall i)\,[(yP_i z \to xP_i z)\ \&\ (yI_i z \to xR_i z)]$ so that by Lemma 6.1 we have $(yRz \to xRz)$.

Similarly we have $(zRx \to zRy)$. Thus

$$(xRy\ \&\ yRz\ \&\ zRx) \to (xRy\ \&\ yIz\ \&\ zIx).$$

Consider now the hypothesis yRx. Since $(\forall i)\,(xR_i y)$, clearly the Strict Pareto Criterion implies that $(\forall i)\,(xI_i y)$. Hence

$$yRx \to (\forall i)\,[\{(xP_i z \to yP_i z)\ \&\ (xI_i z \to yI_i z)\}\ \&\ \{(zP_i y \to zP_i x)$$
$$\&\ (zI_i y \to zI_i x)\}]$$
$$\to [(xRz \to yRz)\ \&\ (zRy \to zRx)],\ \text{by Lemma 6.1.}$$

Thus $(yRx\ \&\ xRz\ \&\ zRy) \to (yRx\ \&\ xIz\ \&\ zIy)$. R cannot violate quasi-transitivity without at least one of the two R-cycles $(xRy\ \&\ yRz\ \&\ zRx)$ and $(yRx\ \&\ xRz\ \&\ zRy)$ holding, and if either of them holds then at least two of the Rs must be Is. This means that violation of quasi-transitivity is imposssible which completes the proof.   Q.E.D.

Given Theorem 1.3, the following theorem follows immediately from Theorems 6.1 and 6.3.

THEOREM 6.4. *If S is finite, then a sufficient condition of Type II for a set of individual orderings to be in the domain of very binary, decisive, neutral, and non-negatively responsive Rule satisfying the Strict Pareto Criterion and viewed as SDF is that every permissible set of orderings should satisfy VR or LA over every triple of alternatives belonging to S.*

Of the three conditions, VR, ER and LA, VR and LA have already been shown to be sufficient for quasi-transitivity of binary Rules satisfying decisiveness, neutrality, non-negative responsiveness, and the Strict Pareto Criterion. We may now consider ER. In Chapter 5 we have seen that ER is sufficient for transitivity under the MD-Rule. However, it can be easily checked that ER is not a sufficient condition of Type I or Type II, even for quasi-transitivity under certain binary Rules that satisfy decisiveness, neutrality, anonymity, non-negative responsiveness, and the Strict Pareto Criterion.[1] An example of such a binary Rule is the Pareto-inclusive method of non-minority decision.[2] The example below shows that ER is not a sufficient

---

[1] If, in this list of properties, we strengthen non-negative responsiveness into positive responsiveness, then we arrive at the majority decision Rule.

[2] See Definition 3.10.

condition of either type for quasi-transitivity under the Pareto-inclusive method of non-minority decision. Consider the following permissible set of four orderings which satisfies ER over (x, y, z).

$$x\bar{P}_1 y\bar{P}_1 z \qquad z\bar{P}_2 y\bar{P}_2 x \qquad y\bar{P}_3 z\bar{I}_3 x \qquad x\bar{I}_4 z\bar{P}_4 y.$$

Let N_j be the number of individuals holding the ordering $\bar{R}_j$, for $j = 1, 2, 3, 4$. If $N_1 = 2$, $N_2 = 1$, $N_3 = 1$, and $N_4 = 1$, then the Pareto-inclusive method of non-minority decision yields

$$(xPy \; \& \; yPz \; \& \; xIz)$$

which violates quasi-transitivity.

6.4. *The Existence of a Choice Function under MMD-Rules*

The class of MMD-Rules is a subclass of the class of binary group decision Rules satisfying decisiveness, neutrality, non-negative responsiveness, and the Strict Pareto Criterion.[1] The following theorems, therefore, follow as corollaries from Theorems 6.3 and 6.4 respectively.

THEOREM 6.5. *A sufficient condition of Type II for the quasi-transitivity of R over a given triple under any MMD-Rule is that every permissible set of orderings satisfies VR or LA over that triple.*[2]

THEOREM 6.6. *If S is finite, then a sufficient condition of Type II for a set of individual orderings to belong to the domain of every MMD–SDF is that every permissible set of orderings satisfies VR or LA over every triple of alternatives belonging to S.*

Not only is the fulfillment of VR or LA over every triple a sufficient condition of Type II, and therefore a sufficient condition of Type I, for the existence of a choice function under every MMD-Rule, but also it is a necessary condition of Type I for the existence of a choice function under all MMD-Rules.[3]

---

[1] See Chapter 3.

[2] Since the majority decision Rule is also a MMD-Rule, Theorem 6.5 subsumes Theorems 5.1 and 5.2.

[3] Some explanation may be useful here in avoiding a possible confusion. It is *not* being said that given any particular MMD–SDF, fulfillment of VR or LA over every triple is a necessary condition for a set of individual orderings to be in the domain of that MMD–SDF. What is being said is that fulfillment of VR or LA over every triple is a necessary condition for a set of individual orderings to be in the domain of every MMD–SDF.

To show that it is a necessary condition of Type I it is convenient to proceed in two stages. First, it will be shown that it is a necessary condition of Type II for the existence of a choice function under all MMD-Rules. Then it will be shown that it is also a necessary condition of Type I.

THEOREM 6.7. *A necessary condition of Type II for a set of individual orderings to be in the domain of every MMD–SDF is that every permissible set of orderings should satisfy VR or LA over every triple of alternatives.*

PROOF:

Let Π be any permissible set of orderings which violates VR and also LA over a triple (x, y, z). It will be shown that for some set of individual orderings corresponding to a subset of Π, some MMD-Rule yields an empty choice set for $\{x, y, z\}$.[1] This will prove the theorem.

The thirteen possible orderings over (x, y, z) will be labelled in the same way as in Lemma 5.3.

$(1.1)\ x\bar{P}_i y\bar{P}_i z$	$(1.2)\ x\bar{P}_i y\bar{I}_i z$	$(1.3)\ x\bar{I}_i y\bar{P}_i z$
$(2.1)\ y\bar{P}_i z\bar{P}_i x$	$(2.2)\ y\bar{P}_i z\bar{I}_i x$	$(2.3)\ y\bar{I}_i z\bar{P}_i x$
$(3.1)\ z\bar{P}_i x\bar{P}_i y$	$(3.2)\ z\bar{P}_i x\bar{I}_i y$	$(3.3)\ z\bar{I}_i x\bar{P}_i y$
$(4)\ \ \ x\bar{P}_i z\bar{P}_i y$	$(5)\ \ \ z\bar{P}_i y\bar{P}_i x$	$(6)\ \ \ y\bar{P}_i x\bar{P}_i z$
$(7)\ \ \ x\bar{I}_i y\bar{I}_i z.$		

It can be easily checked that Π can violate VR over (x, y, z) only if it has a three-ordering subset which violates VR over (x, y, z). There are two possibilities: (i) there exists a three-ordering subset which violates VR over (x, y, z) and contains a linear ordering over (x, y, z); (ii) there exists a three-ordering subset which violates VR but no such subset contains a linear ordering over (x, y, z).

(i) Consider the case where there is a three-ordering subset that violates VR and also contains a linear ordering over (x, y, z). Without loss of generality we can assume that the linear ordering

---

[1] I shall use this proof in Theorem 7.7, where it is assumed that the number of entries concerned with respect to (x, y, z) is odd for every majority voting operation involved in the MMD-Rule under consideration. Therefore, in constructing the proof here, I shall take care to satisfy this particular assumption though it is not of relevance for Theorem 6.7.

is 1.1. But the only three-ordering sets inclusive of 1.1 that violate VR are given by: [1.1, 2.1 *or* 2.2 *or* 2.3, 3.1 *or* 3.2 *or* 3.3]. There are nine such three-ordering sets. Only one of these nine sets satisfies LA, viz., [1.1, 2.2, 3.3] where $x\bar{R}_i z$ for all the orderings. In all the other eight cases LA is violated in addition to VR. As seen in the proof of Theorem 5.4, in each of these eight cases, there exists a set of individual orderings corresponding to the three-ordering set such that the MD-Rule which is also a MMD-Rule yields an empty $C(\{x, y, z\})$.

Now consider the set [1.1, 2.2, 3.3]. Since Π violates LA it must contain an ordering for which $z\bar{P}_i x$. The only possible orderings which involve $z\bar{P}_i x$ are 2.1, 2.3, 3.1, 3.2 and 5. If one of the orderings 2.1, 2.3, 3.1 and 3.2 is added to those in the set [1.1, 2.2, 3.3], then we arrive at one of the eight three-ordering sets considered above, except for some formal interchange between x, y and z. These cases need not be considered separately. If Π contains 5 in addition to 1.1, 2.2 and 3.3, then take a set of seven individuals corresponding to [1.1, 2.2, 3.3, 5]. Also, assume that 2.2 is true of R_1 and R_2; 3.3 is true of R_3 and R_4; 5 is true for R_5 and R_6; and 1.1 is true of R_7. The MMD-Rule $((((R_1, R_2, R_5)), ((R_3, R_4, R_6)), R_7))$ yields $(xPy \,\&\, yPz \,\&\, zPx)$ which implies an empty choice set for $\{x, y, z\}$.

(ii) Now consider the case where none of the three-ordering subsets violating VR contains a linear ordering over (x, y, z). In this case Π must include at least one of the following three-ordering sets: [1.2 *or* 1.3, 2.2 *or* 2.3, 3.2 *or* 3.3].[1] Consider [1.2, 2.2, 3.2]. Let there be nine individual orderings with 1.2 true for R_1, R_3, and R_7; 2.2 true for R_2, R_4 and R_6; and 3.2 true for R_5, R_8 and R_9. With this set of individual orderings the MMD-Rule $(((((R_1, R_2, R_3)), ((R_4, R_5, R_6)), ((R_7, R_8, R_9)))))$ yields

$$(zPx \,\&\, xPy \,\&\, yPz)$$

which implies an empty choice set for $\{x, y, z\}$. Now consider [1.3, 2.3, 3.3]. Suppose we have nine individual orderings with 1.3 true for R_1, R_3 and R_5; 2.3 true for R_4, R_6 and R_8; and 3.3 true for R_2, R_7 and R_9. The MMD-Rule $(((((R_1, R_2, R_3)), ((R_4, R_5, R_6)), ((R_7, R_8, R_9)))))$ yields $(zPx \,\&\, xPy \,\&\, yPz)$ which implies an empty choice set for $\{x, y, z\}$.

[1] See Erratum, p. 180 below.

Of the eight three-ordering sets [1.2 *or* 1.3, 2.2 *or* 2.3, 3.2 *or* 3.3] we are now left with six. All these six three-ordering sets satisfy LA and the method of proof is similar in all these cases. I shall, therefore, give the proof for only one of these six cases and omit the proof for the rest. Take the set [1.2, 2.2, 3.3]. For all the orderings in this set $x\bar{R}_i z$ is true. Since Π violates LA, there must be at least one ordering in Π for which $z\bar{P}_i x$ is true. Let $\bar{R}_i^*$ be such an ordering. Now consider the set [1.2, 2.2, 3.3, $\bar{R}_i^*$] which, by hypothesis, is a subset of Π. Let there be fifteen individual orderings corresponding to this subset of Π such that 1.2 is true of R_1 and R_2; 2.2 is true of R_3, R_4, R_5 and R_6; 3.3 is true of R_7, R_9, R_{10}, R_{12}, R_{13} and R_{15}; and $\bar{R}_i^*$ is true of R_8, R_{11} and R_{14}. The MMD-Rule $((R_1, R_2, R_3, R_4, R_5, R_6, ((R_7, R_8, R_9)), ((R_{10}, R_{11}, R_{12})), ((R_{13}, R_{14}, R_{15}))))$ yields $(xPy \;\&\; yPz \;\&\; zPx)$ which implies an empty $C(\{x, y, z\})$. The strategy underlying the construction of this example may be explained here. By combining an individual ordering for which $\bar{R}_i^*$ is true suitably with other individual orderings, we can generate a linear ordering for which $z\bar{P}_i x\bar{P}_i y$ is true. Thus in the example given, each of $((R_7, R_8, R_9))$, $((R_{10}, R_{11}, R_{12}))$, and $((R_{13}, R_{14}, R_{15}))$ will give us a linear ordering for which $z\bar{P}_i x\bar{P}_i y$ is true. Once we have generated such a linear ordering, the problem becomes similar to one of the eight cases examined in (i) where the three-ordering set violates VR and LA and includes a linear ordering. The only task that remains is to take a suitable configuration of preference patterns in the next stage of aggregation, so as to get an empty choice set for $\{x, y, z\}$. This can be done by following the procedure outlined in (i).

Thus in all cases whenever Π violates VR and LA, for some set of individual orderings corresponding to a subset of Π, some MMD-Rule yields an empty $C(\{x, y, z\})$. This completes the proof. Q.E.D.

Now for a necessary condition of Type I.

THEOREM 6.8. *A necessary condition of Type I for a set of individual orderings to be in the domain of every MMD–SDF is that every permissible set of orderings should satisfy VR or LA over every triple of alternatives.*

PROOF:

The proof of this theorem will be used again for Theorem 7.8

where it is assumed that the number of entries concerned with respect to any triple of alternatives is odd for every majority voting operation involved. Therefore, as in the case of Theorem 6.7, the proof here will be constructed so as to satisfy this particular requirement.

Suppose the permissible set of orderings Π violates VR and LA over (x, y, z). Then from the proof of Theorem 6.7 we know that Π must include a subset Π' such that for some individual orderings corresponding to Π' and for some MMD-Rule satisfying the condition that the number of concerned entries is odd for every majority voting operation, we shall have

$$(aPb \ \& \ bPc \ \& \ cPa)$$

where a, b and c are three distinct variables each of which can take one of the values, x, y and z. Now construct the following example by suitably increasing the number of individuals. Let there be a MMD-Rule in which the entries in the final stage include fifteen preference patterns of the type

$$(a\bar{P}_i b \ \& \ b\bar{P}_i c \ \& \ c\bar{P}_i a),$$

each of which in turn is arrived at by multi-stage aggregation o, a set of individual orderings corresponding to Π'. (Such multi-stage aggregation, as seen in the proof of Theorem 6.7, can be constructed so as to satisfy the requirement that the number of concerned entries in each majority voting operation is odd.)

The number of concerned orderings in Π cannot be greater than twelve. Assume that there is a set of twelve individual orderings corresponding to the set of concerned orderings belonging to Π such that each of these concerned individual orderings figures only in the final majority voting operation. Also assume that the final majority voting operation has for its entries only the fifteen preference patterns of the type

$$(a\bar{P}_i b \ \& \ b\bar{P}_i c \ \& \ c\bar{P}_i a);$$

the twelve concerned individual orderings of the type mentioned above; and unconcerned individual orderings, if $x\bar{I}_i y\bar{I}_i z$ belongs to Π. It is clear that we shall have $(aPb \ \& \ bPc \ \& \ cPa)$. This completes the proof since we have a set of individual orderings corresponding to Π and a MMD-Rule such that given this set of individual orderings $C(\{x, y, z\})$ is empty.　　Q.E.D.

6.5. The Existence of a Choice Function under the Method of Non-Minority Decision

So far I have been concerned with subclasses of the class of binary, decisive, neutral, and non-negatively responsive Rules. In this section I discuss a particular element of this class, namely, the method of non-minority decision (Pareto-inclusive or otherwise). Since xRy under the method of majority decision implies xRy under the Pareto-inclusive method of non-minority decision which in turn implies xRy under the method of non-minority decision, it is obvious that for any set of alternatives, the existence of a non-empty choice set under the MD-Rule implies the existence of a non-empty choice set under the Pareto-inclusive method of non-minority decision and also under the method of non-minority decision. The following theorem, therefore, follows from Theorem 5.4.

THEOREM 6.9. *If S is infinite, then a sufficient condition of Type II for a set of individual orderings to belong to the domain of the Pareto-inclusive method of non-minority decision and also to the domain of the method of non-minority decision, both the methods being viewed as social decision functions, is that every permissible set of orderings should satisfy VR or LA or ER over every triple of alternatives belonging to S.*

Can we relax any of the Conditions VR, LA, or ER, and still get a choice function under the method of non-minority decision? Indeed, in a certain sense, we can. Dummet and Farquharson have shown that a condition weaker than NW value restriction, if satisfied over every triple of alternatives, is sufficient for the existence of a choice function under the method of non-minority decision. A generalized version of the Dummet and Farquharson theorem will be given below. We first define certain forms of restriction on a set of orderings Π. As in the case of restrictions defined earlier, these restrictions are also defined in terms of a given triple (x, y, z). a, b and c are three distinct variables each of which can assume one of the values, x, y and z.

DEFINITION 6.1. *Not-Strictly-Worst Value Restriction. There exists an alternative in the triple such that it is not strictly worst in any ordering,* i.e.,
$$(\exists a)\,(\exists b)\,(\exists c)\,[\sim(\exists i)\,(b\bar{P}_i a \,\&\, c\bar{P}_i a)].$$

This is equivalent to saying that

$$(\exists a)\,(\exists b)\,(\exists c)\,(\forall i)\,(a\bar{R}_i b \lor a\bar{R}_i c).$$

DEFINITION 6.2. *Not-Strictly-Best Value Restriction. There exists an alternative in the triple such that it is not strictly best in any ordering, i.e.,*

$$(\exists a)\,(\exists b)\,(\exists c)\,[\sim(\exists i)\,(a\bar{P}_i b \,\&\, a\bar{P}_i c)].$$

This is equivalent to the condition that

$$(\exists a)\,(\exists b)\,(\exists c)\,(\forall i)\,(b\bar{R}_i a \lor c\bar{R}_i a).$$

DEFINITION 6.3. *Not-Strictly-Medium Value Restriction. There exists an alternative in the triple such that it is not strictly medium in any ordering, i.e.,*

$$(\exists a)\,(\exists b)\,(\exists c)\,[\sim(\exists i)\,\{(b\bar{P}_i a \,\&\, a\bar{P}_i c) \lor (c\bar{P}_i a \,\&\, a\bar{P}_i b)\}].$$

For the sake of brevity these three restrictions will be called *NSW* value restriction, *NSB* value restriction, and *NSM* value restriction respectively.

DEFINITION 6.4. *Weak Value Restriction (WVR). NSW value restriction or NSB value restriction or NSM value restriction is satisfied over the triple.*

The following lemma is obvious.

LEMMA 6.2.

    (i)   *NW value restriction implies NSW value restriction;*

   (ii)   *NB value restriction implies NSB value restriction;*

  (iii)   *NM value restriction implies NSM value restriction;*

  (iv)   *VR implies WVR,*

DEFINITION 6.5. *For all x, y and z belong to S, $x\overline{W}yz$ if and only if* $(\forall i)\,(yR_i x \lor zR_i x).$

The lemma that follows will be used in Theorem 6.10 below. The proof of the lemma, as well as that of Theorem 6.10, follows closely the proof of Dummet and Farquharson who showed that *NSW* value restriction over every triple of alternatives is sufficient for the existence of a choice function under the method of non-minority decision.[1]

LEMMA 6.3. *For all x, y, and z belonging to S, the following is true under the method of non-minority decision:*

$$\{[(x\overline{W}yz \vee y\overline{W}xz \vee z\overline{W}xy) \,\&\, (xRy \,\&\, yRz \,\&\, zPx)]$$
$$\rightarrow [(x\overline{W}yz \,\&\, yRx) \vee (y\overline{W}xz \,\&\, zRy)]\}.$$

PROOF:

Suppose $z\overline{W}xy$. Then

$$(\forall i)\,[xR_iy \rightarrow \{(xR_iz \vee yR_iz) \,\&\, xR_iy\}]$$

therefore $\quad(\forall i)\,[xR_iy \rightarrow \{(xR_iy \,\&\, yR_iz) \vee xR_iz\}]$

therefore $\quad(\forall i)\,[xR_iy \rightarrow xR_iz]$ by the transitivity of R_i

therefore $\quad[N(xR_iy) \geqslant N/2] \rightarrow [N(xR_iz) \geqslant N/2],$

where N is the total number of individuals

therefore $\qquad\qquad xRy \rightarrow xRz.$

Thus $\qquad\qquad (z\overline{W}xy \,\&\, xRy) \rightarrow xRz$

therefore $\qquad (xRy \,\&\, zPx) \rightarrow \sim (z\overline{W}xy). \qquad\qquad (1)$

Similarly it can be shown that

$$(x\overline{W}yz \,\&\, yRz) \rightarrow yRx. \qquad\qquad (2)$$

$y\overline{W}xz \rightarrow (\forall i)\,(xR_iy \vee zR_iy)$

$\qquad \rightarrow (\forall i)\,[zR_iy \vee \{xR_iy \,\&\, \sim (zR_iy)\}]$

$\qquad \rightarrow (\forall i)\,[zR_iy \vee (xR_iy \,\&\, yR_iz)],$ by the connectedness of R_i

$\qquad \rightarrow (\forall i)\,[zR_iy \vee xR_iz]$

$\qquad \rightarrow [(N(zR_iy) \geqslant N/2) \vee (N(xR_iz) \geqslant N/2)]$

$\qquad \rightarrow (zRy \vee xRz)$

---

[1] Strictly speaking, what is proved by Dummet and Farquharson is that if *NSW* value restriction is satisfied over every triple of alternatives belonging to any set A, then there exists x in A such that for all $y(y \in A)$,

$$[\{N(xR_iy) > N/2\} \vee \{(N(xR_iy) = N/2) \,\&\, xR_1y\}].$$

Such an alternative is called a 'top' of the set A, by Dummet and Farquharson. Since $[\{N(xR_iy) > N/2\} \vee \{(N(xR_iy) = N/2) \,\&\, xR_1y\}]$ implies $[N(xR_iy) \geqslant N/2]$, the result cited above necessarily follows.

therefore $\qquad (y\overline{W}xz \ \& \ zPx) \to zRy.$ $\qquad$ (3)

$[(x\overline{W}yz \lor y\overline{W}xz \lor z\overline{W}xy) \ \& \ (xRy \ \& \ yRz \ \& \ zPx)]$

$\to [(x\overline{W}yz \lor y\overline{W}xz) \ \& \ (xRy \ \& \ yRz \ \& \ zPx)]$, by (1)

$\to [(x\overline{W}yz \ \& \ yRz) \lor (y\overline{W}xz \ \& \ zPx)]$

$\to [(x\overline{W}yz \ \& \ yRx) \lor (y\overline{W}xz \ \& \ zRy)]$, by (2) and (3).

$\qquad\qquad\qquad\qquad\qquad\qquad\qquad\qquad\qquad\qquad$ Q.E.D.

Now for the theorem.

THEOREM 6.10. *If S is finite, then a sufficient condition of Type II for a set of individual orderings to be in the domain of the method of non-minority decision viewed as a SDF is that every permissible set of orderings should satisfy NSW value restriction over every triple of alternatives belonging to S or NSB value restriction over every triple of alternatives belonging to S.*

PROOF:

If some permissible set of orderings satisfies *NSW* value restriction over every triple of alternatives then any set of individual orderings which corresponds to a subset of this permissible set also satisfies *NSW* value restriction over every triple. In this case Dummet and Farquharson have shown that a choice function will exist under the method of non-minority decision. We need, therefore, consider only *NSB* value restriction. In this case, any set of individual orderings corresponding to a subset of the permissible set of orderings will satisfy *NSB* value restriction over every triple.

First it will be proved that given *NSB* value restriction over every triple, if every m-membered subset of S has a non-empty choice set, then every $(m+1)$-membered subset of S has a non-empty choice set. Suppose this is false, and the choice set for a $(m+1)$-membered subset D $(D = \{a_1, a_2, ..., a_{m+1}\})$ is empty though every m-membered subset of S has a non-empty choice set.

Let $\theta^0 a_p = a_p$. Let θa_p belong to the choice set corresponding to $(D - \{a_p\})$; similarly $\theta^2 a_p$ belongs to the choice set corresponding to $(D - \{\theta a_p\})$ and so on.

Since $C(D)$ is empty, it can be easily shown that no single element can belong to the choice sets of two *different* m-membered subsets of D for in that case it will belong to $C(D)$ itself.

Since D has $(m+1)$ elements there exist g and h such tha $0 \leqslant g < h \leqslant m+1$ and $\theta^g a_p = \theta^h a_p$.

$\theta^g a_p$ belongs to the choice set corresponding to $(D - \{\theta^{g-1} a_p\})$ and $\theta^h a_p$ belongs to the choice set corresponding to $(D - \{\theta^{h-1} a_p\})$.

Since no single element can belong to the choice sets of two different m-membered subsets, if $\theta^g a_p = \theta^h a_p$, then

$$D - \{\theta^{g-1} a_p\} = D - \{\theta^{h-1} a_p\}.$$

Hence $\theta^{g-1} a_p = \theta^{h-1} a_p$. Continuing thus we get $a_p = \theta^{h-g} a_p$.

Let t be the smallest positive number for which $a_p = \theta^t a_p$. Then $a_p, \theta a_p, ..., \theta^{t-1} a_p$ are all distinct. It can now be shown that $\theta^g a_p R \theta^h a_p \leftrightarrow g \not\equiv h+1 \pmod{t}$.[1]

Let $g \not\equiv h+1 \pmod{t}$. Then $g-1 \not\equiv h \pmod{t}$. Hence

$$\theta^{g-1} a_p \neq \theta^h a_p,$$

and therefore $\theta^g a_p R \theta^h a_p$.

Now suppose $g \equiv h+1 \pmod{t}$. Then $\theta^{g-1} a_p = \theta^h a_p$. In this case $(\theta^g a_p R \theta^h a_p)$ would imply that $(\theta^g a_p \in C(D))$ which contradicts our hypothesis that $C(D)$ is empty. Therefore

$$[\{g \equiv h+1 \pmod{t}\} \to {\sim} (\theta^g a_p R \theta^h a_p)].$$

Thus $\qquad \theta^g a_p R \theta^h a_p \leftrightarrow g \not\equiv h+1 \pmod{t}. \qquad (1)$

It can be easily shown that $t \neq 1$ and $t \neq 2$.

Now consider any three non-negative integers d, e and g such that $d \equiv g+1 \pmod{t}$, and $e \equiv g+2 \pmod{t}$.

By (1) $\theta^e a_p R \theta^g a_p$ & $\theta^g a_p R \theta^d a_p$ & ${\sim}(\theta^e a_p R \theta^d a_p)$, since $t \neq 1$ and $t \neq 2$.

Therefore by Lemma 6.3, $(\theta^d a_p R \theta^g a_p \vee \theta^e a_p \overline{W} \theta^g a_p \theta^d a_p)$. By (1) $\qquad\qquad {\sim}(\theta^d a_p R \theta^g a_p).$

Therefore $\qquad\qquad \theta^e a_p \overline{W} \theta^g a_p \theta^d a_p.$

Therefore $\qquad (\forall i)(\theta^g a_p R_i \theta^e a_p \vee \theta^d a_p R_i \theta^e a_p).$

Putting $g = t-k-1$, $d = t-k$, and $e = t-k+1$, where $k < t$, we get $\qquad (\forall i)(\theta^{t-k-1} a_p R_i \theta^{t-k+1} a_p \vee \theta^{t-k} a_p R_i \theta^{t-k+1} a_p). \qquad (2)$

---

[1] $g \equiv h+1 \pmod{t}$ if and only if $\dfrac{g-(h+1)}{t} = k$ where k is an integer (i.e., if and only if the difference between g and $(h+1)$ is exactly divisible by t).

Consider the series $\theta^{t-1}a_p, \theta^{t-2}a_p, ..., \theta a_p, \theta^0 a_p (= a_p)$. By (2),

$$(\forall i)\ (\theta^{t-2}a_p R_i \theta^{t-1}a_p \vee \theta^{t-3}a_p R_i \theta^{t-1}a_p).$$

Again by (2),

$$(\forall i)\ (\theta^{t-3}a_p R_i \theta^{t-2}a_p \vee \theta^{t-4}a_p R_i \theta^{t-2}a_p).$$

Hence by the transitivity of R_i,

$$(\forall i)\ (\theta^{t-3}a_p R_i \theta^{t-1}a_p \vee \theta^{t-4}a_p R_i \theta^{t-1}a_p).$$

Proceeding thus we ultimately have

$$(\forall i)\ (\theta a_p R_i \theta^{t-1}a_p \vee a_p R_i \theta^{t-1}a_p).$$

Therefore $\qquad (\forall i)\ (a_p R_i \theta a_p \rightarrow a_p R_i \theta^{t-1}a_p).$

Therefore $\qquad a_p R\theta a_p \rightarrow a_p R\theta^{t-1}a_p.$

But by (1), $a_p R\theta a_p$ (since $t \neq 1$ and $t \neq 2$) & $\sim (a_p R\theta^{t-1}a_p)$. Thus we have arrived at a contradiction. Therefore $C(D)$ cannot be empty.

Therefore if every m-membered subset of S has a non-empty choice set, then every $(m+1)$-membered subset of S will also have a non-empty choice set.

Since by the decisiveness of the method of non-minority decision, every subset of two alternatives has a non-empty choice set, it follows by mathematical induction that the choice set for every subset of S is non-empty. $\qquad$ Q.E.D.

Two points may be noted here. Firstly, although *NSW* value restriction over every triple or *NSB* value restriction over every triple is sufficient for the existence of a choice function, under the method of non-minority decision, such a choice function does not necessarily exist if each triple satisfies at least one of the two restrictions, but the nature of the restriction is allowed to vary from triple to triple. Consider the following set of three individual orderings:

$$xI_1 zP_1 yI_1 w, \qquad yP_2 xP_2 wP_2 z, \qquad wP_3 zP_3 yP_3 x.$$

NSB value restriction with respect to x is fulfilled over (x, y, z); *NSW* value restriction with respect to w is fulfilled over (y, z, w); *NSB* value restriction with respect to z is fulfilled over (z, w, x); and *NSW* value restriction with respect to y is fulfilled over (w, x, y). However, $C(\{x, y, z, w\})$ is empty under the method of non-minority decision, since we have

$$(yPx\ \&\ xPw\ \&\ wPz\ \&\ zPy).$$

112

Secondly, as noted earlier, *NSW*, *NSB* and *NSM* value restrictions are weaker forms of *NW*, *NB* and *NM* value restrictions respectively. Since *NSW* value restriction over every triple or *NSB* value restriction over every triple is sufficient for the existence of a choice function under the method of non-minority decision, the question arises as to whether a similar result holds for *NSM* value restriction. That it does not hold can be seen from the example given above. In that example, alternatives z, y, x, and w are not given the strictly medium value in the triples (x, y, z), (y, z, w), (z, w, x), and (w, x, y) respectively. But $C(\{x, y, z, w\})$ is empty.

However, if the number of alternatives is restricted to three,[1] *NSM* value restriction becomes sufficient for the existence of a choice function under the method of non-minority decision.

THEOREM 6.11. *If S has only three elements, then a sufficient condition of Type II for a set of individual orderings to be in the domain of the method of non-minority decision viewed as a SDF is that every permissible set of orderings satisfies WVR over the triple.*

PROOF:

Sufficiency of *NSW* value restriction and also that of *NSB* value restriction follows from Theorem 6.10. We have therefore to consider only the case of *NSM* value restriction.

Let (x, y, z) be the given triple of alternatives. Let *NSM* value restriction be fulfilled over it. Since R is always reflexive, and connected under the method of non-minority decision it follows that every subset of $\{x, y, z\}$, that has exactly one element or exactly two elements will have a non-empty choice set. All that we have to prove is that $C(\{x, y, z\})$ is non-empty. $C(\{x, y, z\})$ can be empty only if one of the following two conditions is satisfied:

$$(xPy \ \& \ yPz \ \& \ zPx), \tag{i}$$

$$(yPx \ \& \ xPz \ \& \ zPy). \tag{ii}$$

Suppose (i) is true. Then, by definition,

$$N(xP_iy) > N/2, \tag{1}$$

$$N(yP_iz) > N/2, \tag{2}$$

$$N(zP_ix) > N/2, \tag{3}$$

[1] With less than three alternatives, a choice function necessarily exists since the method of non-minority decision satisfies decisiveness.

where N is the total number of individuals. From (1) and (2) we have

$$(\exists i)\ (xP_iyP_iz).\tag{4}$$

From (2) and (3) we have

$$(\exists i)\ (yP_izP_ix).\tag{5}$$

From (3) and (1) we have

$$(\exists i)\ (zP_ixP_iy).\tag{6}$$

If some permissible set of orderings satisfies *NSM* value restriction, then any set of individual orderings which corresponds to a subset of this permissible set will also satisfy *NSM* value restriction over (x, y, z). It can be easily checked that if the set of individual orderings satisfies *NSM* value restriction, then at least one of (4), (5) and (6) is ruled out.

Therefore (i) cannot be true.

Similarly it can be shown that (ii) cannot be true.

Since (i) and (ii) are both false $C(\{x, y, z\})$ is non-empty.

Q.E.D.

In view of the restrictive assumptions made about the number of alternatives, the usefulness of Theorem 6.11 seems to be limited.

By Lemma 3.5, a choice function over S is defined under the method of non-minority decision if and only if it is defined under the Pareto-inclusive method of non-minority decision. Therefore the sufficient conditions given in Theorems 6.10 and 6.11 for a set of individual orderings to belong to the domain of the method of non-minority decision viewed as a SDF, also prove to be sufficient in the context of the Pareto-inclusive method of non-minority decision viewed as a SDF.

6.6 *The Existence of a Best Alternative in a Given Set of Alternatives*

In Chapter 5 we have seen that if, under the MD-Rule, we are interested in the existence of socially best alternatives for a given subset A of S and not in the existence of a social choice function either over S or A, then we can concentrate only on the Pareto-optimal alternatives in A. The Pareto-inoptimal alternatives need not be considered since the existence of a non-empty choice set for the set of Pareto-optimal alternatives in a given set is a necessary and sufficient condition for the existence of a non-empty choice set for the entire set of alternatives. It will now be shown that this is true not only of the MD-Rule but of binary, decisive, neutral, and non-negatively responsive Rules in general.

LEMMA 6.4.   *For all x, y and z belonging to S, the following are true under any binary, decisive, neutral, and non-negatively responsive Rule:*

(i) $(xPy \ \& \ yQz) \to xPz,$

(ii) $(xIy \ \& \ yQz) \to xRz,$

(iii) $(xQy \ \& \ yPz) \to xPz,$

(iv) $(xQy \ \& \ yIz) \to xRz.$

PROOF:

Let yQz. By definition $[yQz \to (\forall i) \ (yR_i z)]$. Therefore, by the transitivity of R_i, $(\forall i) \ [(xP_i y \to xP_i z) \ \& \ (xI_i y \to xR_i z)]$. Hence by Lemma 6.1, $(xPy \to xPz)$ and $(xIy \to xRz)$.

Thus

$$[(xPy \ \& \ yQz) \to xPz] \quad \text{and} \quad [(xIy \ \& \ yQz) \to xRz].$$

Similarly it can be proved that

$$[(xQy \ \& \ yPz) \to xPz] \quad \text{and} \quad [(xQy \ \& \ yIz) \to xRz].$$

Q.E.D.

LEMMA 6.5.   *A necessary and sufficient condition for any given finite set of alternatives to have a non-empty choice set under a binary, decisive, neutral, and non-negatively responsive Rule is that the set of Pareto-optimal alternatives in the given set should have a non-empty choice set under the same Rule.*

PROOF:

Given Lemma 6.4, the proof of sufficiency is exactly similar to the proof of sufficiency in Lemma 5.7. We need, therefore, prove only the necessity. Let A be the given set of alternatives, and let A^* be the set of Pareto-optimal alternatives in A. Suppose $C(A^*)$ is empty. We shall show that $C(A)$ is empty.

Since $C(A^*)$ is empty,

$$(\forall y) \ [(y \in A^*) \to (\exists x) \ \{(x \in A^*) \ \& \ \sim (yRx)\}]. \tag{1}$$

Therefore

$$(\forall y) \ [(y \in A^*) \to (\exists x) \ \{(x \in A^*) \ \& \ (xPy)\}], \tag{2}$$

by the decisiveness of the Rule.

By Lemma 5.6,

$$(\forall z)\,[\{z \in (A - A^*)\} \to (\exists y)\,\{(y \in A^*)\ \&\ y\bar{Q}z\}]. \tag{3}$$

From (2) and (3),

$$(\forall z)\,[\{z \in (A - A^*)\}$$
$$\to (\exists x)\,(\exists y)\,\{(x \in A^*)\ \&\ (y \in A^*)\ \&\ xPy\ \&\ y\bar{Q}z\}].$$

Therefore by Lemma 6.4,

$$(\forall z)\,[\{z \in (A - A^*)\} \to (\exists x)\,\{(x \in A^*)\ \&\ xPz\}]. \tag{4}$$

From (1) and (4),

$$(\forall a)\,[(a \in A) \to (\exists b)\,\{(b \in A^*)\ \&\ \sim (aRb)\}].$$

Therefore $(\forall a)\,[(a \in A) \to (\exists b)\,\{(b \in A)\ \&\ \sim (aRb)\}],$

Therefore $C(A)$ is empty. \hfill Q.E.D.

Given Lemma 6.5, Theorems 6.12 and 6.13 stated below follow from Theorems 6.2 and 6.4 respectively. The proofs of these theorems will be omitted since the proof in each case is similar to that used in deriving Theorem 5.6 with the help of Lemma 5.7.

THEOREM 6.12. *A sufficient condition of Type II for a finite set of alternatives A to have a non-empty choice set under a binary, decisive, neutral, and non-negatively responsive Rule is that every permissible set of orderings* Π *should satisfy VR over every triple of alternatives belonging to* A^*_{Π}.

THEOREM 6.13. *A sufficient condition of Type II for a finite set of alternatives A to have a non-empty choice set under a binary, decisive, neutral, and non-negatively responsive Rule satisfying the Strict Pareto Criterion is that every permissible set of orderings* Π *should satisfy VR or LA over every triple of alternatives belonging to* A^*_{Π}.

7

THE EXISTENCE OF
A COMPLETE SOCIAL ORDERING[1]

7.1.   *Introduction*

In the last two chapters I have discussed several conditions in terms of restricted individual preferences for the existence of a social choice function under different types of group decision Rules. But not only we may require that our group decision Rule should generate a choice function, but also we may require the choice function to satisfy the Arrow condition of rationality.[2] In that case, we shall be back to the Arrowian problem of a complete social ordering.[3] In this chapter I discuss sufficient conditions for several group decision Rules to generate choice functions satisfying the Arrow condition of rationality, i.e., to generate a complete social ordering. In particular, I shall consider the class of binary group decision Rules satisfying decisiveness, neutrality, and positive responsiveness, and the class of MMD-Rules which includes as a subclass the class of binary, decisive, neutral, and positively responsive group decision Rules. I shall also discuss the problem of a complete social ordering under the MD-Rule which belongs to both the classes mentioned above.

7.2.   *Some More Conditions on Sets of Preference Ordering*

In Chapter 4 several conditions such as VR, ER and LA were defined. We define below some further restrictions on a set of orderings $\Pi (= \{\bar{R}_1, ..., \bar{R}_n\})$. As in the case of VR, ER and LA, the following restrictions are defined with reference to a given triple (x, y, z). a, b and c are three distinct variables each of which can assume one of the values x, y and z. Similarly, a', b' and c' are three distinct variables each of which can assume one of the values x, y and z.

---

[1] This chapter is based on Pattanaik and Batra.   [2,3] See Chapter 3.

DEFINITION 7.1.

(i) *Extremal Agreement (EA).* There exist a, b, and c such that for all concerned $\bar{R}_i$, $(a\bar{P}_i b \ \& \ a\bar{P}_i c)$, or for all concerned $\bar{R}_i$, $(b\bar{P}_i a \ \& \ c\bar{P}_i a)$.

(ii) *Extremal Conflict (EC).* There exist a, b and c such that the set of concerned $\bar{R}_i$, if non-empty, can be partitioned into two non-empty subsets Π_1 and Π_2, satisfying the following condition: $(a\bar{P}_i b \ \& \ a\bar{P}_i c)$ for every $\bar{R}_i \in \Pi_1$, and $(b\bar{P}_i a \ \& \ c\bar{P}_i a)$ for every $\bar{R}_i \in \Pi_2$.

(iii) *Strong Extremal Conflict (SEC).* There exist a, b and c such that the set of concerned $\bar{R}_i$, if non-empty, can be partitioned into two non-empty subsets Π_1 and Π_2, satisfying one of the following conditions: (1) $a\bar{P}_i b\bar{I}_i c$ for every $\bar{R}_i \in \Pi_1$, and $c\bar{I}_i b\bar{P}_i a$ for every $\bar{R}_i \in \Pi_2$, or (2) $a\bar{P}_i b\bar{P}_i c$ for every $\bar{R}_i \in \Pi_1$ and $c\bar{P}_i b\bar{P}_i a$ for every $\bar{R}_i \in \Pi_2$.

(iv) *Weak Extremal Conflict (WEC).* EC holds but not SEC.

The following lemma will be useful:

LEMMA 7.1. (i) *EC is equivalent to the union of SEC and WEC.* (ii) *The condition of NM value restriction is equivalent to the union of EA, SEC and WEC.*

PROOF:

The proof of (i) follows immediately from the definitions of EC, SEC and WEC. We have only to prove (ii). Suppose the set Π of orderings satisfies *NM* value restriction over (x, y, z). Without loss of generality we can assume that Π satisfies *NM* value restriction with respect to x. Then

$$(\forall i) \left[\sim (x\bar{I}_i y\bar{I}_i z) \rightarrow \{(x\bar{P}_i y \ \& \ x\bar{P}_i z) \vee (y\bar{P}_i x \ \& \ z\bar{P}_i x)\} \right].$$

It follows that either

$$(\forall i) \left[\sim (x\bar{I}_i y\bar{I}_i z) \rightarrow (x\bar{P}_i y \ \& \ x\bar{P}_i z) \right]$$

or $\qquad (\forall i) \left[\sim (x\bar{I}_i y\bar{I}_i z) \rightarrow (y\bar{P}_i x \ \& \ z\bar{P}_i x) \right]$

or the set of concerned orderings can be partitioned into two subsets such that for every $\bar{R}_i$ belonging to one subset

$$(x P_i y \ \& \ x P_i z)$$

is true and for every $\bar{R}_i$ belonging to the other $(y\bar{P}_i x \ \& \ z\bar{P}_i x)$ is true. In the first two cases EA will be satisfied, and in the last case EC will be satisfied. Since EC is equivalent to the union of SEC and WEC it follows that Π satisfies EA or SEC or WEC. From the proof above it is also clear that if Π satisfies EA or SEC or WEC, then Π will satisfy *NM* value restriction. Q.E.D.

One more definition will complete our list of restrictions on sets of orderings.

DEFINITION 7.2. *Weakly Echoic Preferences* (*WEP*). *If there is an ordering antisymmetric over* (x, y, z), *then there exists an ordering* $\bar{R}_k$ *antisymmetric over* (x, y, z) *such that the alternative which is given the worst value in* $\bar{R}_k$ *is never strictly preferred in any ordering to the alternative which is given the best value in* $\bar{R}_k$, *i.e.,*

$$\{[(\exists a)\,(\exists b)\,(\exists c)\,(\exists i)\,(a\bar{P}_i b\bar{P}_i c)]$$
$$\rightarrow [(\exists a')\,(\exists b')\,(\exists c')\,\{(\exists k)\,(a'\bar{P}_k b'\bar{P}_k c')\ \&\ \sim (\exists i)\,(c'\bar{P}_i a')\}]\}.$$

WEP may be compared with EP.[1] If a set of preference orderings satisfies EP, it also satisfies WEP. But the converse is not necessarily true. Consider the following set of orderings over (x, y, z):

$$x\bar{P}_1 y\bar{P}_1 z \qquad y\bar{P}_2 x\bar{P}_2 z \qquad x\bar{P}_3 z\bar{P}_3 y \qquad y\bar{P}_4 x\bar{I}_4 z.$$

This set satisfies WEP since $x\bar{P}_i y\bar{P}_i z$ is in the set and z is not strictly preferred to x in any ordering belonging to the set. But it can be seen that EP is not satisfied since $y\bar{P}_2 x\bar{P}_2 z$ and $z\bar{P}_3 y$ are both in the set. In terms of individual orderings the non-trivial fulfillment of EP implies that there are some individuals in the group who have linear orderings over (x, y, z), and that the preference of *each* of those individuals is 'echoed' by everybody else in the group in the sense that the alternative considered 'worst' in the triple by any of these individuals is not strictly preferred by anybody to the alternative considered 'best' in the triple by that individual. The non-trivial fulfillment of WEP only requires that there should be some individuals in the group, having a linear ordering over the three alternatives, and that the preference of *at least one* of these individuals is 'echoed' by everybody else in the group.

7.3. *Transitivity of R under Binary, Decisive, Neutral, and Positively Responsive Rules*

In the last chapter a sufficient condition of Type II was established for the existence of a social choice function under a binary Rule satisfying decisiveness, neutrality and non-negative respon-

[1] See Definition 5.5.

siveness. We now strengthen the property of non-negative responsiveness into positive responsiveness and establish a sufficient condition of Type II for the existence of complete social orderings under binary Rules satisfying decisiveness, neutrality, and positive responsiveness. We proceed to the theorem via the following lemmas.

LEMMA 7.2. *Let* $R = f(R_1, ..., R_N)$ *where f is a binary, decisive, neutral, and positively responsive Rule, then for all x, y, z and w belonging to S,*

$$[\{(\forall i)\,[(xP_iy \to zP_iw)\;\&\;(xI_iy \to zR_iw)]$$
$$\&\;(\exists j)\,[(xI_jy\;\&\;zP_jw)\lor(yP_jx\;\&\;zR_jw)]\}\to(xRy\to zPw)].$$

PROOF:
Since the Rule is binary and neutral,

$$(\forall i)\,[(xR_iy \leftrightarrow zR_iw)\;\&\;(yR_ix \leftrightarrow wR_iz)]\to(xRy\leftrightarrow zRw).$$

Lemma 7.2 follows immediately from this, given positive responsiveness and decisiveness. Q.E.D.

LEMMA 7.3. *Let* $R = f(R_1, ..., R_N)$ *where f is a binary, decisive, neutral, and positively responsive Rule. Then for all x, y, and z belonging to S,*

$$(\forall i)\,[\sim(xI_iyI_iz)\to\{(xP_iy\to zP_iy)\;\&\;(xI_iy\to zR_iy)$$
$$\&\;(yP_iz\to yP_ix)\;\&\;(yI_iz\to yR_ix)\}]$$

implies that either $\sim(xRy\;\&\;yRz)$ *or the set of individual orderings satisfies NM value restriction over* (x, y, z).

PROOF:

$$(\forall i)\,[\sim(xI_iyI_iz)\to\{(xP_iy\to zP_iy)\;\&\;(xI_iy\to zR_iy)$$
$$\&\;(yP_iz\to yP_ix)\;\&\;(yI_iz\to yR_ix)\}]$$
$$\to(\forall i)\,[(xP_iy\to zP_iy)\;\&\;(xI_iy\to zR_iy)\;\&\;(yP_iz\to yP_ix)$$
$$\&\;(yI_iz\to yR_ix)]$$
$$\to[\{(\forall i)\,[(xP_iy\to zP_iy)\;\&\;(xI_iy\to zR_iy)\;\&\;(yP_iz\to yP_ix)$$
$$\&\;(yI_iz\to yR_ix)]\;\&\;(\exists j)\,[(yR_jx\;\&\;zP_jy)$$
$$\lor(zR_jy\;\&\;yP_jx)]\}\lor(\forall i)\,\{\sim(xI_iyI_iz)$$

120

$\rightarrow [(xP_iy \; \& \; zP_iy) \vee (yP_ix \; \& \; yP_iz)]\}]$

$\rightarrow \{[(xRy \rightarrow zPy) \; \& \; (yRz \rightarrow yPx)] \vee (\forall i) [\sim (xI_iyI_iz)$

$\rightarrow \{(xP_iy \; \& \; zP_iy) \vee (yP_ix \; \& \; yP_iz)\}]\}$ by Lemma 7.2

$\rightarrow \{\sim (xRy \; \& \; yRz) \vee (\forall i) [\sim (xI_iyI_iz) \rightarrow \{(xP_iy \; \& \; zP_iy)$

$\vee (yP_ix \; \& \; yP_iz)\}]\}.$

From this the required result follows by the definition of *NM* value restriction.   Q.E.D.

LEMMA 7.4. *Let* $R = f(R_1, ..., R_N)$ *where* f *is a binary, decisive, neutral, and non-negatively responsive Rule. A sufficient condition for the transitivity of R over any triple of alternatives* (x, y, z) *is that* $\{R_1, ..., R_N\}$ *satisfies SEC over* (x, y, z).

PROOF:

SEC is satisfied. Therefore without loss of generality we can assume that one of the following conditions holds:

(1) $(\forall i) [\sim (xI_iyI_iz) \rightarrow \{xP_iyP_iz \vee zP_iyP_ix\}] \; \& \; (\exists i) (xP_iyP_iz)$
     $\& \; (\exists i) (zP_iyP_ix).$

(2) $(\forall i) [\sim (xI_iyI_iz) \rightarrow \{xP_iyI_iz \vee zI_iyP_ix\}] \; \& \; (\exists i) (xP_iyI_iz)$
     $\& \; (\exists i) (zI_iyP_ix).$

(3) $(\forall i) (xI_iyI_iz).$

Suppose (1) holds. Then

$$(\forall i) [\{(xP_iy \vee yP_iz \vee xP_iz) \rightarrow xP_iyP_iz\}$$
$$\& \; \{(zP_iy \vee yP_ix \vee zP_ix) \rightarrow zP_iyP_ix\}$$
$$\& \; \{(xI_iy \vee yI_iz \vee xI_iz) \rightarrow xI_iyI_iz\}].$$

Then by Lemma 6.1

$$[\{(xPy \vee yPz \vee xPz) \rightarrow (xPy \; \& \; yPz \; \& \; xPz)\}$$
$$\& \; \{(zPy \vee yPx \vee zPx) \rightarrow (zPy \; \& \; yPx \; \& \; zPx)\}].$$

Therefore it follows that

$$[(xIy \; \& \; yIz \; \& \; xIz) \vee (xPy \; \& \; yPz \; \& \; xPz) \vee (zPy \; \& \; yPx \; \& \; zPx)].$$

R is thus transitive over (x, y, z).

Suppose (2) holds. Then

$$(\forall i) (yI_iz) \; \& \; (\forall i) [(xP_iy \leftrightarrow xP_iz) \; \& \; (zP_ix \leftrightarrow yP_ix)].$$

By Lemma 3.3 (iv) it follows that (yIz). Also by Lemma 6.1,

$$(xPy \leftrightarrow xPz) \ \& \ (zPx \leftrightarrow yPx).$$

Therefore

$$[(xPy \ \& \ xPz \ \& \ yIz) \lor (zPx \ \& \ yPx \ \& \ yIz) \lor (xIy \ \& \ yIz \ \& \ xIz)].$$

R is thus transitive over (x, y, z).

Suppose (3) holds. Then by Lemma 3.3 (iv), $(xIy \ \& \ yIz \ \& \ zIx)$. This completes the proof of Lemma 7.4. Q.E.D.

THEOREM 7.1.   *A sufficient condition of Type I for a set of individual orderings to be in the domain of every binary, decisive, neutral, and positively responsive group decision Rule viewed as a SWF is that every permissible set of orderings satisfies VR or LA over every triple of alternatives but no permissible set satisfies WEC over any triple.*

PROOF:

Reflexivity and connectedness of R follows from the decisiveness of the Rule. All that we have to prove is, therefore, the transitivity of R. For R to be intransitive over (x, y, z) one and only one of the following two conditions must be satisfied:

(i) $(xRy \ \& \ yRz \ \& \ zRx)$,

(ii) $(yRx \ \& \ xRz \ \& \ zRy)$.

It will be proved that under the postulated conditions it is impossible that one of (i) and (ii) will be satisfied without the other being satisfied.

A. First we consider a permissible set of orderings which satisfies VR over (x, y, z) but does not satisfy WEC. Let there be a set of individual orderings $\{R_1, ..., R_N\}$ which corresponds to this set. Clearly $\{R_1, ..., R_N\}$ satisfies VR over (x, y, z) but not WEC.

Suppose $(\forall i) [\sim (xI_i y I_i z) \to \sim (xR_i y \ \& \ yR_i z)]$. Then

$$(\forall i) [\sim (xI_i y I_i z) \to \{(xR_i y \to zP_i y) \ \& \ (yR_i z \to yP_i x)\}].$$

By Lemma 7.3 either $\sim (xRy \ \& \ yRz)$ or the set of individual orderings satisfies NM value restriction.

If $\sim (xRy \ \& \ yRz)$, then (i) does not hold. Suppose NM value restriction holds. Then by Lemma 7.1, EA or SEC or WEC is satisfied. WEC is ruled out by hypothesis. Therefore EA or SEC is satisfied. If SEC holds, then by Lemma 7.4, R is transitive which implies that (i) cannot be true without (ii) being true.

Suppose EA holds. If $(\forall i)\, (xI_i y I_i z)$, then EA holds trivially. But in this case SEC is also satisfied. This case, therefore, need not be considered again. If $\sim (\forall i)\, (xI_i y I_i z)$, and EA holds, then by the definition of EA it follows that there exist a, b and c in $\{x, y, z\}$ such that $[(a\bar{Q}b \,\&\, a\bar{Q}c) \vee (b\bar{Q}a \,\&\, c\bar{Q}a)]$. By Lemma 3.3 (vi) it follows that there exist a, b and c in (x, y, z) such that

$$[(aPb \,\&\, aPc) \vee (bPa \,\&\, cPa)].$$

But in this case it can be easily checked that (i) cannot be true.

Thus, given that WEC does not hold over (x, y, z), a sufficient condition for ruling out the possibility of (i) being true without (ii) being true is:

$$(\forall i)\, [\sim (xI_i y I_i z) \rightarrow \sim (xR_i y \,\&\, yR_i z)]. \tag{1}$$

Similarly, given that WEC does not hold, each of (2) and (3) rules out the possibility of (i) being true without (ii) being true, and also each of (4), (5), and (6) rules out the possibility of (ii) being true without (i) being true.

$$(\forall i)\, [\sim (xI_i y I_i z) \rightarrow \sim (yR_i z \,\&\, zR_i x)] \tag{2}$$

$$(\forall i)\, [\sim (xI_i y I_i z) \rightarrow \sim (zR_i x \,\&\, xR_i y)] \tag{3}$$

$$(\forall i)\, [\sim (xI_i y I_i z) \rightarrow \sim (yR_i x \,\&\, xR_i z)] \tag{4}$$

$$(\forall i)\, [\sim (xI_i y I_i z) \rightarrow \sim (xR_i z \,\&\, zR_i y)] \tag{5}$$

$$(\forall i)\, [\sim (xI_i y I_i z) \rightarrow \sim (zR_i y \,\&\, yR_i x)]. \tag{6}$$

It can be easily checked that VR over (x, y, z) implies at least one of (1), (2) and (3), and also at least one of (4), (5) and (6).

Since the set of individual orderings satisfies VR over (x, y, z) but not WEC, transitivity of R over (x, y, z) follows.

B. We now consider a permissible set of orderings which satisfies LA over (x, y, z) but not WEC. Let there be a set of individual orderings $\{R_1, ..., R_N\}$ corresponding to this set. Clearly $\{R_1, ..., R_N\}$ satisfies LA over (x, y, z) but not WEC. Without loss of generality we can assume that $(\forall i)\, (xR_i y)$.

Therefore

$$(\forall i)\, [(yP_i z \rightarrow xP_i z) \,\&\, (yI_i z \rightarrow xR_i z) \,\&\, (zP_i x \rightarrow zP_i y)$$
$$\&\, (zI_i x \rightarrow zR_i y)].$$

Therefore by Lemma 7.3 either $\sim (yRz \,\&\, zRx)$ or *NM* value restriction holds.

Therefore as in the case of VR above, it can be shown that (i) cannot be true without (ii) also being true.

Now consider (ii). By Lemma 3.3 (vi)

$$[(\forall i)\,(xR_iy)\;\&\;(\exists i)\,(xP_iy)] \rightarrow xPy.$$

Hence, given that $(\forall i)\,(xR_iy)$, $[yRx \rightarrow (\forall i)\,(xI_iy)]$.

$(yRx\;\&\;xRz\;\&\;zRy)$

$\rightarrow (\forall i)\,(xI_iy)$

$\rightarrow (\forall i)\,[(xP_iz \rightarrow yP_iz)\;\&\;(xI_iz \rightarrow yR_iz)\;\&\;(zP_iy \rightarrow zP_ix)$
$$\&\;(zI_iy \rightarrow zR_ix)].$$

By Lemma 7.3, this implies that either $\sim (xRz\;\&\;zRy)$ or NM value restriction holds. As in the earlier case, it follows that (ii) cannot be true without (i) being true.

Thus if LA is satisfied over (x, y, z) but not WEC, then one of (i) and (ii) cannot be true without the other being true.

Therefore, if LA is satisfied over (x, y, z) but not WEC, then R cannot be intransitive over (x, y, z). This completes the proof of Theorem 7.1. Q.E.D.

The condition that WEC does not hold over any triple of alternatives is crucial for Theorem 7.1. Consider the set of individual orderings $\{xP_1yP_1z,\; yP_2zP_2x\}$. The implied permissible set of orderings satisfies WEC besides satisfying VR and LA. In this case the MD-Rule which is binary, decisive, neutral, and positively responsive, yields the intransitive results

$$(xIy\;\&\;yPz\;\&\;zIx).$$

It should also be noted that fulfillment of VR or LA and non-fulfillment of WEC over a triple, together, do not constitute a sufficient condition of Type II for a set of individual orderings to be in the domain of every binary, decisive, neutral, and positively responsive group decision Rule viewed as a SWF. Consider the following set of permissible orderings:

$$x\bar{P}_1y\bar{P}_1z \qquad y\bar{P}_2z\bar{P}_2x \qquad y\bar{P}_3z\bar{I}_3x.$$

Both VR and LA are satisfied and WEC is not satisfied. However, for the set of individual orderings $\{xP_1yP_1z,\; yP_2zP_2x\}$ which corresponds to a subset of this permissible set of orderings, the MD-Rule yields the intransitive results $(xIy\;\&\;yPz\;\&\;zIx)$.

7.4. *The Existence of a Complete Social Ordering under the MD-Rule*

We have seen above that WEC is not a sufficient condition for the transitivity of the MD-Rule. However, if the number of concerned individuals is assumed to be odd[1] over a triple then EC which is weaker than WEC becomes a sufficient condition for the transitivity of the MD-Rule over that triple.

THEOREM 7.2. *Given that the number of concerned individual orderings is odd for every triple of alternatives, a sufficient condition of Type II for a set of individual orderings to be in the domain of MD–SWF is that every permissible set of orderings satisfies EC over every triple of alternatives.*

PROOF: A set of individual orderings which corresponds to any subset of a permissible set of orderings satisfying EC over a triple (x, y, z) will also satisfy EC over (x, y, z). Without loss of generality we can assume that

$$(\forall i) [\sim (xI_iyI_iz) \rightarrow \{(xP_iy \ \& \ xP_iz) \vee (yP_ix \ \& \ zP_ix)\}].$$

Since $N(\sim [xI_iyI_iz])$ is odd it is clear that $N(xP_iy \ \& \ xP_iz) > N*/2$ or $N(yP_ix \ \& \ zP_ix) > N*/2$ where $N(\sim [xI_iyI_iz]) = N*$. It follows that $(xPy \ \& \ xPz)$ or $(yPx \ \& \ zPx)$. In neither case can R be intransitive, since for R to be intransitive over (x, y, z) one and only one of the following two conditions must be satisfied:

(i) $xRy \ \& \ yRz \ \& \ zRx$, and (ii) $(yRx \ \& \ xRz \ \& z \ Ry)$,

and this is impossible if

$$[(xPy \ \& \ xPz) \vee (yPx \ \& \ zPx)]. \qquad \text{Q.E.D.}$$

It may be noted that even if the number of individual orderings concerned with respect to a triple of alternatives (x, y, z) is assumed to be odd, WEC, and therefore EC, is not sufficient for every binary, decisive, neutral, and positively responsive Rule to yield transitive results. Consider the set of individual orderings $\{xP_1yP_1z, xP_2yP_2z, yP_3zP_3x\}$ corresponding to the permissible set of orderings $\{x\bar{P}_1y\bar{P}_1z, y\bar{P}_2z\bar{P}_2x\}$. Here the number of concerned

---

[1] For a discussion of this assumption see below. Since by Lemma 7.1 EC implies VR, by Theorem 5.1 it is true that EC is sufficient for quasi-transitivity of R under the MD-Rule irrespective of whether the number of individuals is odd or not.

individual orderings is odd and the permissible set satisfies WEC over (x, y, z). Now consider the following MMD-Rule under which $R = ((R_1, R_2, R_3, R_3))$. This MMD-Rule is clearly binary, decisive, neutral and positively responsive. But it yields the intransitive results $(yPz \& zIx \& yIx)$ given the set of individual orderings. The following theorem can be deduced from Theorems 7.1 and 7.2.

THEOREM 7.3.   *Given that the number of concerned individual orderings is odd for every triple of alternatives, a sufficient condition of Type II for a set of individual orderings to be in the domain of MD–SWF is that every permissible set of orderings should satisfy VR or LA over every triple of alternatives.*

PROOF:

Let the set of permissible orderings satisfy VR or LA over a triple of alternatives (x, y, z). Let Π be any subset of this set of permissible orderings. It is clear that Π satisfies VR or LA over (x, y, z). Let the set of individual orderings correspond to Π. Given that the number of individuals concerned with respect to (x, y, z) is odd, from Theorems 7.1 and 7.2 it is clear that for this set of individual orderings the MD-Rule will yield transitive results over (x, y, z). Since Π was assumed to be any subset of the set of permissible orderings satisfying VR or LA over (x, y, z), Theorem 7.2 now follows immediately.   Q.E.D.

Theorem 7.3. is almost equivalent to Sen's[4] theorem on value restriction and Inada's[3] Theorem 8 taken together. Sen's[4] theorem proves the sufficiency of VR for the transitivity of the MD-Rule when the number of concerned individuals is odd.[1] Inada's Theorem 8 proves the sufficiency of his condition of Taboo Preferences for the transitivity of the MD-Rule when the number of individuals is odd.[2]

We now derive certain necessary and sufficient conditions for a set of individual orderings to belong to the domain of MD–SWF. Theorem 7.4 establishes a necessary and sufficient condition of Type II when the number of concerned individuals is

[1] For an alternative proof of Sen's[4] theorem, see Majumdar[2].

[2] Theorem 7.3, however, is not exactly equivalent to these two theorems taken together. This is because, as noted in Chapter 5, Inada's Condition of Taboo Preferences is stronger than LA in so far as it rules out indifference between all the alternatives in a triple.

assumed to be odd. Theorem 7.5 establishes a similar condition for the general case where no restriction is imposed on the number of concerned individuals.

THEOREM 7.4. *Given that the number of concerned individuals is odd for every triple of alternatives, a necessary and sufficient condition of Type II for a set of individual orderings to be in the domain of MD–SWF is that every permissible set of orderings should satisfy VR or LA or ER over every triple of alternatives.*

PROOF:

Sufficiency of the condition follows from the proofs of Theorems 5.3 and 7.3. The proof of necessity follows exactly the same pattern as the proof of necessity in Theorem 5.4. In Theorem 5.4 it was shown that if a permissible set of orderings violates VR, LA and ER over a triple (x, y, z), then for some set of individual orderings corresponding to a subset of the permissible set, the MD-Rule yields an empty $C(\{x, y, z\})$. Following the same procedure it can be shown that if a permissible set of orderings violates VR, LA and ER over a triple (x, y, z), then for some set of individual orderings which contains an odd number of concerned individual orderings and which corresponds to a subset of the permissible set, the MD-Rule yields intransitive results Q.E.D.

THEOREM 7.5. *A necessary and sufficient condition of Type II for a set of individual orderings to belong to the domain of MD–SWF is that every permissible set of orderings should satisfy ER over every triple of alternatives.*

PROOF:

Sufficiency of the condition follows from the proof of Theorem 5.3. We have to prove only necessity. Suppose a permissible set of orderings Π violates ER over (x, y, z). This means that there is (say) some $\bar{R}_i$ belonging to Π such that $x\bar{P}_iy\bar{P}_iz$ while there is an $\bar{R}_j$ such that either (1) $z\bar{P}_jx\bar{R}_jy$ or (2) $y\bar{R}_jz\bar{P}_jx$. Suppose there are two individuals 1 and 2. Suppose individual 1 has the ordering xP_1yP_1z. If zP_2xR_2y then the MD-Rule yields $(xPy \,\&\, yIz \,\&\, xIz)$. If yR_2zP_2x, then we have $(xIy \,\&\, yPz \,\&\, xIz)$ by the MD-Rule. Thus Π has a subset such that for some set of individual orderings corresponding to this subset, the MD-Rule yields intransitive results. This completes the proof.   Q.E.D.

Theorem 7.4 subsumes Sen's [4] theorem on value restricted preferences and also the following theorems of Inada [3]: Theorem 1 (sufficiency of DP), Theorems 2 and 2′ (sufficiency of EP), Theorem 3 (sufficiency of AP), Theorem 8 (sufficiency of 'taboo preferences'), and Theorem 9 (necessity of satisfying VR or DP or EP or AP or 'Taboo Preferences'). Theorem 7.4 is almost equivalent to all these theorems taken together.[1] Theorem 7.5 subsumes the following theorems of Inada [3]: Theorem 1 (sufficiency of DP), Theorems 2 and 2′ (sufficiency of EP), Theorem 3 (sufficiency of AP) and Theorem 4 (necessity of satisfying one of the three). While there is some gain in economy, there is, in this case, no gain in generality, since Theorem 7.5 can also be derived from Inada's [3] Theorems 1, 2, 3, and 4.

Theorems 7.4 and 7.5 establish necessary conditions of Type II. They do not establish any necessary condition of Type I.[2] In fact, in the case of Theorem 7.5 it can be shown with the help of the following theorem that fulfillment of ER over every triple of alternatives is *not* a necessary condition of Type I for a set of individual orderings to be in the domain of MD–SWF.

THEOREM 7.6.　*A sufficient condition of Type I for a set of individual orderings to be in the domain of MD–SWF is that every permissible set of orderings satisfies WEP over every triple of alternatives.*

PROOF:

As before we have to prove only the transitivity of R under the MD-Rule. We have already seen that for R to violate transitivity over (x, y, z), one and only one of the following conditions must be satisfied:

$$(xRy \ \& \ yRz \ \& \ zRx) \tag{i},$$

$$(yRx \ \& \ xRz \ \& \ zRy) \tag{ii}.$$

If there does not exist any ordering in the permissible set, which is antisymmetric over $\{x, y, z\}$, then WEP is trivially satisfied. But in this case ER is also satisfied. By Theorem 5.3 R will be transitive over $\{x, y, z\}$ in this case.

Suppose there does exist an ordering in the permissible set which is antisymmetric over $\{x, y, z\}$. Let $\{\bar{R}_1, ..., \bar{R}_N\}$ be a set of

---

[1] Again, the difference arises because of the difference between LA and Inada's condition of Taboo Preferences.

[2] I have been unable to establish necessary and sufficient conditions of Type I for these cases.

individual orderings corresponding to the set of permissible orderings. Then without loss of generality we can assume that

$$[(\exists i)\,(xP_iyP_iz)\;\&\;\sim(\exists j)\,(zP_jx)]r.$$

However $\quad[(\exists i)\,(xP_iyP_iz)\;\&\;\sim(\exists j)\,(zP_jx)]$

$$\rightarrow[(\forall i)\,(xR_iz)\;\&\;(\exists i)\,(xP_iz)]\rightarrow(xPz).$$

The possibility of (i) holding good is, therefore, ruled out. All that we have to show is that (ii) also cannot be true.

Suppose (ii) is true. Then yRx, which implies that

$$N(yP_ix)\geqslant N(xP_iy). \tag{1}$$

Since $\qquad(\forall i)\,(xR_iz),\,(\forall i)\,(yP_ix\rightarrow yP_iz),$

by the transitivity of R $\tag{2}$

By hypothesis, $\quad(\exists i)\,[\sim(yP_ix)\;\&\;yP_iz]. \tag{3}$

From (2) and (3), $\; N(yP_iz)>N(yP_ix). \tag{4}$

Since $(\forall i)\,(xR_iz)$, it follows that

$$(\forall i)\,(zP_iy\rightarrow xP_iy).$$

Therefore $\qquad N(xP_iy)\geqslant N(zP_iy). \tag{5}$

From (1), (4) and (5), $N(yP_iz)>N(zP_iy).$

Therefore $\qquad\qquad\sim(zRy).$

But this contradicts the hypothesis that (ii) is true. Thus both (i) and (ii) are ruled out. R is, therefore, transitive over (x,y,z).

Q.E.D.

We can now show that the fulfillment of ER over every triple is *not* a necessary condition of Type I for a set of individual orderings to be in the domain of MD–SWF. A counterexample will suffice. Suppose we have a set of three alternatives $\{x,y,z\}$ for which the permissible set of orderings is:

$$x\bar{P}_1y\bar{P}_1z\qquad y\bar{P}_2x\bar{P}_2z\qquad x\bar{P}_3z\bar{P}_3y\qquad y\bar{P}_4x\bar{I}_4z\qquad x\bar{I}_5z\bar{P}_5y.$$

This permissible set of orderings violates ER since $y\bar{P}_2x\bar{P}_2z$ and $x\bar{P}_3z\bar{P}_3y$ are both in the set. But the set of orderings satisfies WEP. Therefore, by Theorem 7.6 the MD-Rule yields transitive results for any set of individual orderings corresponding to the set.

7.5. *Transitivity of MMD-Rules*

Every MMD-Rule is a binary Rule satisfying decisiveness, neutrality, and non-negative responsiveness. But every MMD-Rule does not necessarily satisfy positive responsiveness. It is not, therefore, surprising that the sufficient condition stated in Theorem 7.1 does not work in the context of some MMD–SFWs. Take the following examples:

1. $((((xI_1yP_1z, xP_2yI_2z)), yP_3zP_3x)) = (xIy \ \& \ yPz \ \& \ xIz)$,

2. $((((xP_1yI_1z, xI_2yP_2z)), zP_3yI_3x)) = (xPy \ \& \ yIz \ \& \ xIz)$.

In the first example we have a set of individual orderings which satisfies NB value restriction with respect to z. In the second example we have a set of individual orderings which satisfies LA. In neither case is WEC satisfied. Nevertheless, multi-stage majority decisions are intransitive in each case. Theorem 7.7 below establishes sufficient conditions for a set of individual orderings to be in the domain of a MMD–SWF. The following lemma is useful in proving Theorem 7.7.

LEMMA 7.5. *Let $\{\bar{R}_1, ..., \bar{R}_n\}$ be a set of complete preference orderings defined over S. Let $\bar{R} = f(\bar{R}_1, ..., \bar{R}_n)$ where f is the majority voting operation. Let (x, y, z) be any triple of alternatives belonging to S, and N^* be the number of orderings concerned with respect to (x, y, z). If N^* is odd, then*

(i) $(\forall i) [\sim (x\bar{I}_iy\bar{I}_iz) \rightarrow (x\bar{P}_iy \lor x\bar{P}_iz)] \rightarrow (x\bar{P}y \lor x\bar{P}z)$,

(ii) $(\forall i) [\sim (x\bar{I}_iy\bar{I}_iz) \rightarrow (y\bar{P}_ix \lor z\bar{P}_ix)] \rightarrow (y\bar{P}x \lor z\bar{P}x)$,

(iii) $(\forall i) [\sim (x\bar{I}_iy\bar{I}_iz) \rightarrow \{(x\bar{P}_iy \ \& \ x\bar{P}_iz) \lor (y\bar{P}_ix \ \& \ z\bar{P}_ix)\}]$
$$\rightarrow [(x\bar{P}y \ \& \ x\bar{P}z) \lor (y\bar{P}x \ \& \ z\bar{P}x)].$$

PROOF:

A. $(\forall i) [\sim (x\bar{I}_iy\bar{I}_iz) \rightarrow (x\bar{P}_iy \lor x\bar{P}_iz)]$
$$\rightarrow [\{N(x\bar{P}_iy) > N^*/2\} \lor \{N(x\bar{P}_iz) > N^*/2\}],$$
since N^* is odd
$$\rightarrow [x\bar{P}y \lor x\bar{P}z].$$

B. The proof of (ii) is exactly analogous to that of (i).

C. $(\forall i)\,[\sim (x\bar{I}_i y\bar{I}_i z) \to \{(x\bar{P}_i y\ \&\ x\bar{P}_i z) \lor (y\bar{P}_i x\ \&\ z\bar{P}_i x)\}]$

$\to [\{N(x\bar{P}_i y\ \&\ x\bar{P}_i z) > N^*/2\}$

$\lor\ \{N(y\bar{P}_i x\ \&\ z\bar{P}_i x) > N^*/2\}],$

since N^* is odd

$\to [(x\bar{P}y\ \&\ x\bar{P}z) \lor (y\bar{P}x\ \&\ z\bar{P}x)].$　　　　Q.E.D.

THEOREM 7.7. *Given that the number of entries concerned with respect to any triple of alternatives is odd for every majority voting operation involved, a necessary and sufficient condition of Type II for a set of individual orderings to be in the domain of every MMD–SWF is that every permissible set of orderings satisfies VR or LA over every triple of alternatives.*

PROOF:

Proof of Sufficiency. Since every MMD-Rule is decisive, we need concern ourselves only with transitivity.

A. Consider first the case where the set of individual orderings corresponds to a subset of a permissible set of orderings which satisfies VR over a triple (x, y, z). In this case the set of individual orderings must satisfy VR over (x, y, z).

For all i and j, $R_{ij}^{(0)}$ is an individual ordering.

Therefore the set of all $R_{ij}^{(0)}$ satisfies value restriction. Also, by hypothesis, the number of $R_{ij}^{(0)}$ concerned with respect to (x, y, z) is odd for every j.

From Theorem 7.3. it is clear that $R_j^{(0)}$ is a complete ordering for every j. Also by Lemma 7.5, the set of $R_j^{(0)}$ is subject to the same type of value restriction with respect to the same alternative in (x, y, z) as the set of individual orderings.

Every $R_{ij}^{(1)}$ is either an individual ordering or a $R_j^{(0)}$. It is therefore clear that every $R_{ij}^{(1)}$ is a complete ordering over (x, y, z) and that the set of $R_{ij}^{(1)}$ satisfies the same type of value restriction with respect to the same alternative as the set of individual orderings. Thus from Lemma 7.5. and the Theorem 7.3. again, every $R_j^{(1)}$ is a complete ordering over (x, y, z) and the set of $R_j^{(1)}$ satisfies the same type of value restriction with respect to the same alternative as the set of individual orderings.

Continuing like this we shall ultimately arrive at R which will be a complete ordering, and will satisfy transitivity over (x, y, z).

B. Now consider the case where the set of individual orderings satisfies LA. Without loss of generality we can assume that $(\forall i)\,(xR_i y)$.

For all i and j, $R_{ij}^{(0)}$ is an individual ordering. Hence $xR_{ij}^{(0)}y$ for every $R_{ij}^{(0)}$.

Also, by hypothesis the number of $R_{ij}^{(0)}$ concerned with respect to (x, y, z) is odd for every j.

Hence from Theorem 7.3 it is clear that $R_j^{(0)}$ is an ordering over (x, y, z) for all j. Also it is obvious that $xR_j^{(0)}y$ for all j.

Every $R_{ij}^{(1)}$ is either an individual ordering or a $R_j^{(0)}$.

Hence every $R_{ij}^{(1)}$ is a complete ordering and $xR_{ij}^{(1)}y$ for every $R_{ij}^{(1)}$. By hypothesis the number of concerned $R_{ij}^{(1)}$ is odd for all j.

Therefore again, every $R_j^{(1)}$ is a complete ordering. Also $xR_j^{(1)}y$ for all j.

Continuing like this we shall ultimately arrive at R which will be a complete ordering, and will satisfy transitivity over (x, y, z).

Proof of necessity. To prove the necessity it is enough to prove that if a permissible set of orderings Π violates VR and also LA over a triple (x, y, z), then there exists a set of individual orderings corresponding to a subset of Π such that R is intransitive over (x, y, z) under some MMD-Rule in which every majority voting operation involved has an odd number of entries concerned with respect to (x, y, z). An inspection of the proof of Theorem 6.7 shows that we have already proved this. This completes the proof of Theorem 7.7.   Q.E.D.

Since the MD-Rule is also an MMD-Rule, Theorem 7.7 is a generalization of Theorem 7.3. We can also establish a necessary and sufficient condition of Type I for a set of individual orderings to be in the domain of every MMD-Rule.

THEOREM 7.8.   *Given that the number of entries concerned with respect to any triple of alternatives is odd for every majority voting operation involved, a necessary and sufficient condition of Type I for a set of individual orderings to be in the domain of every MMD–SWF is that every permissible set of orderings satisfies VR or LA over every triple of alternatives.*

PROOF:

Since a sufficient condition of Type II is also a sufficient condition of Type I the proof of sufficiency follows from the proof of sufficiency in Theorem 7.7. Just as the proof of necessity in

Theorem 7.7 follows from the proof of necessity in Theorem 6.7, the proof of necessity here follows from the proof of necessity in Theorem 6.8.   Q.E.D.

7.6. *Some observations on restrictions on the number of concerned individuals*

A remarkable feature of some of the theorems proved in this chapter as distinguished from those proved in the last two chapters is that they assume the number of individuals (or entries in a majority voting operation) concerned with respect to any triple of alternatives, to be odd. This is a restrictive assumption since in actual practice the number of concerned individuals (or concerned entries in a majority voting operation) for a given triple of alternatives is just as likely to be even as odd. To quote Williamson and Sargent: '...the requirement that the number of non-indifferent individuals expressing themselves with respect to *every* triple be odd is rather severe. Indeed, we should expect that on the average, the number of individuals expressing such preferences would, for any triple selected at random, be even 50 % of the time. In the absence of additional restrictions the probability that an even number of individuals will be involved in the voting in at least one out of the total of all such triples can obviously approach unity very rapidly.'

Note that no such assumption was used in the theorems regarding the existence of a social choice function. Restriction on the number of individuals (or entries in a majority voting operation) concerned with respect to any triple of alternatives figures only in Theorems 7.2, 7.3, 7.4, 7.7, and 7.8, all of which are concerned with the existence of a complete social ordering. Theorem 7.2 shows the sufficiency of EC for transitivity under the MD-Rule given that the number of concerned individuals is odd for every triple. Given the same assumption, Theorem 7.3 shows the sufficiency of VR and also LA for the transitivity of R under the MD-Rule, and Theorem 7.4 establishes a necessary and sufficient condition for the transitivity of R under the MD-Rule. If we drop the restriction on the number of concerned individuals in these theorems, only the results concerning sufficiency change and they change only in so far as R, though still quasi-transitive under the MD-Rule, does not necessarily remain transitive.[1] Theorems 7.7 and 7.8 establish necessary and sufficient conditions of Type II and Type I respectively for all MMD-Rules to yield transitive results under the assumption that the number of entries concerned with respect to any triple is odd for every majority voting operation involved. If we drop this assumption regarding the number of concerned entries, then the results concerning sufficiency change in so far as R, though still quasi-transitive, does not necessarily remain transitive.[2]

Thus in all these theorems the restriction on the number of concerned individuals (or concerned entries) is relevant for the sufficiency of certain conditions for the transitivity of R: relaxation of this restriction weakens the result to the extent that the conditions on permissible sets of preference patterns continue to be sufficient for the quasi-transitivity of R, but not necessarily for the transitivity of R. Since the reflexivity, connectedness, and quasi-transitivity of R are together sufficient for the existence of a choice function defined over a finite S, if our emphasis is on the existence of a choice function rather than on the existence of a complete social ordering, then the restriction on the number of concerned individuals (or concerned entries in a majority voting operation) is not required in the context of the group decision Rules that we have discussed earlier.

If, however, we are interested in the existence of complete social ordering, say, under the MD-Rule,[3] then the assumption that the number of concerned individuals is odd for every triple of alternatives does become relevant. It may be thought that the difficulty can be easily overcome by nominating one of the concerned individuals as the chairman whose preference enters into the social decision like that of anybody else, but has the added significance that it is used to break a tie in case there is one. And this is true. But two points should be noted here. Firstly, different persons may have to be elected chairmen for different triples. For the election of a chairman having a tie-breaking capacity does not help in any way so far as the transitivity of majority decisions over a particular triple is concerned, if the chairman happens to be an individual not concerned with respect to that

---

[1] See p. 125 note 1 above, and also Theorems 5.1 and 5.2.

[2] See Theorem 6.5.

[3] In what follows I discuss the MD-Rule; but similar considerations arise in the case of MMD-Rules also.

triple. Secondly, it should be noted that whoever is elected a chairman will enjoy a privileged status: if there is a tie between x and y and if the chairman is not indifferent between x and y[1] then the preference of the chairman will have twice as much weight as the preference of anybody else. This clearly violates May's condition of 'anonymity'. This would not be disturbing if there were some 'satisfactory' way of selecting the chairman. In the absence of any such principle the choice of a chairman, and therefore the social decision in the case of a tie, will remain arbitrary. It may, however, be argued that when the number of concerned individuals is large, there is unlikely to be an exact half-and-half division in any pairwise comparison.[2] In all such cases, therefore, we may discard the assumption of the oddness of the number of concerned individuals without any serious danger of intransitivity.

[1] The chairman may be indifferent between any two 'alternatives in the triple under consideration. All that is required is that he should not be indifferent between *all* the alternatives of the triple.

[2] As noted above, even if we drop the assumption that the number of concerned individuals is odd, the relevant conditions on permissible sets of preference patterns still continue to be sufficient for the quasi-transitivity of R under the MD-Rule. Since R continues to be quasi-transitive, there must be ties in two out of the three pairwise comparisons for the triple of alternatives, if R is to violate transitivity. This is even less likely to occur than a tie in only one pairwise comparison.

8

INTRANSITIVE INDIVIDUAL
PREFERENCES AND SOCIAL CHOICE

8.1. *Intransitivity of Individual Preferences*

One of the basic assumptions underlying the analysis so far is the assumption that the individual weak preference relation is a complete ordering, i.e., each R_i satisfies reflexivity, connectedness, and transitivity over S. The property of reflexivity cannot be questioned seriously since all that it shows is that R_i is a *weak* preference relation. It would also seem reasonable to assume the property of connectedness since one would expect that normally an individual would be able to compare any two alternatives. The position, however, is not so clear so far as the transitivity of R_i is concerned. There has been a growing scepticism about the validity of this assumption.[1] Several experiments have revealed what has been interpreted as the intransitivity of individual preferences.[2] It is true that in many of these experiments the alleged intransitivity, instead of being genuine, might have arisen because of defects in the process of experiment itself. But intuitively also several plausible explanations may be suggested for the possible intransitivity of individual preferences.

One of the most widely known explanations for intransitive individual preferences has been given by May[2]. Basically May's thesis is that 'intransitivity is a natural result of the necessity of choosing among alternatives according to conflicting criteria'. The individual while comparing multi-dimensional objects is faced with a large number of simultaneously relevant criteria and the ranking of different objects on the basis of different criteria will differ. This is held to be responsible for intransitive preferences in such a context. May's analysis here takes advantage of the formal framework of Arrow's General

---

[1] For an exception see Tullock.
[2] For a discussion of some of these experiments see Edwards ([1], [2]).

Possibility Theorem. The individual, according to May, reaches his ultimate preference pattern over the set of multi-dimensional objects by aggregating the different orderings reached on the basis of the different criteria of evaluation. The method of aggregation is assumed to satisfy conditions formally identical with Conditions 1' (ii), 2, 3, 4 and 5 of Arrow [1]. Therefore, by the General Possibility Theorem of Arrow, Condition 1' (i) is violated and the final preference pattern of the individual often turns out to be intransitive.

It may, however, be pointed out that May's application of the General Possibility Theorem in this context, while ingenious and elegant, lacks intuitive appeal. For, as we have seen in the context of social choice, the formal structure of Arrow rules out the possibility of taking into account intensities of individual preferences as distinguished from individual orderings, in deriving the social preferences. Something similar happens in the case of May's individual; the assumptions rule out the possibility of the individual's taking into account the intensity of desirability according to different criteria of evaluation in forming his final preference pattern. There is, however, a basic difference between the two types of situations which seems to have been overlooked by May. Basing social preferences on individual *orderings* only and not on intensities of preferences may have a certain appeal in view of the difficulties of ascertaining intensities of individual preferences and of making interpersonal comparisons of utility. But it may not be insuperably difficult for the single individual to take into account the *intensity* of desirability according to different criteria and to weight them in assessing overall desirability of the objects; certainly the difficulty in this case is not comparable with that arising in the context of interpersonal comparison of utility.

Other more plausible explanations can be given for the intransitivity of individual preferences. One explanation based on the notion of limited human power of perception has been advanced by Armstrong.[1] The individual may *express* indifference between two alternatives x and y not because x and y occupy the same position in his scale of preference, but because the difference between x and y in his scale of preference is so small that he

---

[1] For a somewhat similar argument see Georgescu-Roegen.

cannot perceive the difference.[1] If this possibility is admitted, then the indifference relation I_i may be intransitive. This may be explained with the help of the following simple diagram:

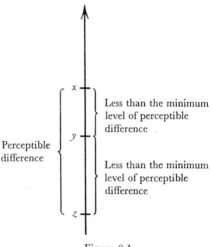

Figure 8.1

The individual's scale of preference is represented along the arrow. As we move up we reach alternatives occupying higher and higher positions in the individual's scale of preference. x stands higher than y in his scale of preference, and so does y as compared to z. The individual's power of perception being limited, if the difference between two alternatives in his preference scale is less than a certain minimum level, he cannot perceive it, and therefore he declares the two alternatives to be indifferent. It is assumed that the difference between x and y as well as the difference between y and z is less than the minimum

---

[1] It may be thought that this is really an intransitivity of the indifference that is *expressed*; the 'true indifference' of the individual, however, is transitive. If we interpret I_i as referring to this 'true indifference' of the individual then the Armstrong type of reasoning does not affect the transitivity of I_i. This line of argument, however, is not very fruitful. For, if the individual himself cannot perceive the difference between x and y, then even if x really stood higher than y in the individual's 'true' scale of preference, there is no way of taking this into account in making social choice. I shall therefore interpret R_i as referring to the individual preference as the individual himself thinks it to be.

perceptibile level of difference.[1] He, therefore, expresses indifference between x and y and also between y and z. However the difference between x and z is perceptible; this is perfectly possible since the difference between x and z is equal to the sum of the difference between x and y and that between y and z. He, therefore, expresses his preference for x over z. Thus we have

$$(xI_iy \ \& \ yI_iz \ \& \ xP_iz).$$

Note that the notion of limited power of perception can explain only the intransitivity of I_i and not that of P_i. For if the individual expresses his preference for x over y, and for y over z, then x stands higher than y by at least the minimum level of perceptible difference, and y stands higher than z by at least the minimum level of perceptible difference, and therefore x must stand higher than z by more than the minimum level of perceptible difference. Thus if only the Armstrong type of explanation of intransitive individual preferences is operative, then R_i will be quasi-transitive but not necessarily transitive.

It has also been suggested that it may sometimes be rational for the individual to behave 'irrationally' in the sense of violating transitivity. If the trouble of weighing different alternatives is considered too much, the individual will be perfectly rational to choose at random.[2] In this case the individual's preferences as reflected in his choice may be clearly intransitive.

In view of these and many other reasons[3] that have been given in the literature, the assumption of transitive individual preferences does not seem to be unassailable. It is, therefore, of some interest to consider the implications for our theory of a relaxation of this assumption. This is what I seek to do in the following sections of this chapter. I shall, however, continue to assume that every individual weak preference relation is reflexive and connected over S.

8.2. *Some 'Possibility' and 'Impossibility' Results*

It is natural to expect that the relaxation of the assumption of transitive individual preferences will make it more difficult to have a reasonable SDF with unrestricted domain. It is, therefore,

---

[1] All this of course assumes the meaningfulness of the concept of preference intensity.   [2] See Clark and Edwards [1].   [3] For a lucid survey see Weinstein.

worth noting that even if we assume only acyclicity of individual strict preference and do not assume either transitivity or quasi-transitivity of individual weak preference, there still exists a SDF with unrestricted domain[1] that satisfies Arrow's Conditions *2, 3, 4 and 5*.[2] In fact a stronger proposition is true:

THEOREM 8.1. *Given that S is finite, if every individual weak preference relation is reflexive and connected over S and at least one individual strict preference relation is acyclic over S, then there exists a SDF with unrestricted domain, that fulfills non-negative responsiveness, neutrality, and anonymity, in addition to Arrow's Conditions 3 and 4.*[3]

PROOF:

The proof consists of an example. Consider the Extended Weak Pareto Criterion. It satisfies decisiveness, non-negative responsiveness, neutrality, and anonymity in addition to Arrow's Conditions *3 and 4*. It can be shown that P under this Rule is acyclic. Suppose P violates acyclicity. Then

$$[x_1 P x_2 \,\&\, x_2 P x_3 \,\&\, ... \,\&\, x_{n-1} P x_n \,\&\, x_n P x_1]$$

for some $x_1, x_2, ..., x_n$ belonging to S. By the definition of the Extended Weak Pareto Criterion it follows that

$$(\forall i)\,(x_1 P_i x_2 \,\&\, x_2 P_i x_3 \,\&\, ... \,\&\, x_{n-1} P_i x_n \,\&\, x_n P_i x_1)$$

which violates our assumption that for some i, P_i is acyclic over S. Hence P must be acyclic. Since R is reflexive and connected, and P is acyclic, by Lemma 1.3 and Theorem 1.1, there exists a choice function over S given that S is finite.

Q.E.D.

If, however, we require our SDF to satisfy the Strict Pareto Criterion, then it becomes impossible to find a SDF with un-

---

[1] In this context the term 'unrestricted domain' refers to a domain that contains every set of individual weak preference relations satisfying our assumption regarding the properties of these relations.

[2] In Chapter 3, these and other properties of a group decision Rule were defined with reference to sets of individual orderings. Since we no longer make the assumption of transitive individual weak preference relations, for the purpose of this chapter these definitions are to be understood in terms of sets of reflexive and connected (but not necessarily transitive or even acyclic) individual weak preference relations.

[3] As noted earlier, non-negative responsiveness implies Arrow's Condition 2, and anonymity implies his Condition 5.

restricted domain even if all individual weak preference relations are quasi-transitive.

THEOREM 8.2. *If individual weak preference relations are quasi-transitive but not necessarily transitive, then there does not exist any SDF with unrestricted domain that satisfies the Strict Pareto Criterion.*

PROOF:

The proof consists of an example. Let there be three individuals having the following preference patterns over a triple of alternatives (x, y, z).

$$xP_1y \; \& \; yI_1z \; \& \; zI_1x,$$
$$xI_2y \; \& \; yP_2z \; \& \; zI_2x,$$
$$zI_3y \; \& \; yI_3x \; \& \; zP_3x.$$

By the Strict Pareto Criterion we have $(xPy \; \& \; yPz \; \& \; zPx)$ which implies that $C(\{x, y, z\})$ is empty. Therefore, the set of quasi-transitive individual weak preference relations, given above, cannot belong to the domain of a SDF satisfying the Strict Pareto Criterion.   Q.E.D.

Though logically this result is not very exciting, it is fairly disturbing if we believe that intransitive indifference relations are not very uncommon among individuals. This is because the Strict Pareto Criterion is an almost universally accepted value judgment. The only way of escaping the dilemma would, therefore, seem to lie in restricting the domain of the SDF. This approach is explored in the next section.

8.3. *A Theorem on the Existence of a Choice Function under Binary, Decisive, Neutral, and Non-negatively Responsive Rules*[1]

Faced with the problem posed by Theorem 8.2, it is of some consolation to find that some of the conditions which were shown to be sufficient for a set of individual orderings to be in the domain of any binary, decisive, neutral, and non-negatively responsive Rule are also sufficient for a set of reflexive, connected, and quasi-transitive, individual weak preference relations to be in the domain of any binary, decisive, neutral, and non-negatively responsive Rule. The conditions discussed earlier were conditions on sets of orderings. They will now be reinterpreted as being conditions on sets of reflexive, connected, and

---

[1] This section is based on Pattanaik [5].

quasi-transitive weak preference relations. The definitions of the conditions, however, remain exactly the same.[1] Two new conditions will now be introduced. As in the case of the conditions stated earlier, these conditions are stated with reference to a given triple of alternatives (x, y, z). As before, a, b, and c are three distinct variables each of which can assume one of the values x, y and z.

DEFINITION 8.1.

(i) *NM* Value Restriction.*

$$(\exists a)\,(\exists b)\,(\exists c)\,(\forall i)\,[(a\bar{P}_i b \,\&\, a\bar{P}_i c) \vee (b\bar{P}_i a \,\&\, c\bar{P}_i a) \vee (a\bar{I}_i b \,\&\, a\bar{I}_i c)].$$

(ii) *VR*.*   At least one of the following three types of value restriction is satisfied—*NW, NB* and *NM**.

It is clear that if every $\bar{R}_i$ is an ordering, then *NM** value restriction is equivalent to *NM* value restriction, and VR* is equivalent to VR. If, however, every $\bar{R}_i$ is reflexive, connected, and quasi-transitive, but not necessarily transitive, then *NM** value restriction is weaker than *NM* value restriction, and therefore VR* is weaker than VR. For example if

$$(x\bar{P}_i y \,\&\, y\bar{I}_i z \,\&\, z\bar{I}_i x)$$

is true of some i and $(y\bar{P}_i x \,\&\, y\bar{I}_i z \,\&\, z\bar{I}_i x)$ is true of the rest, then *NM** value restriction, and therefore VR*, is satisfied though VR is not satisfied.

THEOREM 8.3.   *If individual weak preference relations are reflexive, connected, and quasi-transitive, then a sufficient condition of Type II for a binary, decisive, neutral, and non-negatively responsive Rule to yield quasi-transitive results over a triple is that every permissible set of preference patterns satisfies VR* over that triple.*

PROOF:

As noted earlier, a necessary condition for R to violate quasi-transitivity over a triple of alternatives (x, y, z) is that at least one

---

[1] Note that with a set of reflexive, connected, and quasi-transitive weak preference relations, ER is no longer equivalent to the union of DP, AP and EP. Consider the set $\{\bar{R}_1,\ \bar{R}_2\}$ where $\bar{R}_1$ and $\bar{R}_2$ are two reflexive, connected, and quasi-transitive weak preference relations such that

$$x\bar{P}_1 y \,\&\, yP_1 z \,\&\, x\bar{P}_1 z \qquad z\bar{P}_2 x \,\&\, x\bar{I}_2 y \,\&\, yI_2 z.$$

It can be easily checked that $\{\bar{R}_1,\ \bar{R}_2\}$ satisfies ER but does not satisfy either AP or EP or DP.

of the following two conditions should be satisfied with at least two of the Rs being Ps.

$$(xRy \ \& \ yRz \ \& \ zRx) \tag{i},$$

$$(yRx \ \& \ xRz \ \& \ zRy) \tag{ii}.$$

Let $\{R_1, \ldots, R_N\}$ be any set of individual weak preference relations corresponding to a subset of a permissible set of preference patterns satisfying VR* over (x, y, z). Then $\{R_1, \ldots, R_N\}$ satisfies VR* over (x, y, z).

$$(\forall i) \left[\sim (xP_iy \ \& \ yR_iz) \ \& \ \sim (xR_iy \ \& \ yP_iz) \right]$$

$$\rightarrow (\forall i) \left[\{(xP_iy \rightarrow zP_iy) \ \& \ (yI_iz \rightarrow yR_ix)\} \right.$$
$$\left. \& \ \{(yP_iz \rightarrow yP_ix) \ \& \ (xI_iy \rightarrow zR_iy)\} \right]$$

$$\rightarrow (\forall i) \left[\{(xP_iy \rightarrow zP_iy) \ \& \ (xI_iy \rightarrow zR_iy)\} \right.$$
$$\left. \& \ \{(yP_iz \rightarrow yP_ix) \ \& \ (yI_iz \rightarrow yR_ix)\} \right]$$

$$\rightarrow \left[(xPy \rightarrow zPy) \ \& \ (yPz \rightarrow yPx) \right] \text{ by Lemma 6.1.}[1]$$

Therefore a sufficient condition for ruling out the possibility of (i) holding with at least two of the Rs being Ps is

$$(\forall i) \left[\sim (xP_iy \ \& \ yR_iz) \ \& \ \sim (xR_iy \ \& \ yP_iz) \right]. \tag{1}$$

Similarly each of (2) and (3) rules out the possibility of (i) holding with at least two of the Rs being Ps, and each of (4), (5) and (6) rules out the possibility of (ii) holding with at least two of the Rs being Ps.

$$(\forall i) \left[\sim (yP_iz \ \& \ zR_ix) \ \& \ \sim (yR_iz \ \& \ zP_ix) \right]. \tag{2}$$

$$(\forall i) \left[\sim (zP_ix \ \& \ xR_iy) \ \& \ \sim (zR_ix \ \& \ xP_iy) \right]. \tag{3}$$

$$(\forall i) \left[\sim (yP_ix \ \& \ xR_iz) \ \& \ \sim (yR_ix \ \& \ xP_iz) \right]. \tag{4}$$

$$(\forall i) \left[\sim (xP_iz \ \& \ zR_iy) \ \& \ \sim (xR_iz \ \& \ zP_iy) \right]. \tag{5}$$

$$(\forall i) \left[\sim (zP_iy \ \& \ yR_ix) \ \& \ \sim (zR_iy \ \& \ yP_ix) \right]. \tag{6}$$

If NB value restriction with respect to x is satisfied, then (1) holds. For, if $(\exists i) \left[(xP_iy \ \& \ yR_iz) \lor (xR_iy \ \& \ yP_iz) \right]$, then by the quasi-transitivity of R_i it will follow that

$$(\exists i) \left[\sim (xI_iy \ \& \ yI_iz \ \& \ zI_ix) \ \& \ (xR_iy \ \& \ xR_iz) \right]$$

[1] It can be checked that the proof of Lemma 6.1 does not depend on the assumption that R_i is transitive.

which is impossible if we have NB value restriction with respect to x. In general, it can be easily checked that VR^* over (x, y, z) implies at least one of (1), (2) and (3) and also at least one of (4), (5) and (6). Therefore, neither (i) nor (ii) can hold with at least two of the three Rs being Ps. Hence R must be quasi-transitive.   Q.E.D.

The following theorem follows from Theorems 8.3 and 1.3.

THEOREM 8.4.   *If S is finite and if individual weak preference relations are reflexive, connected and quasi-transitive, then a sufficient condition of Type II for a set of individual weak preference relations to be in the domain of any binary, decisive, neutral, and non-negatively responsive Rule viewed as SDF is that every permissible set of preference relations should satisfy VR^* over every triple of alternatives.*

In Chapter 6, LA was shown to be sufficient for quasi-transitivity under any binary, decisive, neutral, and non-negatively responsive Rule satisfying the Strict Pareto Criterion when individual preferences are transitive. If, however, individual preferences are assumed to be quasi-transitive and not necessarily transitive, then as can be seen from the example in the proof of Theorem 8.2, LA fails to be sufficient[1] even for acyclicity of P, and, therefore, for the existence of a choice function, under any Rule satisfying the Strict Pareto Criterion.

8.4.   *Choice Under the MD-Rule*

The following theorem due to Fishburn can be deduced as a special case from Theorem 8.3.

THEOREM 8.5.(Fishburn).   *If individual weak preference relations are reflexive, connected, and quasi-transitive, then a sufficient condition of Type II for the MD-Rule to yield quasi-transitive results over a triple is that every permissible set of preference patterns satisfies VR^* over that triple*

Given the assumption that every R_i is a complete ordering over S, it has been shown earlier[2] that fulfillment of VR or La over a triple of alternatives is a sufficient condition of Type II for quasi-transitivity of R over that triple, under the MD-Rule, and

---

[1] This is true of sufficiency in Type I as well as Type II sense.
[2] See Chapter 5.

also that fulfillment of ER over a triple of alternatives is a sufficient condition of Type II for transitivity of R over that triple, under the MD-Rule. When individual weak preference relations are assumed to be reflexive, connected, and quasi-transitive, but not necessarily transitive, by Theorem 8.5, VR still continues to be a sufficient condition of Type II for the quasi-transitivity of the MD-Rule. From what has been said in the last section, it is clear that if individual weak preference relations satisfy reflexivity, connectedness, and quasi-transitivity but not necessarily transitivity, then LA is not sufficient even for the acyclicity of P under MD-Rule. The following examples show that under the changed assumption none of the conditions AP, EP and ER is a sufficient condition of Type I or Type II for the acyclicity of P under the MD-Rule.

$$xP_1y \ \& \ yP_1z \ \& \ xP_1z \qquad xI_2y \ \& \ zP_2y \ \& \ zI_2x$$

$$xI_3y \ \& \ zP_3y \ \& \ zI_3x \qquad yP_4x \ \& \ yI_4z \ \& \ zI_4x$$

$$yP_5x \ \& \ yI_5z \ \& \ zI_5x.$$

The permissible set of preference patterns corresponding to this set of individual preference patterns satisfies AP, EP and ER.[1] The MD-Rule, however, yields the results

$$(xPz \ \& \ zPy \ \& \ yPx).$$

Similarly, the example in the proof of Theorem 8.1. shows that DP is no longer sufficient even for the acyclicity of P under the MD-Rule. Thus under the changed assumption regarding individual preferences, of all the conditions discussed in Chapter 5 only VR survives as a sufficient condition for the acyclicity of P under the MD-Rule; in fact under the changed assumptions VR* which is weaker than VR is sufficient for the quasi-transitivity of R under the MD-Rule, which is a stronger requirement than the acyclicity of P.

[1] As pointed out in note on p. 142, when individual weak preferences are assumed to be quasi-transitive but not necessarily transitive, a set of individual preference patterns may satisfy ER without satisfying DP or AP or EP.

9

INTENSITY OF INDIVIDUAL
PREFERENCES

9.1. *Preference Intensity and Independence of Irrelevant Alternatives*

So far I have discussed the possibility of resolving Arrow's paradox through modifications of his Condition 1'. I now consider his Condition 3. As observed in Chapter 3, Arrow's Condition 3 rules out the influence of irrelevant alternatives. In Chapter 3 it was also argued that it is the formal structure within which Arrow's problem is posed rather than his Condition 3, which rules out the possibility of social decisions being influenced by changes in intensities of individual preferences so long as the preference orderings remain the same. The significance of Condition 3, however, is closely linked with the problem of preference intensities. Firstly, even if we redefine the group decision Rule so as to allow for the influence of changes in preference intensities on the social weak preference relation R, such influence will still be ruled out if we retain Condition 3. In this case Condition 3 will impose a further constraint in addition to ruling out the influence of irrelevant alternatives. Secondly, as regards the irrelevant alternatives, there does not seem to be any reason why we should feel disturbed by the fact that the preferences for the irrelevant alternative are not allowed to influence social decisions in a pairwise comparison except so far as these preferences give us some insight into the intensities of individual preferences between the two alternatives involved. If the individual orderings all remained the same so far as alternatives x and y are concerned, and if somehow or other we knew that the intensities of individual preferences between x and y also remained the same,[1] then it would be difficult to justify any

---

[1] The problem as to how we get this information need not bother us here. It is enough for our argument if it is accepted that the individual orderings over $\{x, y\}$ and the intensities of individual preferences between x and y can remain the same even if individual preferences involving the 'irrelevant alternatives' z, w, etc. can change, and vice versa.

change in the social decision between x and y even if the individual preferences involving the other alternatives might have undergone change.

Thus acceptability of Condition 3 boils down to the questions as to whether social decisions should be influenced by changes in the intensities of individual preferences and whether the irrelevant alternatives give us any information regarding these intensities. In many ways the first question is a more fundamental one; the answer to it also determines the very relevance of Arrow's logical structure which bases the social weak preference relation on individual orderings alone.[1] This problem of taking into account preference intensities is discussed in the following sections.

9.2. *Preference Intensity and Interpersonal Comparison of Utility*

Should preference intensities count in social choice? If, for example, a change from x to y makes John only slightly happier but reduces enormously the happiness of Tom, should we ignore this asymmetry in the intensities of effects on the two individuals, in making social choice? Note that in stating the problem itself we have implicitly assumed that it is meaningful to compare the preference intensities of different individuals. Whether such comparison can be made is a problem of facts, while the desirability of taking into account preference intensities is an ethical problem, but the ethical problem can be posed only if it is meaningful to ask the factual question.

The problem of interpersonally comparing preference intensities is part of the broader and controversial problem of the possibility of knowing other minds. It has often been held that we cannot possibly have any knowledge of other persons' sensations and feelings. These cannot be directly observed. All that we can observe is the behaviour of the other person. But from the behaviour of an individual we cannot deduce anything about his comparative sensations or feelings. Without entering into any philosophical depths it may only be remarked that this view leads to the position that the connection between outward

---

[1] It is being assumed here that the individual weak preference relations are complete orderings. The argument, however, applies even if this assumption is not made, since a group decision Rule specifies one and only one R for a set of individual weak preference relations.

behaviour and the sensations and feelings is absolutely unique for every individual, and that though I might have observed certain relations between my feelings and my behaviour, I cannot attribute them to any other individual. This seems to be extremely arbitrary.

In fact, there is reason to believe that in real life interpersonal comparisons are fairly widespread and that when somebody makes statements of the type 'An additional dollar means more to John than to Tom', he usually means something different from the statement than an additional dollar to John would produce certain outward signs (e.g., smiles) to a greater extent than an additional dollar to Tom. What he really implies is a comparison between the sensations of the two individuals. Such comparisons are admittedly not precise. But, whatever be the margin of error, we can always find some cases where there will be general agreement about the interpersonal comparisons involved. If this is true and if, therefore, it does make sense to compare the intensities of different individuals' preferences, should we then ignore any knowledge we may have in this respect, in making social decisions? The precise way in which the preference intensities are to be incorporated into the social decision process need not detain us here. If we are utilitarians, we would probably like to maximize the sum of utilities. Or, instead of abiding solely by the utilitarian criteria we may like to introduce certain extra-utilitarian considerations. But whatever be the precise method, it can hardly be denied that ethically it is desirable to take into account preference intensities, that in a two-person society if a change from x to y makes one individual only slightly happier but throws the other individual from happiness to abject misery, then we would, in general, decide to remain in x rather than changing over to y.

The case for allowing changes in preference intensities to influence social decisions would become much stronger if we could find some satisfactory method of constructing cardinal utility functions for different individuals and for interpersonally comparing the preference intensities revealed by such functions. In terms of the methodology outlined in Chapter 2 all that we have tried to show so far is that the value judgment regarding intensity of individual preferences, implicit in Arrow's framework, is a non-basic value judgment since there are at least some cases where we can have a fairly good idea of the relative preference intensities, and where we would like to introduce this additional consideration as a relevant factor in social decision. But the practical importance of this non-basicness will become much greater if there exists a sufficiently accurate method of interpersonally comparing preference intensities.

Does there exist any such method? A large number of models have been proposed for constructing cardinal utility functions of individuals, as the basis of social decisions.[1] In the following sections of this chapter we shall discuss the model of Goodman and Markowtiz and also those of Vickrey and Harsanyi ([1], [2]). We shall show that these models do not provide a satisfactory solution to the problem of introducing preference intensities into the social decision process. Nor do we know of any formal model which does. But it must be emphasized that even if all these attempts to incorporate preference intensities as an ingredient of social choice are found to be deficient in some respect or other, it does not remove the non-basicness of the value judgment regarding preference intensities, implicit in Arrow's formulation of the problem of social choice. It only demonstrates that in the present state of our knowledge there does not exist any *precise* method of measuring and interpersonally comparing the intensities of individual preferences.[2]

9.3. *Individual Rankings and Preference Intensity*

In Chapter 8 we referred to Armstrong's hypothesis that because of limited power of perception an individual can perceive a difference in utility from two objects only if this difference is not less than a certain minimum. A similar notion underlies the formulation of Goodman and Markowitz. It is assumed 'that each individual has only a finite number of indifference levels or "levels of discretion".... A change from one level to the next represents the minimum difference which is discernible to an individual.'[3] A cardinal utility index is then provided by repre-

---

[1] See, for example, Hildreth, Kemp and Asimakopulos, Armstrong, Goodman and Markowitz, Harsanyi ([1], [2]), and Vickrey.

[2] For a discussion of different degrees of interpersonal comparability of utility, see Sen[8].

[3] Goodman and Markowitz, p. 259.

senting the utility of a given social state by the number of discretion levels below the level at which the given social state is placed. Interpersonal comparison is introduced through the assumption that the social significance of a movement from one discretion level to the next is the same for all individuals and that it is independent of the initial level from which the change is made. Given this assumption, the method of social decision takes the simple form of maximizing the sum of individual utilities as defined above.

This model involves two basic difficulties. Firstly, objection can be raised against the ethical assumption that the social significance of a movement from one discretion level to another is the same for all individuals. Assume that there are two persons with equal capacity for feeling in the sense that the range between the two extreme levels of wellbeing—for the sake of convenience we may call these bliss and abject misery—is the same for both persons. But assume that one of the persons has a fine sense of discrimination so that he has a large number of discretion levels between bliss and abject misery whereas the other person has only a few discretion levels between these two extremes. In this case to declare that the social significance of a movement from one discretion level to another is the same for both individuals will be regarded by many as being unfair to the person with fewer discretion levels.[1]

Another difficulty which is in some respects more fundamental arises from the fact that we cannot really observe the number of discretion levels lying below the level corresponding to a given social state. Goodman and Markowitz recognize this when they point out that in actual practice what we can observe is not the discretion level L_{ij} at which the individual i places the jth social state, but the rank α_{ij} which individual i attaches to the jth social state in a given set of alternatives.[2] They however suggest that α_{ij} can be used as an approximation for L_{ij}. The rank numbers α_{ij} now serve as utility indices. The method of social decision takes the form of maximizing the sum of individual utilities as

---

[1] See Rothenberg. See also Arrow ([1], second edition), who shows that in this model even a small difference in sensitivity will lead to great inequality in distribution.

[2] It is assumed that $\alpha_{ij} \geq \alpha_{ik}$ if and only if individual i considers the jth alternative to be at least as good as the kth alternative.

measured by the rank numbers attached by the individuals to different elements of a given set of social states. This, however, introduces a very high degree of arbitrariness. For under this method it is possible that even when individual orderings and also the intensities of individual preferences, as between x and y, remain the same, social decision between x and y may change because of a change in the individual ranking of x and y among the alternatives under consideration. Suppose we have two individuals 1 and 2, and three alternative social states, x, y and z. Suppose initially the orderings of the two individuals are xP_1yP_1z and yP_2zP_2x respectively. On the basis of the rule suggested by Goodman and Markowitz society prefers y to x since the rank numbers of x and y are 3 and 2 respectively for individual 1; and 1 and 3 respectively for individual 2. Now assume that the first individual continues to prefer x to y and the second individual continues to prefer y to x. Also assume that the intensities of individual preferences as between x and y (measured by the number of discretion levels separating x and y) also remain the same. But assume that individual orderings of x, y and z now becomes xP_1yI_1z and yP_2xI_2z. Under the Goodman–Markowitz rule, the society is now indifferent between x and y. This would seem to be highly arbitrary since one feels that if all the individual orderings and also the intensities of individual preferences as between x and y remain the same, then social decision between x and y should also remain the same. From the example given above, it is clear that the Goodman–Markowitz method of social decision violates Arrow's Condition 3. However, what is really disturbing is not the violation of Arrow's Condition 3 as such but the ethically objectionable form in which this violation takes place.

9.4. *Neumann–Morgenstern Utility Indices and an Alternative Interpretation of Ethical Preference*[1]

One possible way of approaching the problem of measuring and interpersonally comparing preference intensities is through the von Neumann–Morgenstern utility indices. These utility indices were originally introduced to rationalize individual choice among risky prospects. Von Neumann and Morgenstern showed that if the behaviour of an individual satisfies certain plausible

---

[1] This section as well as the next is based on Pattanaik[4].

assumptions, then there exists a utility index unique up to linear transformation such that the individual's choice among alternative probability distributions of certain alternatives conforms to the principle of maximizing expected utility.[1]

One difficulty in using the individual Neumann–Morgenstern utility functions for the purpose of interpersonal comparison is clear. The Neumann–Morgenstern utility function is unique only up to linear transformation, i.e., we can arbitrarily fix the origin as well as the scale. The arbitrariness of the origin does not create any problem. However, it is necessary to reduce the scales to a comparable basis before we can aggregate the individual utilities so as to arrive at social preference. For each individual there exists an infinite set of von Neumann–Morgenstern indices, all linear transforms of each other; the crucial problem is that of choosing one from the set of indices for each individual. Whatever practical procedure we may follow is likely to be more or less arbitrary, and it is difficult to see how one can escape this arbitrariness.[2]

Some writers[3], however, have raised a more fundamental objection against the use of Neumann–Morgenstern utility indices in the context of social choice. It has been argued that these utility indices are constructed in a situation involving risk and, since the choices offered to the individual are risky prospects, the utility numbers attached to these alternatives will inevitably reflect attitude to risk. From this it is concluded that the cardinalism of these indices has no relevance for social choice of non-risky social states. Arrow ([1], p. 10), for example, writes: 'This theorem does not, as far as I can see, give any special ethical significance to the particular utility scale found.

[1] For an extremely lucid discussion of the Neumann–Morgenstern utility indices see Luce and Raiffa.

[2] Cf. Arrow [1] and Vickrey. Vickrey makes a detailed investigation into the undesirable consequences of the different practical procedures that can be followed to render the scales comparable. Arrow [1] illustrates these difficulties in the specific case where the utility numbers 1 and 0 are assigned to the best and worst alternatives, respectively, for each individual. The examples given by Arrow are meant to illustrate how the use of the Neumann–Morgenstern index leads to violation of his Condition of Independence of Irrelevant Alternatives. However, it is not the violation of this condition as such but the nature of such violation which is disturbing.

[3] See, for example, Arrow [1] and Friedman and Savage.

Intensity of Individual Preferences

For instead of using the utility scale found by von Neumann and Morgenstern, we could use the square of that scale; then behavior is described by saying that the individual seeks to maximize the expected value of the square root of his utility... it has nothing to do with welfare considerations, particularly if we are interested primarily in making a social choice among alternative policies in which no random elements enter. To say otherwise would be to assert that the distribution of the social income is to be governed by the tastes of individuals for gambling.'

The passage quoted above gives two reasons why the von Neumann–Morgenstern utility indices of individuals should not be used as the basis of social choice. The first reason is that no special ethical significance attaches to such an index since we could as well rationalize the individual's behaviour by taking the square of the scale adopted. This is no doubt true. But as Arrow himself recognizes, one of the tests for judging among alternative scientific hypotheses is that of simplicity. If two hypotheses serve equally well to explain, it is scientific practice to accept the simpler of the two and reject the other. It is on this ground that we accept the von Neumann–Morgenstern scale rather than its square or square root. But once we accept a certain hypothesis as 'correct' in this sense in positive economics, it is difficult to see why one should have qualms in using it as the basis of welfare judgments *provided* it is not objectionable in any other way.

The second reason given by Arrow is the one which we have cited earlier, namely, that the von Neumann–Morgenstern index will reflect the individual attitude towards risk ('tastes for gambling') and is therefore irrelevant for social choice among sure prospects. That this objection is not as decisive as it seems to be, comes out quite clearly in the models of Vickrey and Harsanyi ([1], [2]).[1]

There are two remarkable features of the formulations of Vickrey and Harsanyi ([1],[2]). Firstly, in contrast to the argument of Arrow[1] quoted above, it is held that not only are individual preferences among risky prospects and, therefore,

---

[1] Harsanyi[2] has two models. One of them is different from that in Harsanyi[1]. For convenience this will be called Model A. The other is identical with that in Harsanyi[1]. This will be called Model B.

Neumann–Morgenstern utility indices, relevant, but also they serve to explicate our intuitive concept of ethical preference,[1] and hence are closely interlinked with the problem of social choice. The interpretation of ethical preferences underlying the formulations of Vickrey and Harsanyi ([1], [2]) is based on the notion of impersonality, a notation similar to (though not identical with) that of universalizability discussed in Chapter 2. Impersonality is defined in terms of individual's choice in a certain type of risky situation, and this involves the use of Neumann–Morgenstern utility indices.

Secondly, it is claimed that all individuals have identical ethical preferences. This is an important claim. For the identity of ethical preferences implies at least that the ethical orderings, i.e., the orderings implied by ethical preferences, must be the same for all individuals. Therefore, if ethical preferences under this interpretation are identical and if the interpretation is persuasive enough for us to accept the ethical preferences, so interpreted, as the basis of social preference,[2] then the problem of aggregating the individual ethical preferences will be practically eliminated since the ethical ordering common to all the individuals can be adopted as the social ordering. We shall, however, see that while the interpretation of ethical preference that is provided in the formulations of Vickrey and Harsanyi ([1], [2]), is fairly persuasive, the conclusion that ethical orderings will be identical for all individuals cannot be maintained except under restrictive assumptions.

Vickrey's model is simpler than that of Harsanyi. Vickrey considers a prospective immigrant weighing the relative attractiveness of different communities into which he can immigrate. The preference pattern of all individuals in all communities is exactly similar to that of the immigrant. Individuals, however, differ in talents (although each community enjoys the same distribution of talents), and this produces inequality in the dis-

---

[1] It may be noted that Vickrey does not explicitly use the notion of 'ethical preference'. However, I believe that no great injustice will be done to Vickrey's ideas if we interpret his model in terms of ethical preference.

[2] The decision to base social choice on ethical preferences rather than subjective preferences does not mean that we shall be rejecting the principle of basing social preferences on individual evaluations; all that we shall be doing is to adopt one type of individual evaluation rather than another.

tribution of income within each community. The immigrant is uncertain of the position that he can occupy in the various communities. Under these conditions, 'he may, ..., make his decisions on the basis of maximizing his expected utility, the alternative utilities in question being those of the various members of a given community...If we identify the social welfare with the attractiveness of the various communities to this prospective immigrant, we see that the social welfare function takes the form of a weighted sum of the individual utilities. If the immigrant is completely ignorant as to what role he will fill in the new community and weighs the roles of all individuals equally, we get the Benthamite summation of individual utilities with the utilities being Bernoullian.'[1] Let the social state, represented by the ith community having N individuals, be x_i. Let X_{ij} be the social position of the jth individual in x_i. Let $\hat{x}_i$ be the uncertain prospect composed of the positions X_{ij} $(j = 1, ..., N)$, all having equal probability. If the individual preferences are assumed to satisfy the von Neumann–Morgenstern axioms, the utility W_i of the uncertain prospect $\hat{x}_i$ for this immigrant (this utility is identified with social welfare from x_i) will be

$$W_i = \frac{1}{N} \sum_{j=1}^{N} U(X_{ij}),$$

where $U(X_{ij})$ refers to the immigrant's evaluation of X_{ij}. Since all the individuals involved (including the prospective immigrant) are assumed to have exactly the same preference patterns,[2]

$$W_i = \frac{1}{N} \sum_{j=1}^{N} U_j(X_{ij}),$$

where $U_j(X_{ij})$ refers to the jth individual's evaluation of his position in the social state x_i. In other words, except for a multiplicative constant, social welfare is equal to the sum of the individual Neumann–Morgenstern utility indices for the social state under consideration.

But, of course, the assumption of identical preference patterns is drastic; any genuine attempt at evaluating social welfare must take into account the differences in preference patterns of

---

[1] Vickrey, pp. 524–5.

[2] As will be seen below, it is necessary to interpret 'preference patterns' to include attitude toward risk.

individuals. And it is precisely here that Harsanyi's Model B differs from that of Vickrey. Harsanyi does not make the restrictive assumption of identical preferences. Still Harsanyi's 'social welfare function'[1] gives social welfare as a weighted sum of what Harsanyi calls[2] the individual utilities. Just as in the case of Vickrey social welfare is identified with the evaluation of the prospective immigrant, in Harsanyi also social welfare is identified with an individual's evaluation of the social state viewed as an uncertain prospect. Each social state is presented to the evaluating individual as an uncertain prospect composed of equal chances of the individual's being each of the individuals in their respective positions. To make the concept more precise, let the social state x_i be a set of 'N' positions X_{ij} $(j = 1, 2, ..., N)$ corresponding to the 'N' individuals respectively in the society. Let $(X_{ij}Y_j)$ refer to the sure prospect of being the jth individual in the *objective position* X_{ij}. Y_j may be interpreted as the aggregate of *subjective features* of the jth individual. Social welfare of x_i is identified with the individual's evaluation of the risky prospect $\bar{x}_i$ composed of the alternatives $(X_{i1}Y_1)$, $(X_{i2}Y_2)$, ..., $(X_{iN}Y_N)$, all the alternatives having equal probability. If now it is assumed that individual preferences among alternatives of the type $(X_{ij}Y_j)$ satisfy the Marschak axioms,[3] it follows that the individual's evaluation of the uncertain prospect $\bar{x}_i$ will be equal to the arithmetic mean of

$$U(X_{ij}Y_j) \quad (j = 1, 2, ..., N)$$

where $U(X_{ij}Y_j)$ indicates the utility attached by the *evaluating individual* to $(X_{ij}Y_j)$. This, Harsanyi thinks, is the same as saying that social welfare of a particular social state is the arithmetic mean of the utilities of different individuals in that state provided the evaluating individual has some 'objective criterion for comparing his fellows' utilities with one another and with his own'. As a corollary it follows that if such an objective criterion for interpersonal comparison of utility were available, social welfare evaluation arrived at by each individual will be the same.

---

[1] The phrase 'social welfare function', as used by Harsanyi, refers to 'preferences based on a given individual's value judgments concerning "social welfare"...' (Harsanyi [2], p. 310 n. 4). This point will be further discussed below.

[2] The meaning of this qualifying phrase will be clear later.

[3] See Marschak.

In the next section I attempt to clarify the ethical basis of this formulation and to show that while the ethical foundation is appealing, in general one cannot derive from it the conclusion that social welfare in Harsanyi's sense is the arithmetic mean of the individual utilities or that, given full factual information about other people's utility, the process outlined above gives us social welfare as a magnitude which will be the same irrespective of whoever happens to be the evaluator. It will also be seen that this remark does not apply to Vickrey's model.

9.5. *Harsanyi's Concept of Ethical Preference: An Appraisal*

A point which has caused some misunderstanding is the nature of the uncertain prospects involved in Harsanyi's Model B. As pointed out above, the elements of the uncertain prospect $\bar{x}_i$ are not $X_{i1}, X_{i2}, ..., X_{iN},$ but $(X_{i1}Y_1), (X_{i2}Y_2), ..., (X_{iN}Y_N)$, i.e., the alternatives involved comprise not only the objective positions but also the subjective features of the respective individuals. This seems to have created some confusion. Rothenberg (pp. 268–9), for example, writes '...why should he *become* some other concrete individual in order to experience one position or another? No one individual is uniquely suited to any one social niche... If the evaluator must *become* others, then the procedure is purely and simply one in which the choice criterion is the average of everybody's payoff in some particular social state. There is no uncertainty about anybody's position—certainly not the evaluator's. But if there is no uncertainty, then the evaluator's choice has nothing to do with maximization of *his* utility. So the assumption of von Neumann–Morgenstern rationality does not suffice to determine his choice.' This criticism seems to involve two propositions: (1) if the individuals are not 'uniquely suited' to their respective positions, it is not necessary for any individual to undergo a transformation of personality so as to experience another individual's position; (2) if on the other hand we assume that the different individuals are 'uniquely suited' to their respective positions so that a transformation of personality is necessary for the individual to experience another individual's position, there is no uncertainty and therefore the question of maximizing utility does not arise. But what is meant by an individual's being 'uniquely suited' to his position? The only reasonable meaning one can assign to it is that it is inconceivable that a particular individual should occupy the position of another individual while remaining himself. But this is obviously absurd. And the first proposition is true. If the individuals can be conceived to occupy a position different from what they are occupying now while retaining their own identity, it is certainly not necessary for them to undergo a transformation of personality to experience it. But Harsanyi's purpose is *not* merely to put several *objective* positions as the uncertain outcomes before the evaluating individual, but to present a combination of the objective positions and the subjective features of the respective individuals. In fact, the entire criticism seems to be based on a misunderstanding of the elements involved in the uncertain prospects and a failure to appreciate their full significance. Since being a particular individual means possessing the features of his personality, it is clear that the procedure implies putting the subjective characteristics of an individual on the same basis as the more 'objective' items in his possession.[1] Once we consider the possession of an individual to comprise not only his 'objective' position but also his subjective features, it becomes self-evident why a transformation of personality is required so as to experience another individual's possessions (as defined above). Nor is this requirement of the imaginative perception of utility that can be realized in the other man's position with the other man's personality 'gratuitous and destructive of the sense of the procedure', as Rothenberg would like us to believe. On the contrary, it serves a definite purpose and increases the ethical appeal of the formulation. This will be discussed later, but before that it is necessary to analyse the role of risk in this type of model.

Risk here is intimately linked up with the concept of impersonality or objectivity which is explicitly postulated in Harsanyi's discussion of the social welfare function and which seems to be implicit in Vickrey's formulation. In Harsanyi particularly, the social welfare function is visualized as a process of second-order evaluation of social alternatives by the individual, its crucial characteristic being 'impersonality' or 'impartiality'. The first-order evaluation expresses 'subjective preferences' of the evalu-

---

[1] Cf. Arrow ([1], p. 115) for an interesting discussion of what he calls 'extended sympathy' meaning thereby a comparison between alternatives of the type $(X_{ij} Y_j)$.

ating individual, being based on the utility of that one individual, while the second-order evaluation expresses the 'ethical preferences', being based on an impartial attitude, or a 'fair compromise' of the utilities of all individuals.[1]

Harsanyi's Model B is an attempt to provide a precise meaning of this impersonality. Harsanyi's reasoning seems to be that the subjective preferences of an individual have no moral force at all (and, therefore, cannot be elevated to the height of a 'social welfare function') since they may be based on judgments like 'Slavery is good, I being a slave-owner'. It is only when the individual can say, 'Slavery is good, even though I do not know whether I am going to be a slave or a slave-owner' that his statement acquires a moral sanctity.

The similarity of all this to the concept of morality explained earlier is quite clear. According to the view adopted in Chapter 2, moral judgments are essentially universalizable, prescriptive judgments: my statement that slavery is good becomes a moral judgment only if I can say it irrespective of my position. Harsanyi's concept of 'impersonality', though characterized by something very similar to universalizability, differs from this in so far as he tries to distil this impersonality through individual attitudes to risk. For Harsanyi, the statement 'Slavery is good' expresses 'ethical preferences' not when I can say it irrespective of my position, but when I can say it even though I do not know what my position is going to be or, to be more precise, even though I know that there is an equal chance of my being a slave or a slave-owner.[2] Thus risk and universalizability together give

[1] 'Even if both an individual's social welfare function and his utility function in a sense express his own individual preferences, they must express preferences of different sorts: the former must express what this individual prefers (or rather would prefer) on the basis of impersonal social considerations alone, and the latter must express what he actually prefers, whether on the basis of his personal interests or on any other basis. The former may be called his "ethical" preferences, the latter his "subjective" preferences.' (Harsanyi [2], p. 315.) This is reminiscent of Kant's distinction between pragmatic and moral imperatives.

[2] One is reminded of Rawls [2] who elaborates the concept of justice as fairness by visualizing a group of rational egoists deliberating as to the rules of decision-making in the case of conflicts, when they are uncertain about the relation in which they will stand to others in the conflicts that are likely to occur in the future. In particular, compare the following remark of Rawls ([2], pp. 172–3): '...having a morality is analogous to having made a firm commitment in advance; for one must acknowledge the principles of morality even when to one's disadvantage'.

us Harsanyi's concept of impersonality which he holds to be the defining feature of the social welfare evaluation by the individual.

But the question can further be asked as to why extended sympathy should have been brought in. Is it not enough for the evaluating individual to be presented with an uncertain prospect where the elements are only the objective positions $X_{i1}, X_{i2}, ..., X_{iN}$? Some such question seems to be implied in the passage quoted from Rothenberg above. But there seem to be good reasons why it is not enough to take uncertain prospects having X_{i1}, X_{i2}, etc. for their elements. It can be seen that without sympathetic identification or some such assumption the analysis may lead to some odd results. Take, for example, a situation where individual 1 (who hates oranges but likes peaches) gets ten peaches and individual 2 (who in turn hates peaches and loves oranges) gets ten oranges. If individual 1 were to evaluate the positions in terms of his own subjective preferences, his 'social welfare function' may prescribe that individual 2 (who hates peaches) should get some peaches and he himself should get some oranges!

But what is more important, this formulation does not correspond to our idea of justice as much as Harsanyi's. For we would not surely call somebody a good judge if in deciding cases he takes into account only the facts of the objective situation and does not consider the subjective states of the individuals by means of some kind of sympathetic identification. Similarly, an evaluation which completely ignores other people's attitudes could hardly be called either an ethical evaluation or an evaluation of social welfare.[1]

Harsanyi's concept of ethical preferences is a persuasive one, but it does not in itself solve Arrow's problem of constructing a social preference pattern by aggregating individual preferences. It should be noted that the term social welfare function is used

---

[1] It is interesting to note the similarity between Harsanyi's concept of impersonality in this respect and the concept of a 'competent judge' as given by Rawls ([1], p. 179): '...he must not consider his own *de facto* preferences as the necessarily valid measure of the actual worth of those interests which come before him, but that he be both able and anxious to determine, by imaginative appreciation, what those interests mean to persons who share them, and to consider them accordingly'. This imaginative appreciation, however, is only one of the features of Rawls' competent judge.

by Harsanyi in a sense different from ours. Harsanyi is concerned with the social welfare function in the sense of some given individual's evaluation of social welfare, whereas social welfare function as defined in Chapter 1 essentially refers to the process by which a social ordering of the alternatives is arrived at on the basis of individual orderings.[1] There can, therefore, be as many social welfare functions, in Harsanyi's sense, as there are individuals in the community. The problem of aggregating these individual 'social welfare evaluations' so as to arrive at a unique social preference pattern has not been undertaken by Harsanyi. In fact, this further problem of aggregation would be superfluous if Harsanyi's conclusions are accepted. For Harsanyi thinks that his Model B gives social welfare as an arithmetic mean of individual utilities, and that if full factual information were available to the evaluating individual about other people's utility, this would be the same irrespective of the evaluator.

As noted earlier, the conclusion that the social welfare indices constructed in Harsanyi fashion will be the same for different individuals implies at least that ethical orderings (i.e., the orderings corresponding to ethical preferences) will be identical for all individuals. This conclusion, however, cannot be sustained: even when perfectly objective criteria are available to the evaluating individual for making interpersonal comparisons of utility,[2] the ethical ordering will not necessarily be the same. This is due to the simple reason that the risk attitudes of different individuals will, in general, be different, and that the Neumann–Morgenstern utility indices are affected by attitudes to risk. This can be seen as follows. Consider a society of two individuals indicated by the subscripts 1 and 2. Let the social states under consideration be x_1 and x_2. Let $\bar{U}_k(X_{ij}Y_j)$ indicate the *introspective* utility of the kth individual from $(X_{ij}Y_j)$ and $U_k(X_{ij}Y_j)$ indicate the Neumann–Morgenstern utility index for $(X_{ij}Y_j)$ with respect to the kth individual. Now consider the introspective utilities from the basic alternatives $(X_{11}Y_1)$, $(X_{12}Y_2)$, $(X_{21}Y_1)$ and $(X_{22}Y_2)$. These will be exactly identical for the two individuals. There would be no meaning in distinguishing, for example, between $\bar{U}_1(X_{11}Y_1)$

---

[1] It is being assumed here that individual weak preference relations are complete orderings.

[2] This, of course, is an ideal condition which will rarely be satisfied in actual life.

and $\bar{U}_2(X_{11}Y_1)$. All possible grounds of distinction are irrelevant because of the presence of Y_1 (standing for the subjective features of individual 1) in the alternatives. The introspective utility of individual 2 from $(X_{11}Y_1)$ must be the same as that of individual 1 since to experience the alternative $(X_{11}Y_1)$ at all, individual 2 has to transform himself through imagination into individual 1. The subscripts of $\bar{U}$ are therefore superfluous and we can simply write $\bar{U}(X_{ij}Y_j)$. But from this it does not follow that the preference orderings (among all the prospects, risky as well as certain) will be the same for both individuals. Let us suppose that

$$\bar{U}(X_{11}Y_1) = \bar{U}(X_{12}Y_2) = \bar{U}'.$$

Let $\bar{U}(X_{21}Y_1)$ be very much higher than $\bar{U}'$ and $\bar{U}(X_{22}Y_2)$ be very much lower than $\bar{U}'$. Now present $\bar{x}_1$ and $\bar{x}_2$ (i.e., the uncertain prospects derived from x_1 and x_2 in the Harsanyi fashion) before each individual. Will the ordering of the two individuals between $\bar{x}_1$ and $\bar{x}_2$ be the same? Not necessarily. For the ordering of each individual will depend not only on his introspective utilities from the basic alternatives involved but also on his risk attitude. Although the introspective utilities from the basic alternatives are identical for both individuals, their risk attitudes, in general, will be different. Suppose one of the individuals is a risk-lover and the other is a risk-averter. It is likely that the risk-lover will prefer $\bar{x}_2$ to $\bar{x}_1$ and the risk-averter will prefer $\bar{x}_1$ to $\bar{x}_2$. Thus, even though the introspective utilities (and, therefore, the orderings) of the two individuals are exactly identical for the basic (certain) alternatives, their orderings of the uncertain prospects will differ if their risk attitudes are different. Therefore, if the choices of the individuals can at all be rationalized in terms of Neumann–Morgenstern utility indices, it can be done only by assigning to them different sets of indices implying different orderings of the prospects.[1] This stricture, however, does not apply to Vickrey's

---

[1] The ethical preference index W_{ik} of the kth individual for the ith social state will, indeed, be equal to

$$\frac{1}{N}\sum_{j=1}^{N} U_k(X_{ij}Y_j).$$

But, as is clear from what has been said above, this is quite different from saying that

$$W_{ik} = \frac{1}{N}\sum_{j=1}^{N} U_j(X_{ij}Y_j).$$

result. For Vickrey's immigrant by assumption has a preference pattern (which presumably includes risk attitudes) exactly similar to that of any other individual involved. In Vickrey's model, therefore, social welfare evaluations will be the same for all individuals (in the sense explained above) and there would be no problem of aggregation. But the very problem of group preference loses most of its significance if we assume all the individuals to be of identical preferences.

Once we allow differences in risk attitudes, ethical preferences no longer remain the same for different individuals even if we introduce sympathetic identification as in Harsanyi, and the problem of aggregation crops up again. How to aggregate the ethical preferences so as to get a unique social welfare evaluation? As noted above, there is an alternative model (which we call Model A) in Harsanyi[2]. By combining the results of Model A with that of Model B it seems possible to utilize Harsanyi's highly appealing concept of ethical preferences to derive the social preferences. Model A is based on the following postulates: (*a*) social preferences satisfy the axioms of expected utility, as given by Marschak; (*b*) individual preferences also satisfy the same axioms; and (*c*) if two prospects *a* and *b* are indifferent from the standpoint of every individual, they are also indifferent from the social standpoint. On the basis of these postulates, the conclusion is deduced that the social welfare function of the Bergson type is of the form $W_i = \sum_{j=1}^{N} \lambda_j U_{ij}$ where U_{ij} refers to the utility of the *j*th individual corresponding to the social state x_i and λ_j to the weight to be attached to a unit change in the *j*th individual's utility. With full factual information about different persons' utilities and with complete individualistic ethics we get $W_i = \sum_{j=1}^{N} U_{ij}$. This is an interesting result in view of the fact that the ethical judgment embodied in Postulate (*c*) is a weak one and is likely to be generally acceptable. It should, however, be noted that the individual preferences and social preferences mentioned in the postulates both refer to individual evaluations although of a different order; they correspond to the subjective preferences and ethical preferences respectively. What I want to suggest here is that the individual preferences in

Postulate (*b*) should be interpreted as ethical preferences and the social preferences referred to in Postulate (*a*) be interpreted to mean social preferences in the sense in which we have defined it. Thus social preferences are to be derived by aggregating ethical preferences of individuals and not their subjective preferences. It will be seen below that this interpretation has an inherent attractiveness due to the persuasive quality of the concept of ethical preference.

There are thus three distinct concepts: (1) subjective preferences of the individuals, (2) ethical preferences of the individuals, and (3) social preferences. Three different problems of derivation are particularly interesting:

(*a*) Subjective preferences
↓
Ethical preferences

(*b*) Subjective preferences
↓
Social preferences

(*c*) Ethical preferences
↓
Social preferences

Derivation (*a*) corresponds to Harsanyi's Model B. The framework in terms of which the problem of social choice was posed in Chapter 1 corresponds to derivation (*b*). Derivation (*c*) is the one under consideration here.

Derivations (*b*) and (*c*) both refer to the aggregation of individual preferences into social preference. But if the required information regarding ethical preferences is available, then it would seem more reasonable to base social evaluation on the balanced and impersonal evaluations of individuals rather than on the subjective preferences which may reflect the extreme egoism of selfish individuals. In other words, what is being argued is that individual preferences may be at different levels of objectivity and that it seems more reasonable to base social preferences on a higher-order evaluation—ethical preferences, rather than on a lower-order evaluation—subjective preferences. Without some such procedure, the interests of the egoistic individuals will have too great a weight in a social welfare function based on cardinal individual utilities, than is desirable and the more altruistic individuals are likely to be penalized because of their altruism. The following example will illustrate the point. Let *1*, *2* and *3* be the three individuals in the society; let x_1, x_2, x_3 and x_4 be four social states; and let there be a single commodity. The individual preferences are represented by utility indices, the best and the worst alternatives for each individual being given the values 100 and 0 respectively for that individual. The following table summarizes the choice situation:

Social states	Shares of individuals in terms of units of the commodity			Utilities of individuals			Sum of utilities	Social choice
	1	*2*	*3*	*1*	*2*	*3*		
x_1	80	10	10	0	0	0	0	
x_2	$33\frac{1}{3}$	$33\frac{1}{3}$	$33\frac{1}{3}$	100	50	80	230	x_4
x_3	40	35	25	80	60	50	190	
x_4	15	50	35	50	100	100	250	

x_4 is the social state to be selected. But in x_4 individual *1* gets only 15 units. As can be seen from the example, *2* and *3* are the more egoistic individuals and *1* is more altruistic. Had *1* been egoistic like *2* and *3* and given the lowest valuation to x_4, some other alternative might have been chosen. But thanks to the altruism of individual *1*, he ends up with only 15 units. It is, of course, possible to fix up (by additional value judgments) what relative social weight a unit change in the utility of different individuals should have in the social preference. But such value judgments are extremely difficult to make and a much more palatable procedure would be to take the ethical preferences of all individuals, which are more or less on the same level of objectivity, and to aggregate them into social preferences.

It can be seen that Arrow's objection that Neumann–Morgenstern individual utility indices reflect the individual's

[1] These indices are assumed to reflect *introspective* utilities corresponding to subjective preferences of the individuals. It is also assumed that the scales have been standardized so as to make interpersonal comparisons possible. The question as to how we could arrive at such indices need not concern us here.

tastes for gambling does not apply here. For in the context of our specific problem it would mean that the preference intensities revealed by such an index constructed for ethical preferences are affected by the individual's attitude to risk. This is true; but all the same, such attitude towards risk *is* relevant for social choice among sure prospects provided we accept the contention that it is more reasonable to base social preferences on ethical preferences of Harsanyi type rather than on subjective preferences. Risk here is the device through which an impersonal evaluation is distilled from the subjective preferences of individuals; the attitude to risk cannot therefore be rejected in the context of social choice among sure prospects simply because it is attitude to risk. More convincing arguments would seem to be required to justify such rejection.

The real difficulty with Harsanyi's Model A seems to lie somewhere else. The mere construction of a cardinal utility index to represent the ethical preferences of each individual is not enough. It is necessary to reduce the scales to a comparable basis. In view of the uniqueness only up to linear transformation of the Neumann–Morgenstern utility indices this presents a serious problem. As Sen [5] shows, the ordering which results from the aggregation of individual preferences by means of Harsanyi's Model A will differ, depending on the procedure followed to standardize the scales of different individuals. Sen [5] is concerned with the problem of aggregating subjective preferences into social preferences in Harsanyi's sense. But his conclusion regarding non-uniqueness of the result of aggregation applies equally well to our problem namely, that of deriving social preferences from the ethical preferences of individuals.

So far it has been implicitly assumed that sufficient information is available for constructing Neumann–Morgenstern utility functions for the different individuals involved. In actual practice, however, the difficulties of constructing such a utility function for each individual are likely to be formidable; this is true especially when the preferences under consideration are the ethical preferences in Harsanyi's sense, which involve 'sympathetic identification'.

10

CONCLUSION

The paradox of collective choice thrown up by Arrow's analysis has been the main theme of this book. The inconsistency of values underlying the paradox presents a problem for anybody concerned with normative aspects of group choice.[1] Is there a satisfactory solution to the problem? This is the question with which we have been mostly concerned in the earlier chapters.

One of the possible solutions discussed was in terms of restrictions on individual preferences, these restrictions being treated as empirically testable hypotheses. It was argued that if a group decision Rule defined a complete social ordering for every set of individual orderings that was likely to occur in real life, then there was no reason why we should feel depressed even if it did not define a complete social ordering for every logically conceivable set of individual orderings.

A suggestion was also made for modifying the requirement of a complete social ordering itself. It was held that in some respects the crucial problem was the existence of a social choice function and not the existence of a complete social ordering. It was shown that the necessary and sufficient condition for the existence of a social choice function was that R should be reflexive and connected, and P should be founded. If the set of alternative social states was infinite, then this condition might not be satisfied even if there existed a complete social ordering. On the other hand, if the set of alternative social states was finite, as we assumed it

---

[1] There has been a tendency among some welfare economists (e.g., Little [2], Mishan ([1], [2]), Bergson [3]) to reject Arrow's analysis altogether as something not coming within the domain of Welfare Economics. This, it should be clear by now, is unjustified. For, if policy prescription is to have any place in Welfare Economics, then it is difficult to see how Arrow's problem regarding criteria of social decision is excluded from Welfare Economics. In fact, the familiar Pareto criteria and the compensation principles of Kaldor and Scitovsky ([1], [2]), which are universally regarded as belonging to the domain of Welfare Economics, are concerned primarily with the criterion for social decision. Arrow's search for a suitable criterion of social decision, therefore, seems to be in conformity with the main tradition in welfare analysis.

to be, the necessary and sufficient condition for the existence of a choice function turned out to be considerably weaker than the condition that R should be a complete ordering.

Following the two lines of approach mentioned above, necessary and sufficient conditions were established in terms of restricted individual preferences for the existence of a social choice function under the MD-Rule. Though the MD-Rule has several attractive properties and has been the subject of a considerable volume of literature, in actual practice, several group decision Rules are frequently used, which fulfill some but not all the properties of the MD-Rule. The analysis was extended to some of these Rules. In particular, conditions were formulated for the existence of a social choice function under (1) binary, decisive, neutral, and non-negatively responsive Rules; (2) binary, decisive, neutral, and non-negatively responsive Rules satisfying the Strict Pareto Criterion; (3) MMD-Rules; and (4) the method of non-minority decision. Though the main focus of the discussion was on the existence of a choice function, conditions were also derived for the existence of a complete social ordering under (1) MMD-Rules; (2) binary, decisive, neutral, and positively responsive Rules; and (3) the MD-Rule.

A basic assumption underlying most of the analysis was that individual weak preference relations were complete orderings. Some of the implications of relaxing this assumption were considered. It was shown that even if individual weak preference relations were only reflexive, connected, and acyclic, but not necessarily transitive or quasi-transitive, there still existed a binary, decisive, neutral, and non-negatively responsive Rule that satisfied the Weak Pareto Criterion and anonymity, and defined a choice function over any finite set of alternatives for all logically possible sets of individual weak preference relations fulfilling the properties assumed. It was, however, shown that if individual preferences were quasi-transitive but not necessarily transitive, then there did not exist any group decision Rule that satisfied the Strict Pareto Criterion and defined a choice function for every logically possible set of individual weak preference relations fulfilling the properties assumed. A sufficient condition was established for the existence of a choice function under any binary, decisive, neutral, and non-negatively responsive Rule,

Conclusion

when individual preferences were reflexive, connected, and quasi-transitive, but not necessarily transitive.

I have been mainly concerned with the logical problem of formulating necessary and sufficient conditions for the existence of a choice function and also for the existence of a complete social ordering under various group decision Rules. To what extent these conditions are actually fulfilled is a problem which I have not pursued in this book. This is essentially a factual question, and in the absence of empirical evidence no conclusive answer can be given. In this connection it is interesting to note the contention that has been often made that if we interpret individual preferences as ethical preferences rather than subjective preferences, then they will be found to be identical. This raises the problems as to whether ethical preferences or subjective preferences should constitute the basis of social choice, and whether ethical preferences are identical for all individuals.

With respect to the first problem it may be pointed out that the individual preferences are likely to differ depending on the frame of reference in response to which the individual indicates his preference,[1] and the decision to base social decisions on any particular type of preferences involves a value judgment. It will probably be generally agreed that ethical preferences rather than personal likings and dislikings of individuals should constitute the basis of social preference. In some sense or other, we feel that ethical preferences are 'better' than the personal inclinations of individuals. The value of the idealist tradition in social philosophy lies here. It emphasizes that it is ethical preferences which are relevant for social choice. The individual, it is said, can act at several levels of rationality; each higher level includes the lower ones but goes further than those. The ethical preferences belong to an order which comprehends subjective preferences but goes beyond them. According to the definition of value judgments adopted by us, the precise point where ethical preferences transcend personal inclinations is where we take into account the interests of others by seeking to universalize our judgment: the statement 'Apartheid is better than no apartheid' becomes a value judgment only if we are prepared to assert it irrespective of our colour and status.[2]

[1] Cf. Marglin.   [2] See Chapter 2.

Conclusion

Kant seems to have thought that the moral principles which followed from his 'categorical imperatives' would necessarily have interpersonal validity. In other words, according to Kant the ethical preferences will be identical for all individuals. The implication of this is clear. If we have decided to base social preferences on ethical preferences of individuals, and if ethical preferences are necessarily identical for all individuals, then there would not be any further problem of aggregation at all. We, however, no longer accept the conclusion that ethical preferences will necessarily be identical for all individuals. We believe that we are free to hold any value judgment we like, provided, of course, we are prepared to universalize our judgment.[1] It, therefore, follows that the problem of aggregation would still remain there even if the social decision process takes into account not the subjective preferences of individuals but their ethical preferences. It is, however, likely that the ethical preferences, *provided we can discover them*, will exhibit a considerably greater degree of similarity than subjective preferences, which will render the problem of aggregating individual preferences into social preferences easier. The real snag lies in the underlined clause. For, how do we know the ethical preferences?[2] What is the guarantee against cheating—against the possibility that an individual may say '*x* should be done rather than *y*' without really believing so? The problem is to devise a frame of reference such that the individuals will be induced to express their ethical preferences rather than their subjective preferences. Whatever be the appeal of ethical preferences as a basis of social decision, the practical difficulty of devising such a frame of reference seems to be overwhelming. We have, therefore, to fall back on subjective preferences of individuals as the basis of social choice, and any empirical test of the restrictions on individual preferences discussed earlier has to be in terms of subjective preferences.

Apart from the similarity of individual preferences, the possibility of introducing the preference intensities of individuals as a relevant factor also provides a possible route of escape from

---

[1] This, in fact, is the central thesis of Hare [2].

[2] As noted in Chapter 1, it may be extremely difficult to ascertain the 'true' preferences of an individual even when we interpret these preferences as subjective preferences. But the difficulties become immensely greater if what we want to know are the individual's ethical preferences.

Conclusion

Arrow's paradox. This I discussed in Chapter 9. In particular, I examined the model given by Goodman and Markowitz for basing social decisions on cardinal utility functions of individuals. The method suggested by Goodman and Markowitz was found unsatisfactory because the ethical assumption used for interpersonally comparing utilities was objectionable, and also because under this method social decision between two alternatives might change even when the individual orderings, as well as preference intensities, between the two alternatives remained unchanged. I also examined the possible use of Neumann–Morgenstern utility indices as suggested by Vickrey, and Harsanyi ([1], [2]). Vickrey's formulation was found restrictive in so far as it rules out differences in individual preference patterns. Harsanyi's formulation which combines risk and 'extended sympathy' to provide an interpretation of ethical preference was found to be ethically appealing. But it was shown that Harsanyi's formulation, in itself, did not solve the problem of social choice, since the ethical preference of different individuals would be usually different owing to difference in risk attitudes. It was held that in some respects it was more appealing to base social choice on ethical preferences as interpreted by Harsanyi rather than on subjective preferences. Difficulties, however, arose because of the uniqueness only up to linear transformation of Neumann–Morgenstern utility indices. In fact, these difficulties together with the difficulties of constructing Neumann–Morgenstern utility indices for all individuals are likely to be formidable in any attempt to use the Neumann–Morgenstern utility functions of individuals as the basis of social choice.

A general review of the different aspects of the problem leads one to the conclusion that no clear-cut solution has been found for Arrow's paradox. In any case, the problem of social decisions cannot be disposed of once and for all. For the problem is essentially one of ethical exploration into the criteria for aggregating individual preferences. The values involved are numerous and changing. All that we can do is to work out the implications of different values, to assess their acceptability by making clearer their consequences and to strike a balance between them as well as we can. If the analysis of this book has made some contribution in this direction, then I shall not consider my effort to have been futile.

BIBLIOGRAPHY

Archibald, G. C.
'Welfare Economics, Ethics and Essentialism', *Economica*, New Series, Vol. 26 (November 1959), pp. 316–27.

Armstrong, W. E.
'Utility and the Theory of Welfare', *Oxford Economic Papers*, New Series, Vol. 3, No. 3 (October 1951), pp. 259–71.

Arrow, K. J.
[1] *Social Choice and Individual Values*, New York: Wiley, 1st Ed., 1951; 2nd Ed., 1964.

[2] 'Rational Choice Functions and Orderings', *Economica*, New Series, Vol. 26 (May 1959), pp. 121–7.

[3] 'Values and Collective Decision Making', in P. Laslett and W. G. Runciman (ed.), *Philosophy, Politics and Society*, 3rd Series, New York: Barnes and Noble, 1967.

Bergson, A.
[1] 'A Reformulation of Certain Aspects of Welfare Economics', *Quarterly Journal of Economics*, Vol. 52 (February 1938), pp. 310–34.

[2] 'Socialist Economics', in H. S. Ellis (ed.), *A Survey of Contemporary Economics*, Philadelphia: Blakiston, 1948.

[3] 'On the Concept of Social Welfare', *Quarterly Journal of Economics*, Vol. 68, No. 2 (May 1954), pp. 233–52.

Black, D.
[1] 'On the Rationale of Group Decision Making', *Journal of Political Economy*, Vol. 56 (1948).

[2] *The Theory of Committees and Elections*. London: Cambridge University Press, 1958.

Blau, J. H.
'The Existence of Social Welfare Functions', *Econometrica*, Vol. 25 (April 1957), pp. 302–13.

Borda, J.-C. de
Mémoire sur les élections au screutin. Read to the French Academy of Sciences in 1770, printed in *Histoire de l'Académie Royal des Sciences*, 1781 and published in 1784.

Bibliography

Clark, J. M.
'Economics and Modern Psychology', *Journal of Political Economy*, Vol. 26, No. 1 (January 1918), pp. 1–30, and No. 2 (February 1918), pp. 136–66.

Condorcet, M. de
Essai sur l'application de L'analyse à la probabilité des decisions rendues à la pluralité des voix, Paris, 1785.

Dahl, R. A.
A Preface to Democratic Theory. Chicago: The University of Chicago Press, Phoenix Ed., 1963.

Debreu, G.
Theory of Value, New York: Wiley, 1959

Dummet, M. and Farquharson, R.
'Stability in Voting', *Econometrica*, Vol. 29, No. 1 (January 1961), pp. 33–43.

Edwards, W.
[1] 'The Theory of Decision Making', *Psychological Bulletin*, Vol. 51 (1954).
[2] 'Behavioral Decision Theory', *Annual Review of Psychology*, Vol. 5 (1960), pp. 473–98.

Fishburn, Peter C.
'Intransitive Individual Indifference and Transitive Majorities', *Econometrica* (1970), forthcoming.

Friedman, M. and Savage, L. J.
'The Utility Analysis of Choices Involving Risk', *Journal of Political Economy*, Vol. 56 (August 1948), pp. 279–304.

Georgescu-Roegen, N.
'The Pure Theory of Consumer's Behavior', *Quarterly Journal of Economics*, Vol. 50 (August 1936), pp. 545–93.

Goodman, L. and Markowitz, H.
'Social Welfare Functions Based on Individual Rankings', *American Journal of Sociology*, Vol. 58, No. 3 (November 1952), pp. 257–62.

Graaff, J. de V.
'On Making a Recommendation in a Democracy', *Economic Journal*, Vol. 72 (June 1962), pp. 293–8.

Hansson, B.
'On Group Preferences', *Econometrica*, Vol. 37 (1969).

Bibliography

Hare, R. M.
  [1] *The Language of Morals*, London: Oxford University Press: Oxford Paperback Edition, 1964.
  [2] *Freedom and Reason*, London: Oxford University Press: Oxford Paperback Edition, 1965.

Harsanyi, J. C.
  [1] 'Cardinal Utility in Welfare Economics and in the Theory of Risk-taking', *Journal of Political Economy*, Vol. 61, No. 5 (October 1953), pp. 434–5.
  [2] 'Cardinal Welfare, Individualistic Ethics, and Interpersonal Comparisons of Utility', *Journal of Political Economy*, Vol. 63, No. 4 (August 1955), pp. 309–21.

Hildreth, C.
  'Alternative Conditions for Social Orderings', *Econometrica*, Vol. 21 (January 1953), pp. 81–94.

Inada, K.
  [1] 'Alternative Incompatible Conditions for a Social Welfare Function', *Econometrica*, Vol. 23, No. 4 (October 1955), pp. 396–9.
  [2] 'A Note on the Simple Majority Decision Rule', *Econometrica*, Vol. 32, No. 4 (October 1964), pp. 525–31.
  [3] 'On the Simple Majority Decision Rule', *Econometrica*, Vol. 36 (1969).

Kaldor, N.
  'Welfare Propositions of Economics and Interpersonal Comparisons of Utility', *Economic Journal*, Vo. 49 (September 1939), pp. 549–52.

Kant, I.
  'Fundamental Principles of the Metaphysic of Morals', in *Critique of Practical Reason and Other Works on the Theory of Ethics*, English translation by T. K. Abbot. London: Longmans, 6th Ed. 1909.

Kemp, M. C.
  'Arrow's General Possibility Theorem', *Review of Economic Studies*, Vol. 21 (1953–4), pp. 240–3.

Kemp, M. C. and Asimakopulos, A.
  'A Note on "Social Welfare Functions" and Cardinal Utility.' *Canadian Journal of Economics and Political Science*, Vol. 18 (May 1952), pp. 195–200.

Bibliography

Leibenstein, H.
'Notes on Welfare Economics and the Theory of Democracy',
Economic Journal, Vol. 72 (June 1962), pp. 299–317.

Little, I. M. D.
[1] *A Critique of Welfare Economics*. London: Oxford University
Press: Oxford Paperback Edition, 1960.

[2] 'Social Choice and Individual Values', *Journal of
Political Economy*, Vol. 60, No. 5 (October 1952), pp. 422–
32.

Luce, R. D. and Raiffa, H.
Games and Decisions, New York: Wiley, 1957.

Majumdar, T.
[1] 'Choice and Revealed Preference', *Econometrica*, Vol. 24,
No. 1 (January 1956), pp. 71–3.

[2] 'Sen's Theorem on Transitivity of Majority Decisions: An
Alternative Proof', to be published in the forthcoming
volume of essays in honour of Professor U. N. Ghosal.

Marglin, S. A.
'The Social Rate of Discount and the Optimal Rate of
Investment', *Quarterly Journal of Economics*, Vol. 77, No. 1
(February 1963) pp. 95–111.

Marschak, J.
'Rational Behaviour, Uncertain Prospects, and Measurable
Utility', *Econometrica*, Vol. 18, No. 2 (April 1950), 111–41.

May, K. O.
[1] 'A Set of Independent Necessary and Sufficient Conditions for Simple Majority Decision', *Econometrica*, Vol. 20
(October 1952), pp. 680–4.

[2] 'Intransitivity, Utility and the Aggregation of Preference
Patterns', *Econometrica*, Vol. 22, No. 1 (January 1954),
pp. 1–13.

[3] 'A Note on Complete Independence of the Conditions for
Simple Majority Decision', *Econometrica*, Vol. 21 (1953).

Mishan, E. J.
[1] 'An Investigation into Some Alleged Contradictions in
Welfare Economics', *Economic Journal*, Vol. 68 (September
1957), pp. 445–54.

[2] 'A Survey of Welfare Economics, 1939–59', *Economic
Journal*, Vol. 70 (June 1960), pp. 197–265.

Bibliography

[3] 'A Comment' in 'Welfare Criteria: an Exchange of Notes', *Economic Journal*, Vol. 72 (March 1962), pp. 234–44.

Murakami, Y.

[1] 'A Note on the General Possibility Theorem of the Social Welfare Function', *Econometrica*, Vol. 29 (April 1961), pp. 244–6.

[2] 'Some Logical Properties of Arrowian Social Welfare Function', *Journal of Economic Behaviour*, Vol. 1 (April 1961), pp. 77–84.

[3] 'Formal Structure of Majority Decisions', *Econometrica*, Vol. 34 (1966).

[4] *Logic and Social Choice*, New York: Dover, 1968.

Nowell-Smith, P. H.

Ethics, Harmondsworth: Penguin, 1954.

Pareto, V.

Cours d'économie politique. Rouge, Lausanne, 1897.

Pattanaik, P. K.

[1] 'A Note on Democratic Decision and the Existence of Choice Sets', *Review of Economic Studies*, Vol. 35 (January 1968).

[2] 'A Note on Leibenstein's "Notes on Welfare Economics and the Theory of Democracy"', *Economic Journal*, Vol. 77 (December 1967).

[3] 'Sufficient Conditions for the Existence of a Choice Set under Majority Voting', forthcoming, *Econometrica* (1970).

[4] 'Risk, Impersonality and the Social Welfare Function', *Journal of Political Economy*, Vol. 76 (1968).

[5] 'On Social Choice with Quasi-transitive Individual Preferences', forthcoming, *Journal of Economic Theory* (1970).

Pattanaik, P. K. and Batra, R. N.

'Transitivity of Social Decisions under Some More General Group Decision Rules than the Method of Majority Decision', mimeograph.

Popper, K. R.

[1] *Logic of Scientific Discovery*, London: Hutchinson, 1959.

[2] *The Open Society and Its Enemies*, Vol. 2, London: Routledge, 4th Ed., 1962.

Quine, W. v. O.
Set Theory and Its Logic, Cambridge, Mass.: Harvard University Press, 1963.

Rawls, J.
[1] 'Outline of a Decision Procedure for Ethics', *Philosophical Review*, Vol. 60 (April 1951), pp. 177–97.
[2] 'Justice as Fairness', *Philosophical Review*, Vol. 67 (1958), pp. 164–94.

Riker, W.
'The Paradox of Voting and Congressional Rules for Voting on Amendments', *American Political Science Review* (1958).

Robbins, L.
An Essay on the Nature and Significance of Economic Science. London: Macmillan, 2nd Ed., 1935.

Rothenberg, J.
The Measurement of Social Welfare, Englewood Cliffs, N.J.: Prentice-Hall, 1961.

Samuelson, P. A.
Foundations of Economic Analysis, Cambridge, Mass.: Harvard University Press, 1947.

Scitovsky, T.
[1] 'A Note on Welfare Propositions in Economics', *Review of Economic Studies*, Vol. 9 (November 1941), pp. 77–88.
[2] 'A Reconsideration of the Theory of Tariffs', *Review of Economic Studies*, Vol. 9 (November 1941), pp. 89–110.
[3] *Papers on Welfare and Growth*, London: Allen & Unwin, 1964.

Sen, A. K.
[1] 'Distribution, Transitivity and Little's Welfare Criteria', *Economic Journal*, Vol. 73 (December 1963), pp. 771–8.
[2] 'Preferences, Votes and the Transitivity of Majority Decisions', *Review of Economic Studies*, Vol. 31 (April 1964), pp. 163–5.
[3] 'Hume's Law and Hare's Rule, *Philosophy*, Vol. 41, No. 155 (January 1966), pp. 75–9.
[4] 'A Possibility Theorem on Majority Decisions', *Econometrica*, Vol. 34, No. 2 (April 1966), pp. 491–9.
[5] 'Planners' Preferences: Optimality, Distribution and Social Welfare', in J. Margolis and H. Guitton (ed.), *Public Economics.* New York: St Martin's Press, 1969.

Bibliography

[6] 'Nature and Classes of Prescriptive Judgments', *Philosophical Quarterly* (January 1967).

[7] 'Quasi Transitivity, Rational Choice and Collective Decisions', *Review of Economic Studies*, Vol. 36, No. 3 (July 1969).

[8] 'Interpersonal Aggregation and Partial Comparability', Discussion Paper 75, Harvard Institute of Economic Research, 1969.

[9] 'The Impossibility of a Paretian Liberal', Discussion Paper 67, Harvard Institute of Economic Research, 1969.

[10] *Collective Choice and Social Welfare*, forthcoming in the Holden-Day and Oliver and Boyd Series in mathematical economics and econometrics.

Sen, A. K. and Pattanaik, P. K.
'Necessary and Sufficient Conditions for Rational Choice under Majority Decision', *Journal of Economic Theory*, Vol. 1, No. 2 (August 1969).

Suppes, P.
Introduction to Logic, Princeton, N.J.: D. Van Nostrand, 1957.

Tullock, G.
'The Irrationality of Intransitivity', *Oxford Economic Papers*, New Series, Vol. 16 (November 1964), pp. 401–6.

Vickrey, W.
'Utility, Strategy and Social Decision Rules', *Quarterly Journal of Economics*, Vol. 74 (November 1960), pp. 507–35.

Von Neumann, J. and Morgenstern, O.
Theory of Games and Economic Behaviour, Princeton, N.J.: Princeton University Press, 3rd Ed., 1953.

Ward, B.
'Majority Voting and Alternative Forms of Public Enterprises', in J. Margolis (ed.), *2nd Conference in Urban Expenditure* (forthcoming).

Weinstein, A. A.
'Individual Preference Intransitivity', *Southern Economic Journal*, Vol. 34 (January 1968), pp. 335–43.

Williamson, O. E. and Sargent, J. G.
'Social Choice: A Probabilistic Approach', *Economic Journal*, Vol. 77 (1967).

GLOSSARY OF LOGICAL
AND SET-THEORETIC SYMBOLS

& : 'and'

∨ : inclusive 'or'

→ : implication

↔ : logical equivalence

∼ : negation

∀ : universal quantifier

∃ : existential quantifier

∈ : 'element of'

∪ : union of sets

∩ : intersection of sets

⊂ : set inclusion

− : difference between sets

α & β : both statements α and β are true

$\alpha \vee \beta$: at least one of α and β is true

$\alpha \to \beta$: If α is true, then β is true

$\alpha \leftrightarrow \beta$: α is true if and only if β is true

$\sim \alpha$: the statement α is not true

$(\forall x)$ (...) : for all x, statement ... is true

$(\exists x)$ (...) : there exists x such that statement ... is true

$x \in A$: x is an element of A, i.e. x belongs to A

$A \cup B$: the set of all entities belonging to at least one of the sets A and B

$A \cap B$: the set of all entities belonging to both the sets A and B

$A \subset B$: A is a subset (but not necessarily a proper subset) of B

$A - B$: the set of all entities belonging to A, but not to B

ERRATUM

p. 104, line 26: read 'ordering sets: [1.2 *or* 1.3, 2.2 *or* 2.3, 3.2 *or* 3.3] or some other three-ordering set which can be derived from one of these eight three-ordering sets by a formal interchange between x, y, and z and which need not, therefore, be considered separately from these eight cases. Consider [1.2, 2.2, ...'.

INDEX

Index

Index

Index